YouTubers

Chris Stokel-Walker

YouTubers

How YouTube shook up TV
and created a new generation of stars

Chris Stokel-Walker

Canbury Press

First published by Canbury Press 2019

This edition published 2019

Canbury Press

Kingston upon Thames, Surrey, United Kingdom

www.canburypress.com

Cover: Rache Bowie

Printed and bound in Great Britain by
CPI Group (UK) Ltd, Croydon,CR0 4YY

This is a work of non-fiction.

The events and experiences detailed herein are true and have been

faithfully rendered to the best of the author's ability.

ISBN: Hardback: 978-1-912454-21-1

Ebook: 978-1-912454-24-2

Audiobook: 978-1-912454-23-5

Printed on FSC paper

Typeset in Athelas 12pt/14.4pt (body), Futura PT (headings)

CONTENTS

PART I
POWER AND
BEGINNINGS

1.

UPLOADING:
CASEY NEISTAT AND THE
POWER OF YOUTUBE

One spring afternoon Casey Neistat uploaded a video lasting five minutes and twenty-two seconds to YouTube. In the style of so many YouTubers, he looked straight into the camera and aired his opinion on a matter of importance. As the elder statesman on the platform, Neistat's words carry weight. He can make or break products and careers — and this video was no different. Seconds after he uploaded his video to YouTube via his superfast broadband at his creative headquarters in New York, it was available worldwide to four billion people: everyone on Earth with an internet connection. Millions of Neistat's subscribers instantly received a notification telling them that one of YouTube's most influential stars was again speaking directly to them.

Across the world in apartment blocks, restaurants, bedrooms and bathrooms, phones pinged, buzzed and beeped. Hundreds of thousands of people instantly watched what Neistat had to say. Wearing dark glasses, his hair streaked blond, Neistat vented his frustration at the way the media was second-guessing the motivations of YouTubers; and he wanted to single out one journalist in particular. In the comments section underneath his video his fans began discussing the question he posed: did people post videos on YouTube for the fame and fortune — or just to express themselves?

YouTube is a kaleidoscope of visual and audio content that mimics the richness, quirkiness, beauty and madness of human life. Every day its users upload videos on everything from pop music to politics, fashion to plumbing, and cars to fishing. The topics are as diverse (and as random) as the world itself. Want to watch racing pigeons, cut a perfect bob, discuss Che Guevara, speak Mandarin, or play guitar? YouTube can offer that, instantly. Want to relax while seeing boiled sweets made the old-fashioned way? Load up Lofty Pursuits. Have a hankering to watch a man meticulously scratch away the foil on 200 lottery playing cards to see if he can win back his outlay? Type 'moorsey scratchcards' into your search bar and reap the rewards.

Whether giving sex advice, posting football clips or simply splicing together footage to create an action-packed vlog, video makers want to communicate with and be seen by YouTube's 1.9 billion registered users. Some hope that, like Casey Neistat, they too will one day set off pings across the world. For a few, notifications mean that millions of fans are watching them and their view counters are whirring upwards, along with their bank balances. Elite influencers are creative and dynamic and get to do what they want all day long. Unsurprisingly, becoming a YouTuber is the job children most covet.

They understand the platform's extraordinary growth. YouTube is expanding so fast that outsiders can't accurately measure its size. An estimated 576,000 hours of video are added daily to YouTube – vastly more than the new releases on Netflix. In October, November and December 2018, Netflix added 781 hours of original content, while 53 million hours of footage likely went onto YouTube. It would take you 35 days to watch the new Netflix content non-stop. You'd still be watching the YouTube uploads in the year 8069.

YouTube's rise has been swift. In little more than a decade, it has moved from an oddity broadcast on bulky grey computer monitors to mass media entertainment viewed on ultra-thin, wall-mounted 55-inch televisions. In the past five years, YouTube viewing has rocketed from 100 million hours a day to one billion hours a day. It's by far the most-watched video service worldwide, seen by 69% of all internet users every month. It's the internet's second most visited site, behind only Google (whom we ask about life), but ahead of Facebook (with whom we share our lives).

We are addicted. YouTube is the first thing many of us wake up to on our mobile phone screens, and the last thing we watch at night before turning off the television. It's what we watch when we're bored in our lunch hour, when we hear about the latest gossip, or when we want to listen to the latest pop song (or want to know how to get rid of a wasps' nest). In one month alone, November 2017, YouTube was watched by an estimated 91 million Americans and by 21 million people in Britain. Many of them watched for hour after hour. Shortly after 9pm on 1 March

2018, one of them was my friend, Simon Coward. He opened up Facebook Messenger and tapped out a message: 'So you've just been mentioned by one of the biggest YouTubers there is.'

Though only 38, Casey Neistat is something of the grand old man of YouTube. He became a viral sensation in 2003 when he uncovered Apple's attempts to keep people locked into buying its products by making batteries in its iPods irreplaceable – and quick to wear out. He parlayed that into making independent films and an eight-part television show for American cable network *HBO*. He joined YouTube in 2010 and is approached by its executives when they want to publicly admit to and atone for transgressions against the community. He has 10 million subscribers, but his power eclipses even that vast number.

Filmed at 368 Broadway in New York, the location of an independent co-working studio space for YouTubers he set up, Neistat's video discussed a story I had written for Bloomberg explaining how 96% of those who upload to YouTube don't make enough money from adverts alone to break through the US poverty line. As a tech writer fascinated by YouTube – its stars, its ecosystem, its finance, its everything – I wanted to let people know that YouTube is not quite the gold mine that some aspiring vloggers believe it to be. Neistat's beef was that people didn't just go on YouTube to make money – they did it because they wanted to create. And because Neistat is a good human being and acutely aware of the power he holds over his subscriber base he ended with the message: 'Please do not send the author of this article any negativity.'

Some couldn't resist. As I sat in my bedroom 3,332 miles away in Newcastle in Britain, a Canadian basketball coach, Allen Harrington, sent me a private tweet stating that I was a horrible person as well as a horrible reporter. A teenage girl called me a 'pussy' and said she was going to make a YouTube video about me. 'Diss track with Rice comin soon,' she wrote, referencing one of her favourites, YouTuber Brian 'RiceGum' Le. A third fan protested: 'Your look on shit is complete crap. I could make a better counter-argument article.' (He didn't.)

In the end, two million people watched the video. I had learnt some home truths. Among them were just how fast and direct the connection between YouTubers and viewers is, how passionate those fans can be – and how a video can spread around the world in minutes.

YouTube is different to a conventional media company: its reach is wider, its diversity broader, its demographic younger, and its power stronger. All that has caught the attention of big business. Unsurprisingly for such a sweeping force, YouTube has transformed advertising. Corporations from big carmakers like Ford and Audi to toiletries giants like Procter & Gamble no longer have to display their message in the breaks during scheduled TV shows. They can speak personally to a specific audience, either directly through their own YouTube channel or through a creator who has a direct connection with their fans. Want to see a hands-on review of the latest iPhone model? You may have to head to YouTube. Apple has started entrusting the few review copies of its latest devices to YouTubers rather than traditional media. It's a stark (and visual) demonstration of how significantly the balance of power has shifted from traditional broadcasters towards YouTube.

It is, in fact, a revolution. In the past, Hollywood studios, television networks and newspaper publishers were top-down, professionalised industries. 'You were a consumer, not a producer, of content,' points out communication academic Cynthia Meyers, of New York's College of Mount Saint Vincent. No longer, she says:

'Social media makes every single person that participates in it a content producer as well as consumer. Content flow is no longer coming out of TV networks: it's coming out of users.'

Most incredibly, this fundamental change has slipped almost unnoticed and without oversight into our everyday lives. On the few occasions YouTube bursts onto the pages of newspapers, it's in simplistic tones or wonder, with little understanding or analysis as to what its explosive growth means to our economy and to our lives. It's written about primarily in the context of three things: its scandals, the wealth that youngsters have accrued in just a few years (more than most people make in a lifetime), and the impact of fake news, unsavoury content and children's shows.

But YouTube is far more nuanced than media coverage suggests. It's a multi-billion dollar industry that employs hundreds of thousands of talented people across the world. Many of them work at Google, which owns YouTube. Thousands more are employed in the booming associated industries that have sprung up to support these new celebrities. The super-charged growth of production companies, video editors and agents in this new age of individual video makers makes Hollywood's early years seem like a cottage industry.

YouTube has a do-it-yourself ethic; it is punk TV for the 21st century. Opportunities for on-camera talent are democratic (pick up a camera and start talking) and still expanding. People are beginning to make serious money behind the scenes, too. It has created its own norms, businesses and subculture. In 2013, Companies House in the UK didn't know anyone working as a 'vlogger', 'YouTuber' or 'influencer'. Five years later, 74 entrepreneurs used those titles.

Make it big and you are made for life. Some YouTubers live in mansions funded by the merchandise they sell to fans. Jake Paul, PewDiePie and KSI are instantly recognisable names to young people – but not usually to their parents.

So, who are these stars? What kind of lives do they live? What do they want? What does their success mean for the future of the media, and for society?

What role does YouTube itself – which is seen by many as the future of entertainment – have in our daily lives? And what consequences does a self-regulating, private video marketplace have for the spread of extremism and for the creators themselves?

For the first time, this book looks independently at the rise of YouTube, the changes it has wrought to our viewing habits, and its rapidly evolving and growing ecosystem. It also looks at the personal stories – the successes and failures – of some of YouTube's biggest creators, both those on the way up and those on the way down. It investigates the pretenders, the also-rans, and the platforms that were YouTube before YouTube existed.

It's the story of YouTube and YouTubers. It explains how one company's algorithm is powering the world, and how teenagers who have just left school are able to make more money than modern-day industrialists. It is stranger than fiction, and like the best stories, is filled with human drama. Welcome to the amazing, dynamic, controversial, odd – and dazzlingly popular – world of YouTube.

2.

JAKE PAUL:

CARS, MONEY AND

A BURNING SWIMMING POOL

Make your way the 100 metres or so up the gated driveway of a mountainside home in California and your eye is drawn to the rust-coloured statue in the middle of the front yard. Cast in metal, a stick man holds up four large boxes that appear to be toppling out of reach. Look left and you'll see a newly installed skate ramp on the front lawn. To the right of that you'll see the dirt ramp where the owner jumps his luxury cars, among them a Lamborghini Huracán Performante, a Tesla Model X P-100 D (nicknamed Bloodshark), and a tie-dyed Ford Focus RS called Rainbro.

But don't get distracted by the flashy motors and the general hullabaloo taking place in the grounds of this three-and-a-half acre property. Otherwise you'll miss the 15,000-square-foot, eight-bedroom mansion, which has a custom-designed fish tank in the master bedroom and a 'merchandise shop' (which the public can't visit) showcasing a custom line of T-shirts, hoodies and sweatshirts.

The owner of this $6.9 million mansion is a high school dropout with a short attention span. A decade ago Jake Paul might have been consigned to a low-wage future scanning groceries in a supermarket in his native Ohio. Instead he is the modern face of YouTube; a boisterous millionaire with a frenetic lifestyle and a booming business. His story shows how YouTube is throwing jokers into the pack of modern media.

In 2014, Paul left school and the family home in Westlake, Ohio, aged 17, for the West Coast to upload videos to the internet. An early fan of sketch comedy channel *Smosh* (Paul and his older brother's first joint YouTube channel on the platform was called *Zoosh*, inspired by the *Smosh* name), he first came to real fame by doing jokey videos on Vine, the six-second social media video sharing app bought by Twitter. He bounded onto YouTube when Vine closed in late 2016. 'I was a savage from day one,' he boasted in a video hyping his YouTube channel.

Certainly, he was too savage for some neighbours of the $17,000-a-month home he was renting in Beverly Grove, California. For one 15-minute video, uploaded in July 2017, Paul decided to drive around in his newly souped-up truck, honking his extra-loud horn at passersby. One shopper, Ellis Barbacoff, later sued Paul, claiming that 'sustained shock and injuries to his body' had caused longstanding 'pain and suffering' and 'emotional distress'. (When this book went to press, the case was ongoing.) His neighbours threatened a class action lawsuit against him because of his outlandish behaviour – which included setting fire to his own swimming pool. You might wonder how someone would set fire to a swimming pool. The answer is: you throw a load of furniture into the empty pool, toss some lighter fluid over it, then set fire to it. If you have to ask why, then you don't understand Jake Paul.

His YouTube persona is the annoying, puckish person we all know and hate, with a whiny voice, attention-seeking attitude, bleached blond hair and gnat-like attention span – a Jedward for the online generation. This is how he introduces his YouTube channel:

WHATS UP?! Im Jake Paul.
Im 21, live in Los Angeles, & have a crazy life! Keep up :)
The squad 'Team 10' & I are always making comedy vids, acting,
doing action sports, & going on crazy adventures.
Subscribe & watch daily to keep up with the madness

Paul is also – alongside his brother Logan, who is best known for uploading a video of a dead body hanging in a forest in Japan – one of the most successful YouTubers, with 17 million subscribers. He has interviewed a United States senator about gun control. He's been invited to – and illicitly stayed overnight in – the White House (the unexpected sleepover was a dare for a video, of course). He owns two absurdly expensive Audemars Piguet Swiss watches. He is estimated to earn anything between £250,000 ($350,000) and £4 million ($5.6 million) per year from advertising on his YouTube videos alone. He has done more with his life than many 52-year-olds, let alone other 22-year-olds from Ohio.

In many ways, Paul is the most successful postmodern You-Tuber, transparent about the transactional nature of the relationship between him and his fans. He is clear that the reason why he's quite so annoying is that he knows it will gain him notoriety, and consequently lucrative views. He finally moved out of Beverly Grove in October 2017, not because of the fires or the car horns or the savage behaviour, but on a technicality. He was banned from filming in the building without a shooting permit – preventing him from legally creating content without risking a six-month jail sentence.

Paul now lives in the mansion in Calabasas with members of Team 10, a ragtag gang of fellow YouTubers, all of whom are believed to have signed contracts giving him a cut of their earnings from the video sharing website. He is backed by a crew of agents, runners, producers, and general hangers-on, focused on the bottom line and squeezing out every penny from his often young fans.

His constantly shifting Team 10 can range in number from a handful to a dozen – including a toddler called Mini Jake Paul – depending on who's in town and happy to hang out at his Mc-Mansion. All of them know that the quid pro quo for living in his orbit and enjoying the lifestyle is the requirement that they appear in his videos, shot by a cameraman trailing him at every moment and often edited while he sleeps by a British-based video editor, Jack Bell. (Paul's team declined a request to speak to Bell about his life as the person responsible for Jake Paul's inimitable video style.)

Regardless of who the supporting cast members are, his videos have a common theme: chaos. Like many lifestyle vloggers, Paul goes about his life – which just so happens to be wild and wacky – and brings along the viewers for a ride. Sometimes he plays pranks on his friends within his mansion; other times he sets fire to things because he is bored. He has made a habit of taking his colourful cars for a spin to visit the nearest supermarket, where he wanders the aisles picking up supplies for his next stunt. The result is like a scene from *Who Framed Roger Rabbit?*: the cartoon character, dressed head to toe in his own merchandise, or 'merch', stands out like a sore thumb, looking askance at packets of crisps and posters.

For all the antics, viewers are not in any doubt that Paul is running a business as well as living a lifestyle. Spend some time watching the videos he or his older brother Logan produce, and you'll find that they are driven by a messianic urge to make you buy their merch, including $42 shorts, and a windbreaker that costs $90. For this book I analysed 50 videos uploaded by Jake and Logan Paul in February and March 2018 – more than six hours of content – to see how often they mentioned their merchandise. On average, it was once every 142 seconds.

Nowhere is this desire to upsell you on... well, anything, more obvious than in Jake Paul's 2017 Christmas album. *Litmas*, the main track on the 18-minute album, is a vapid two-minute song with an industrial-sounding melody and a chorus that repeats the lines 'Christmas is lit/Christ-mas, lit-mas'. Even in a genre famous for its bad music, the Christmas single is a new low (comments on the video included 'This is easily the worst chorus to any song I have ever heard in my life'). No matter. Less than 24 hours after its release, it had been seen 2.4 million times.

A better glimpse into how modern-day YouTube works is *Fanjoy to the World* – a two-minute 16-second version of the Christmas classic *Joy to the World* with reworked lyrics. It starts by repeating 'Buy dat merch' seven times, adding: 'All I want for Christmas is that Jake Paul merch/All I want for Christmas is a

Jake Paul shirt'. Later, Paul manages to incorporate the URL to his online merchandise store in the song, and tells the listener: 'Get in while you can/Before I sell it all' and 'Go tell your momma/She gotta buy it all'.

His approach is working. In 2018, Paul was the second highest-earning YouTuber, pulling in $21.5 million before management fees and taxes, according to Forbes. (The highest earning, who we'll meet later, was even younger. No, it's not Mini Jake Paul.)

Unsurprisingly, there are thousands of smaller scale Jake Pauls on YouTube, hoping to ape his success. Some of them even forked out $64 to learn more about Paul's business model through a dubious online course he set up called Edfluence.

How did Jake Paul happen? How did YouTube become a site where people create entire conceits so that they can pepper their videos with calls to buy their merchandise every two minutes? Where individual vloggers can command global audiences of millions and live in mansions, surrounded by sports cars and hangers-on? How did YouTubers start living the life which school children most want to lead?

Every story needs to start somewhere – and fittingly for YouTube, which can often seem like a madhouse full of party animals, it started in a zoo.

3.

ME AT THE ZOO:

JAWED KARIM AND

THE WORST VIDEO OF ALL TIME

Me at the zoo is one of the most banal videos ever made. Even by the standards of home movies, it is lo-fi and boring. The narrator looks awkward, the camera work is amateurish, and other than some elephants swaying gently, tails swishing, in the background, nothing really happens. Nobody comes. Nobody goes. It's... well, awful.

Jawed Karim is the 'star' of *Me at the zoo*. Wearing an oversized black windcheater over a dark blue top, Karim looks nervously into the camera. Behind him is the elephant enclosure at San Diego Zoo. He seems to speak off-the-cuff – or is practising the comedy of excruciation. It is a one-take, 19-second video. One scene, with no special effects or change of focus. It is the kind of movie you would make if you had no experience of making films and had just got a new video camera. Haltingly, Karim says:

> 'Alright, so here we are in front of the elephants. [Pause]. Um, and the whole thing with these guys is that they have really, really, really long, um, trunks… and that's cool.'

Karim looks back to the elephants and then back to the camera, then adds: 'And that's pretty much all there is to say.'

The video truly stretches the definition of 'compelling content'. Yet, at the time of writing, 60 million people have seen *Me at the zoo.*

While looking like any other awkward twenty-something man with a degree in computer science when confronted by a pack of pachyderms, Karim was doing something that would be viewed again and again by future generations. He was making the first YouTube video.

At the time, online video was hardly a practical proposition, at least for ordinary people. Download speeds for most people in the western world were slow. Superfast fibre broadband was out of the reach of many, too expensive and too complicated to install in most homes. Apple's touch-screen iPhone was two years away, a sleek, shapely glint in Steve Jobs' eye. Instead, computer users had to make do with a slow broadband connection or an even slower dial-up modem connection, which took minutes or even hours to load dense content like videos.

When 25-year-old Karim was standing in front of the elephants, the internet revolution was transforming the market for information, including financial data such as share prices, and practical information and news, rather than imagery.

California was the beating heart of the startup world, where innovators were exploring the possibilities of this revolution. Typically several companies were battling it out in the same space. In the early 2000s if you wanted to search the internet, you could Ask Jeeves, Google, Altavista or any number of other smaller competitors.

Once the early potential of online video was spotted, the same happened there. Some visionaries grasped that, at least in theory, video, and more specifically, 'video blogs', could be the future of the web. Several video sites were set up between 2003 and 2005. Israeli entrepreneurs launched Metacafe in 2003. Two were started at the end of 2004 – Vimeo established a platform for independent film-makers and Grouper hosted the sharing of photos, video and music.

Vimeo's co-founder Jake Lodwick was among these video visionaries who gave a presentation at the first convention devoted to discussing the possibilities of this visual age. Vloggercon began on the fourth floor of an 11-floor block at 721 Broadway, New York, at 9am on 22 January 2005. Movers and shakers in the new world of video blogging had anticipated the convention for weeks – and the event had spread beyond the small group of digital pioneers. 'Our intimate gathering has become a bit of a spectacle,' remarked organiser Jay Dedman before the event, held at New York University's Interactive Telecommunications Program building.

What's most striking about the discussions those first vloggers held over the course of the one-day meeting was their prescience. Introducing one session, entitled 'Content is King', Dedman, a TV journalist at *CNN International*, outlined what made the new method of broadcast unique. 'The thing about video blogs is it's not television in the sense that it's a one-way thing,' he told the assembled audience of around 50 people – only half of whom he estimated had ever made a video. 'You're doing it because you get comments, you get track-backs, you can start a conversation.' Other discussions revolved around how people could make money from video blogging.

Just three days after the conference, on 25 January 2005, Google, which was winning the lucrative race for search, also entered the fray. With the resources of its wealthy parent, Google Video was the favourite to sweep up the exciting possibilities of the visual age.

Google, however, would find itself competing with three geeky men who had started a challenger company called YouTube. Among them were two immigrants. One was Jawed Karim. Karim had arrived in the United States as a teenager with his German mother and Bangladeshi father. At the University of Illinois, the hardworking Karim combined his bachelor's degree in computer science with work at a new internet payment startup called PayPal. Also working at PayPal was a university friend, Steve Chen, whose family had emigrated to Illinois from Taiwan. There they met Chad Hurley, a fine artist with a sensitive soul, who had designed PayPal's original logo. (In a sign of the interlinking origins of California start-ups, Chen also worked briefly at a new social network, Facebook, started the previous year by another computer programmer, Mark Zuckerberg.)

Late on Valentine's night 2005, the three computer pioneers registered YouTube.com. Two months later the site went live with *Me at the zoo*. The vision of its founders was simple: 'We're the ultimate reality TV,' Hurley told reporters. 'Giving you a glimpse into other people's lives.'

27

Karim, Chen and Hurley were the first YouTubers. Their timing was good. The world was on the cusp of a video revolution that would pivot the text-based internet into a visual one. Digital stills cameras were beginning to replace film-based ones among the general public. Meanwhile, affordable handheld video cameras – camcorders – were being put in the hands of ordinary Joes, too. Nonetheless, the video revolution was jerky and grainy in its early days. One would hook up a laptop to a TV via an HDMI or RGB composite cable to see fuzzy, pixellated videos, poorly shot in questionable lighting, from creators with obscure usernames like DaxFlame, WhatTheBuck? and Wheezy Waiter. Some were downright odd. DaxFlame, for instance, was a character actor, a quirky, oddball teenager with ideas above his station who would smirk with disdain while telling and sometimes acting out creepy stories he said happened in his life. Others, though, would be in the more traditional vein of vlogging: single individuals talking through the camera.

In November 2005, videomakers Anthony Padilla and Ian Hecox launched a new comedy channel: *Smosh*. At first they lip-synced to childhood TV programmes' theme music, then developed their own brand of oddball sketch comedy. Within a few months, *Smosh* was the most popular channel on YouTube, scaling the heights of 2,500 subscribers. There was a significant drop-off in viewers for the next most popular channels.

In 2005, YouTube carried no advertising; it was just running through $3.5 million of investment Sequoia Capital had pumped into the business. Like many tech businesses at the time, such as Amazon and Facebook, the business model was to lose money until there was a way of making some – to enter the digital elevator on the ground floor.

So, content creators who uploaded their videos didn't earn any money. They just had the satisfaction of seeing something they had made being visible to the world, on a platform with great potential. They might become part of the brave future of video sharing, when technology improved, as it surely would.

Other innovators, however, had solved this problem: how to make a living from making videos. In the late 1990s and early 2000s, the file-sharing program Napster had opened up a world of content to anyone who was willing to withstand the painfully slow download times and to flout copyright laws. Ian Clarke and his friends, Steven Starr and Oliver Luckett, had come together in a desire to push the boundaries of the web, creating digital services in the public interest. Together they created Freenet, the world's first decentralised peer-to-peer network.

In October 2005, they founded Revver, a content-sharing website. Its premise was simple – to reward people financially for their creativity. After testing a range of early prototypes, including an online music store that allowed bands to upload their songs and used machine learning to recommend music to users, the trio hit on what they felt best represented the future of creativity online: a website where people could upload videos of themselves, against which adverts would be sold.

'We wanted to create a marketplace for creativity,' says Clarke from his home in Austin, Texas, his Irish accent imbuing his words with bonhomie. 'We concluded that short-form video content was really likely to explode.' He and his co-founders assumed that the internet was spreading so quickly that broadband connections would soon be speedy enough to make streaming video online feasible. At the time many tech pioneers, including Skype's inventors, were working on downloadable software to play videos. But Revver's founders bet that rather than wanting to download a video-playing application, people would happily play videos direct from a website.

The Revver team still had to overcome three issues. Firstly, how to allow people to upload their short-form videos easily. Secondly, how to monetise those videos, and, thirdly, how to share the advertising revenue from them with their creators. They decided early on to split any money 50/50 with creators. Implicitly, videomakers would be responsible for their content, and only they would be able to upload it; it was theirs and they should benefit.

Revver had a public service ethos, innovative ideas and, now, a way of incentivising creators to choose its platform over rivals. It was well-placed to take gold in the race to capitalise on the growth and wealth of the video revolution.

Only one rival could stop it – by finding compelling content unlike *Me at the zoo*.

4.

VIRAL COMEDY:

YOUTUBE LAUGHS

ALL THE WAY TO THE BANK

What could attract more viewers than showing the best TV clips for free?

In December 2005, the US comedy show *Saturday Night Live* broadcast a digital video sketch starring Andy Samberg and Chris Parnell called *Lazy Sunday*. In the two-minute video Parnell and Samberg rap about how they want to buy cupcakes and watch *The Chronicles of Narnia*. Watched with the benefit of hindsight, *Lazy Sunday* is a little dated: the sharp-edged topical jokes have been blunted by time, and the over-the-top delivery is now pat.

But at the time it was a major event. Put up on YouTube, the clip went viral. In its first week it received two million views. There was just one problem: NBCUniversal, which owned the intellectual property, hadn't uploaded it. (This was an issue that *Smosh* faced in its early days: in fact, their existence on YouTube is because they tracked down an unapproved upload to the site, saw what they liked, and stayed.) For Jorma Taccone, who had created the *Saturday Night Live* skit with fellow writer Akiva Schaffer and Samberg and Parnell, that wasn't an issue. 'We were watching numbers on a site we had never heard of. It was this double whammy: we always got associated with the internet, but it was television that made it possible,' he told *Variety* later. But for NBCUniversal's lawyers, that was their content, and it had been illegally uploaded. No matter that the video was an enormous advert for *Saturday Night Live*, or that it was giving what Taccone called 'second life to television'. It wasn't making money for NBCUniversal (nor at the time was it making money for the ad-less YouTube).

Here, however, the different approaches of the video pioneers played out. Grouper and other sites were quick to tackle copyrighted material uploaded to their platforms, partly because they didn't want to unpick who should be paid what in the event of competing claims. Revver had audio fingerprinting and a team of manual reviewers checking for copyright infringement. It didn't allow *Lazy Sunday* because 'it was obviously copyright infringement', according to Clarke. In tune with its public ethos, Revver wanted to reward copyright owners — the creators. It wanted to pay creators with advertising revenue. It had prioritised revenue over reach.

By contrast, YouTube had prioritised reach over revenue. It wanted views. It eventually pulled the *Lazy Sunday* clip in February 2006, placing a short note on its blog stating: 'YouTube respects the rights of copyright holders.' Copyright owners complained that YouTube was slow to take down offending videos, by which point users might have moved on from a sketch show to homegrown content. YouTube tended not to investigate where its content came from until someone complained. YouTube was not taking ads, but its content was highly watchable. In its two months online, *Lazy Sunday* was viewed seven million times.

Viacom, the conglomerate which owned *NBC* and *Nickelodeon*, later sued YouTube, alleging massive copyright piracy was integral to its business. In the deposition, Viacom complained:

'Some entities, rather than taking the lawful path of building businesses that respect intellectual property rights on the Internet, have sought their fortunes by brazenly exploiting the infringing potential of digital technology. YouTube is one such entity.'

Viacom claimed that *Lazy Sunday* was just one of at least 150,000 unauthorised clips of copyrighted programming – viewed 1.5 billion times – that had been shown on YouTube. However, Viacom protested that was only a tiny fraction of the copyright-infringing material on the site, because 'YouTube prevents copyright owners from finding on the YouTube site all of the infringing works from which YouTube profits.' The lawsuit was settled.

Josh Felser, a co-founder of Grouper, later reflected: 'YouTube exploded on the backs of *Saturday Night Live*'s *Lazy Sunday* clip and a ton of "illegally" shared copyrighted content.' Revver's Clarke said: 'A lot of YouTube's early growth was due to content they were distributing without the permission of the copyright holders... If the game is building a website that is solely focused on letting people upload and share video, then YouTube pretty much was winning that game out of the gate.'

As well as its relaxed attitude to copyright, YouTube had other advantages. It was fast and clean. While contemporary competitors could sometimes struggle under the weight of overwrought design, YouTube was slick. Load up the homepage back in 2005 and just like today, a viewer was thrown headlong into the stream of content, with thumbnails of five recently viewed videos presented horizontally and a smattering of featured videos beneath. The idea was obvious: let's get watching – and quickly.

At the time, YouTube was mostly hosting a mishmash of ripped-off TV clips, occasional animation and lo-fi home movies. Although the quality was often poor, it could also be strangely appealing. For the first time, viewers could find an ocean of alternative videos unmediated by television executives. Some were compelling, especially when it was a vlogger speaking directly into the camera, sharing their life. One such early creator was an American girl broadcasting from her bedroom. Uploading her first video to YouTube on 16 June 2006, Bree Avery called herself *lonelygirl15* and explained she was a 16-year-old who was being home-schooled. She would complain about her parents grounding her, how she had to do homework during summer holidays, and how she found out her friend Daniel had a crush on her. All the while she explained how much she loved YouTube and discussed her favourite creators. Her tell-all approach to her audience captivated viewers. Fans would find her MySpace page and send her messages. She would respond. YouTube wasn't just showing reality TV of real people's lives. It was allowing viewers to interact with the real people they were watching.

Another early star in summer 2006 was Michael Buckley, a camp 30-year-old administrative assistant from Connecticut.

He just wanted to post some clips of him presenting so that he could get a job in television. Instead he began to make a name for himself in the small world of YouTube, becoming one of its first true stars alongside actor Lucas Cruikshank, whose voice was digitally manipulated to become the character Fred Figglehorn, a six-year-old with anger management issues.

Buckley's vlog, *WhatTheBuck?*, took an acerbic sideways slant on celebrity news. His show featured Paris Hilton's latest antics, Britney Spears's public breakdown and American footballer Michael Vick's arrest on charges of illegal dog fighting. Buckley's persona was 'a bitchy, rambling pop culture expert talking head' and his quickfire wit and putdowns perfectly fitted the grubby, anarchic medium. He would stand in front of a green screen, passing sly comments as grainy photographs of actors and pop stars appeared over his shoulder then disappeared. Buckley claims he was among the first YouTubers to ask for likes and comments from his fans: 'I made opening credits that said: "Rate it even if you hate it" and the next week everyone was asking for likes and comments.'

At the time, audiences were still relatively small. There was, however, a real feeling of community among the creators. Buckley recalled: 'YouTube in 2006 was people just uploading videos of their pets or very weird comedic sketches they'd shoot with themselves. There was no high quality content. But there were very high, very personal interactions within the community because there were so few of us. We'd go to a YouTube event and there were 10, 20 of us. We were all on a first name basis.'

Such direct-to-camera confessionals and commentary won viewers galore. Within 18 months of launch, YouTube had become a phenomenon. Its traffic quadrupled between January and July 2006, when it broke into the top 50 most-visited websites, with 16 million visitors. Jack Flanagan, an analyst for Comscore, which provided the figures, forecast that advertising dollars would move online 'where consumers can be targeted with efficiency.'

By September 2006, *Smosh*'s subscriber numbers had rocketed to 17,500, making it the fourth most popular channel on the site. Audiences for each individual video were still small. But the potential was vast. YouTube was outclassing its rivals. Metacafe had struggled to fund its producer rewards programme where it gave creators $5 for every 1,000 US views above 20,000. Others moved into niches, such as Vimeo, which hosted high-quality videos by musicians and film-makers.

By now Google Inc, the star performer in California's Silicon Valley, was experiencing exponential growth. Google had floated some of its shares in an Initial Public Offering in 2004, valuing it at $23 billion. With its three-month headstart on YouTube and the backing of its wealthy parent, Google Video should have won the online video war. But some of its content was dull compared to YouTube. Google employees uploaded staid lectures to Google Video, while YouTube hosted viral sensations. Google was deft with data, but less so with visual entertainment.

From its headquarters in a single room above a Japanese restaurant and pizza parlour in San Mateo, YouTube was going from strength to strength. Finally, it started to monetise its fast-growing audience. In September 2006, following much smaller deals involving other firms, it partnered with Cingular Wireless, then America's biggest mobile phone network, to launch a search for unsigned bands. As YouTube's co-founders sat on red beanbags at its HQ in October 2006, they struggled to field calls from media around the world asking them to explain the secret of their success. (Karim often wasn't there: he was studying for a master's degree at nearby Stanford University.)

Google decided that instead of trying to beat the competition, it would buy it and acquired YouTube for $1.65 billion in October 2006. Contemporary reports estimated the deal netted Hurley, Chen and Karim between $100 million and $200 million each, while Sequoia Capital made an unspecified amount.

Every day YouTube was seeing 100 million video views daily and 65,000 new videos uploaded. Even so, Wall Street analysts were sceptical about the acquisition. Josh Martin, a research analyst for Yankee Group Research, said: 'It was a bad business decision for Google.' American investor and entrepreneur Mark Cuban called the purchase 'crazy'.

It was actually a bargain. Today, YouTube is estimated to be worth $140 billion.

When Google ploughed its cash into YouTube, the competition shrivelled. Google started expanding the platform. In June 2007, YouTube went global, setting up national versions of the site in Brazil, France, Italy, Japan, the Netherlands, Poland, Spain, Ireland and the UK.

Google also explored a sustainable commercial future for the platform based on advertising. It meticulously A/B tested ad formats to ensure they did not alienate viewers. Then in August 2007 the first adverts from 1,000 official partners, including BMW and *The Simpsons Movie*, rolled out across the site. Lasting around 10 seconds, an advert popped up translucently on the bottom fifth of a video, normally 15 seconds after the video started. Learning from Revver's approach, Google also gave more than half of the proceeds to videomakers. The money began flowing into creators' accounts. For the first time, becoming a full-time YouTuber became a realistic job option.

5.

GRACE HELBIG
AND THE FIRST STARS
OF VLOGGING

Sharing advertising revenue attracted businesses to YouTube. Among them were multi-channel networks (MCN), a cross between a talent agency, manager and PR firm. One MCN, *MyDamnChannel*, had its own web presence that hosted videos away from YouTube. And in April 2008, it signed up one of the platform's most endearing personalities, Grace Helbig.

Helbig is perhaps the closest thing you can get to YouTube royalty. She uploaded her first videos in 2007 to fill in time as she house-sat for a friend in South Orange, New Jersey. She quickly became popular, her girl-next-door persona appealing to male viewers and her big sisterly advice and quirky humour attracting women. Helbig would embrace her quirks and heroically fail: she had an occasional series of videos in which she cooked poorly and another where she commented on red carpet fashion. Like many of the early forays by now-big YouTubers, her first online videos were amateurish compared to the glossy, confident presentations she would film later. But they all contained the germ of her awkward comedy of embarrassment. Helbig liked to describe herself as 'the internet's awkward older sister'.

After signing with *MyDamnChannel*, Helbig's YouTube videos teased extra content at *MyDamnChannel*. The theory was that those teasers would act as ads for a presence off YouTube that would be wholly controlled by *MyDamnChannel*. Helbig's first video for *MyDamnChannel* was about champagne and toast – emblematic of Helbig's personality, mixing the high and the low. Fast-paced and interspersed with quick cuts and enough swearing for a whole series of *The Sopranos*, Helbig kept to a relatively strict upload regimen: every Monday, she would post videos of her out and about, often at events. On Tuesdays, she'd react to user comments; Wednesdays she would review an odd product; and Thursdays were devoted to how-to videos. Friday was re-branded 'sexy Friday': talking about love and relationships. Each was a way to promote Helbig's presence off YouTube. Over five and a half years, she uploaded more than 1,500 videos between YouTube and *MyDamnChannel*. In return, she received a salary from *MyDamnChannel*. Being a YouTuber, which had started as a lark, was now her full-time job.

Likewise, Michael Buckley started to realise that he could make a living from the platform. Instead of just putting up a few clips, Buckley found himself increasingly busy, juggling his day job at the music promoter Live Nation with shooting, editing and uploading his videos. 'I had a 40-hour-a-week job and I was still spending every waking hour writing and editing and just promoting, really working on building it,' he explained. 'It was a lot of work but it was fun and I didn't know where it was going to lead, but I just saw a great potential.'

Slowly, his carefree attitude to mocking stars gained him success, views and ultimately a share of Google's advertising revenue. By September 2008, Buckley was earning more than $100,000 a year from YouTube for his videos. That might not seem like much a decade later when YouTubers bring in $20 million a year, but back then it was astronomical – not least at a time when traditionally 'safe' jobs were being uprooted by the emerging financial crisis. That month, aged 33, Buckley took the plunge: he gave up his job to become a full-time YouTuber. He felt vindicated. He was astounded. Instead of finding a job as a presenter on someone's else TV channel, he had started his own.

Talking down a crackling phone line in a traffic jam after celebrating a holiday weekend with his parents on Cape Cod, Massachusetts, Buckley, now 43, recalls: 'You start making money on it and think you've tricked the world. How did this happen? I was doing this for fun, and for free, and now I have thousands of dollars in my AdSense account. This is crazy! It's nutty.'

Buckley began exploiting a new form of monetisation in addition to Google ad revenue: direct sponsorship deals. He began shooting videos promoting Pepsi. 'Back in the day there was only a few of us doing sponsored content. Companies would throw you a lot of money to do sponsored content. Now everybody on Instagram and Twitter is monetising their following. It was just such a different time. You see sponsored content all day everywhere. We'd do a couple of sponsored videos and people would say: "What's this?" People are much more receptive and not irritated by the sponsored content anymore.'

With traffic soaring month after month and year after year, YouTubers began to appreciate that they needed to hire professional production staff. For many the realisation came as quite a surprise. Even in 2011, the American author John Green thought the idea was preposterous. By then, Green and his brother Hank (the Vlogbrothers) had set up VidCon, a YouTube industry conference that was later acquired by the American media firm Viacom for an undisclosed amount. (That YouTube can sustain a multi-day industry conference, attended by tens of thousands of people every year which has been held in Anaheim, Amsterdam, London and Melbourne, shows just how much the site has changed.) At its second conference in 2011, Green was listening to two major YouTubers – Philip DeFranco and Freddie Wong – talk about hiring people to help with video production, which at the time was considered 'a crazy idea', John Green says.

Back then, Green thought of YouTube and online video as something done in your basement in your spare time. It was a solitary lifestyle, a one-man creative enterprise. Yet he and Hank were starting to get frustrated by the barriers they came up against. They wanted to include animations in their videos, but didn't have the skills themselves. They wanted to increase the pace of output, but couldn't fact-check or write scripts quickly enough. 'I remember listening to Phil talk about that process, going from one person to two and how it's a big leap,' says Green. When he got home, Green posted an advert on the website Craigslist, where people can find casual workers. One of the respondents to Green was Stan Muller. He joined Green as his first employee, and with the Green brothers co-founded Crash Course, an educational YouTube channel.

'Without him the whole educational video side of our company wouldn't exist, which is the vast majority of the content we make now,' recalls Green. 'That's the thing that really sticks out for me: thinking and hearing those guys talk about how they went from one to two and what becomes possible when you make that leap.'

YouTubers started hiring large teams, including video-graphers, editors, managers and agents to intercede between viewers and creators. At the same time, the talent pool ballooned. Hank Green says: 'In the very early days, [YouTube] was a lot of people doing kind of the same thing, and we had very similar styles and budgets, very similar audiences. Now there is such a huge diversity of kinds of content, kinds of people, kinds of audiences – whether that's four-year-olds or 65-year-olds. Now, you can't know everyone who is making YouTube content. It's too big.'

Green will wander the corridors of VidCon and not know if creators have two million or 20,000 subscribers. 'In a way that doesn't matter as much anymore because there are interesting things being done at all levels,' he says. 'I love that it's gone from being: "YouTube is a genre of video" to "YouTube is an entire new media that has hundreds of genres on it".'

Since that second VidCon back in 2011, YouTube has become a truly global spectacle.

6.

FROM RUSSIA

TO LATIN AMERICA:

YOUTUBE GOES GLOBAL

On the wall of Martin Dominguez's office is a blackboard, two metres wide by one-and-a-half metres tall. Dotted on it are multi-coloured Post-it notes showing his company's different projects, divided into business, administration, development (split into ongoing and to-do projects), pre-production, shooting, post-production, and distribution.

'It keeps me organised, more than anything,' explains Dominguez, a producer at one of the biggest Spanish-language YouTube channels, *Enchufe.tv*. 'As overwhelming as it might seem, it's less overwhelming than not having a physical manifestation in my office.' The board demonstrates the scale and scope of the endeavour he and his colleagues are undertaking – while the YouTube channel, which boasts 20 million subscribers from across the globe, demonstrates just how multinational YouTube is.

Enchufe now employs 20 people in grand offices in a converted mansion on the sweeping outskirts of Ecuador's capital, Quito. What was once an opulent place to live is now a bustling creative hub. In its basement are the editing and recording suites. The wall of the ground-floor reception is full of awards. Upstairs are meeting rooms.

The channel was founded in 2011 by a group of Ecuadorean film students. For their final year project at film school, Dominguez and his friends made a comedy pilot. They hawked it around TV companies but had no luck. The sheer number of layers in the TV bureaucracy meant that they couldn't convince every executive they'd need to in order to make it to the TV screens of the general public. Stung by rejection and frustrated by the standard of television in Latin America, Dominguez and his friends considered another path: YouTube. Spanish-language comedy channels were few and far between. So they did what many other creators have done before them: they started a new channel.

They weren't alone. In 2011, 60% of YouTube's views came from non-English language users. Taking inspiration from American online comedy video series *College Humor*, Dominguez and three friends formed a sketch comedy troupe called *Enchufe* (*little plug* in Spanish). Their first video, *El peor casting* (*the worst casting*), outlined the odd circumstances that surround casting for TV and movies. Dominguez pressed the upload button on a bank holiday weekend. 'My index finger had the sum of all hopes in it,' he says. The video racked up 600 views in a few weeks. At the time that was healthy but not outstanding. But it didn't matter to the film-makers. When had 600 people ever turned up to their university screenings? The video eventually broke 1,000 views.

Enchufe kept uploading new ones. One based around a popular festival in Ecuador where participants carouse while dousing each other with water, *Carnaval*, mimicked the first-person shooting games popular at the time and did even better. *Carnaval* has now been seen by more than nine million people and *Enchufe* is among the top 100 most subscribed channels on YouTube. A majority stake in the company behind *Enchufe* was bought by Spanish MCN-turned-digital media group 2btube in late 2018, with a source close to the negotiations telling me the deal valued *Enchufe* at between $5 million and $10 million. But unless you speak Spanish, you've probably never heard of *Enchufe*. You've also probably never heard of *El Rubius* – even though the Spanish-Norwegian YouTuber, also known as Rubén Doblas Gundersen, has 34 million subscribers.

Indeed, YouTube is widely popular across Europe. A March 2017 survey by ComRes asked adolescents aged between 14 and 18 about their wider social media usage. Some 91% of British 14-18-year-olds checked YouTube more than once a week, but the numbers in other European countries were even higher – 93% in France and 95% or more in Germany, Italy, Poland and Sweden. Mainland Europe can't get enough of YouTube. In 2018, YouTube video views tracked by Tubular Insights, a YouTube analyst, increased by 17% in the UK. They increased by 25% in Spain; 32% in Italy; and 23% in Germany.

Around 100 localised translations of the site display YouTube in the home language of 95% of the internet's users and Google sends paychecks from ad revenue to around 90 countries. It's difficult to quantify exactly how big YouTube's non-English language audience is because Google is notoriously coy about sharing any useful data. But stats from another third-party YouTube database compiled by Paladin, analysed for the first time for this book, show that only three in 10 YouTube channels are based in English-speaking countries. And around a third of YouTubers based in the United States and United Kingdom broadcast in a language other than English.

Creators from the populous, fast-growing BRIC (Brazil, Russia, India and China) nations tend to figure most prominently in any roundup of YouTube's biggest names worldwide. (For this book, Tubular Insights analysed all non-English language videos uploaded in 2018 that attracted more than 10,000 views: one fifth of total views came from Brazil and Russia.)

Take Konrad Cunha Dantas, a 30-year-old music video director in São Paulo, Brazil, who first picked up cinematography when his mother died when he was 18. With the life insurance payout he bought a Canon EOS 5D camera and started directing slick music videos full of private planes, suitcases of cash and impossibly beautiful women. Not much has changed, except the videos are even higher budget and sun-splashed. Posting under the username Kondzilla, Cunha Dantas has the eighth most subscribed YouTube channel in the world, and the sixth most viewed, with more than 23 billion views in seven years. Every month, Kondzilla adds another 600 or 700 million views to his total count. He is surging towards 30 billion views.

A near neighbour of Kondzilla in São Paulo is Whindersson Nunes Batista, with whom he battles for supremacy in the Portuguese language stakes. Nunes Batista wanted to be a YouTuber from the age of 15. Now 24, his comedy sketches are seen by 35 million subscribers. He averages 1.35 million views a day. As well as Kondzilla and Nunes Batista, two brothers – Felipe and Luccas Neto – have 55 million subscribers between them. Felipe, the oldest by three years, founded *Paramaker*, a multi-channel network that has helped legitimize online video in Brazil and South America. He also uploads videos breathlessly talking about shocking, absurd news headlines, testing out wacky inventions and testing what happens if you hold a blow torch to various household items. The breadth of his content choice is typified by his ever-changing shock of blue, green or rainbow-coloured hair.

India's YouTube community is dominated by corporate-run channels such as *T-Series*, run by an eponymous Indian movie and music production company, and *SET India*, the online presence of Sony Entertainment Television, a traditional TV network broadcasting movies and TV shows in Hindi. But it's *T-Series*, which posts vibrant, colourful clips of popular pop songs performed in riotous Bollywood movies, which rules supreme in India – and across YouTube globally, vying with PewDiePie for the title of the world's most subscribed channel.

Like *Smosh*, whose founders were drawn to YouTube when they tried to take down pirated copies of their videos, T-Series also first approached YouTube in anger. The company, which was founded in 1984, filed an injunction similar to Viacom's against YouTube in the Delhi High Court in 2010. In the three years YouTube had been in India, it had been littered with illegally uploaded clips from T-Series' productions. While the court granted T-Series an injunction, the entertainment producer saw an opportunity. 'Through a common friend we engaged with YouTube, and by the third or fourth quarter of

2010 we were executing a licensing agreement,' explains Neeraj Kalyan, president of T-Series.

In 2014, *T-Series* was just one of 16 channels to cross the million subscriber mark (there are now more than 300 million-plus channels in India alone). It is now adding millions to its 90 million subscribers every month – benefiting from the drop in the cost of internet data due to the launch of Jio, a 4G phone network that has expanded into broadband access. *T-Series* uploaded 1,335 videos in 2018 – more than three a day. Its impact is out-sized: it uploaded only 0.05% of all videos in India but they accounted for nearly a quarter of the 648 billion YouTube views recorded in the country by Tubular Insights last year.

Not everyone is a fan of *T-Series*, as we'll learn in a subsequent chapter. However, individual creators still hold significant sway in the world's second most populous country. Amit Bhadana, for instance, is a household name across India, with 14 million subscribers enjoying his wry take on India's societal foibles. A Bhadana video which receives less than 10 million views in a week has underperformed.

In Russia, *FROST* plays video games for his eight million subscribers. He sits on an elite gaming chair in front of Spongebob Squarepants stuffed toys or on a chintzy white leather sofa surrounded by potted plants. His antics include retch-inducing cocktail tastings on an ironing board and gladiatorial battles with giant cotton buds on a frozen lake.

The queen of Russian YouTube is an American-based, Russian-speaking toddler called Nastya, whose two channels (which switch between Russian and English) have a combined 32 million subscribers. Cameras follow Nastya as she does fun activities or performs skits where she plays her dad at cards or ten-pin bowling. There are over-the-top reactions like silent films, all of which play out over a jaunty musical background, full of odd sound effects and *Batman*-esque graphic overlays. The idea is a simple one: to induce envy, and to provide bright, oversaturated, Technicolor content that stimulates the senses of children and keeps them coming back.

But YouTube is not everywhere. The site has become such a crucial way to distribute and disseminate information that it has fallen foul of strict censorship laws in totalitarian regimes. Iran and North Korea have made the site inaccessible except through technological workarounds such as virtual private networks (VPNs), which mask the origin of a web browser. Armenia, Afghanistan, Pakistan, Turkey and Syria have also blocked YouTube for prolonged periods in the recent past due to political sensitivities.

The site is a key platform for free speech in suppressive political regimes. Yuri Dud's long-form video interviews regularly reach millions of people in a week. The 32-year-old sports journalist with expressive eyes, who likes to style his hair in an ostentatious quiff, was born in Germany but has lived in Russia since he was four. He launched his YouTube channel in February 2017, at a time when Russian president Vladimir Putin was cracking down on independent television channels. It quickly grew and now interviews opposition politicians like Alexei Navalny and Mikhail Khodorkovsky, both of whom are outspoken critics of the Putin regime. In countries where the state controls much of the media, YouTube provides a lifeline for independent information like Dud's channel. And its reach is almost as great: 82% of Russians aged 18-44 watch YouTube – nearly the same proportion that watch *Channel One*, Russia's biggest TV channel.

Asia is important for YouTube, too, with its own personalities. Raking in the views by the millions is Hikakin, a 30-year-old YouTuber whose incredible beat-boxing skills went viral. Now, like Felipe Neto, he has parlayed his on-screen success into an off-screen business, founding one of Japan's biggest multi-channel networks. Western viewers watching his videos will notice the incredible amount of graphics, background music and on-screen captions that mark out Japanese television.

In South Korea, Jung Man-soo, better known as Banzz, is a popular face on YouTube. The 29-year-old eats inordinately large amounts of food on camera for people's entertainment. He is a mukbang star. It's an important role in South Korean society, where eating alone is seen as shameful. People like Banzz help people feel connected, but creating videos is hard work for the YouTuber. He often has to exercise 12 hours a day to work off the calories he ingests for viewers.

Characters like Hikakin and Banzz are just two of many in the YouTube ecosystem in Asia. While they may be at the more outlandish end, their existence is replicated over the world. There are western mukbang stars and Asian beauty vloggers and gamers who can bring throngs of fans to stores. In Asia, online video is booming like elsewhere in the world. The amount of time spent in the video players and editors and entertainment categories on mobile app stores has tripled since 2015, according to App Annie. In Europe, the rise is 2.7 times and in the Americas 2.4 times.

Australia's most popular YouTuber is Wengie, a 33-year-old Chinese national with 13.4 million subscribers, who moved to Australia as a child. She's an all-encompassing entertainer, focusing on the latest trends on YouTube, presenting them in bright, Crayola-esque colour, surrounded by succulents and unicorns, looking like a cartoon character. She's previously posted beauty vlogs, pranks and DIY life hacks (such as making crafts for going back to school). In 2019 though, she's slavishly following the trend, making a slew of slime videos and making ASMR (autonomous sensory meridian response) videos, whispering into a microphone while eating popping candy.

The country she left, China, is YouTube's biggest black hole. Pick out a couple of hundred people in the UK, US or elsewhere, and you'll find at least one YouTuber. According to Paladin, China is the country with the lowest proportion of YouTubers in its population. The site is technically banned in the People's Republic, although the internet monitoring firm Alexa estimates that around 4% of visitors worldwide still come from China, making it the 12th most popular website in the country.

'YouTube is part of Google and Google decided to stay away from China seven or eight years ago,' explains Chris Dong, research director and China expert at research agency IDC. The Chinese government asked Google to censor its search results in order to filter out results that portrayed the Communist ruling party in a bad light, or could be used to foment discontent. Google at the time refused to do so (though now, in 2019, Google employees are worried that the company is secretly developing a censored search engine for the country).

But even if Google had decided to play ball with the Chinese government's demands for censorship, it's still unlikely that YouTube would be as dominant as it is in many western nations. For YouTube, Hulu, Netflix and other online media companies, there's a big reason they can't do business in China.

'Online video is one part of online content distribution – it's a publishing business,' says Dong. Foreign-owned companies are all but prohibited from running such businesses in the one-party state, which controls public discourse, in the goal of preserving social stability, national security, and protecting Chinese culture. 'People call it censorship,' he says, 'the government call it content review.'

But just because China doesn't have YouTube, don't think it doesn't have online video stars. Far from it. Instead, China has three big home-grown versions of the site: Youku Tudou, Tencent Video and iQiyi. All three differ little from YouTube. Outwardly, they may look a little different, with colourful, garish designs compared to YouTube's clean, minimalistic layout. But click onto one of the videos and the platform is fundamentally similar to YouTube.

Even without understanding Mandarin, westerners would still be able to fumble their way around the three major video websites without much difficulty: on all three there's a front page with an almost endless scroll of videos, broken down into themed subsections. Once you click on an individual video, there's a large video player with play and pause and volume controls on the bottom left, and subtitle and caption options on the right, while to the right of the video player is a beloved standard of YouTube: the autoplay queue (which, although it seems like a staple of the site, only came to YouTube in 2015). Some other aspects will make western viewers feel right at home: autoplaying video adverts for KFC.

The comparisons aren't just superficial, either: what's broadly popular in one country tends – with few exceptions – to be popular elsewhere. On China's video sharing websites are the same mix of clipped-up mainstream television shows, personal tell-all vlogs and street-shot prank videos as found on YouTube. The formula is the same; just the packaging and language is different. Humans are mostly interested in watching the same things: personality, games, pop music, sport, entertainment and humour.

PART II

ENGINE ROOM:

HOW YOUTUBE WORKS

7.

THE ALGORITHM:
YOUTUBE'S SECRET FORMULA

YouTube's best-known star is PewDiePie, a skinny, fast-talking Swede with an apparent attention deficit disorder. Real name Felix Arvid Ulf Kjellberg, PewDiePie is a quicksilver presence on YouTube; always mutating, with an endlessly changing array of videos which he hopes will go viral and push him ever higher in the rankings. He made his name commenting on video games, but now he does songs (one, *Bitch Lasagna*, has proved oddly popular), social media memes, and book reviews.

Watching his daily uploads is like flicking through TV channels at hyperspeed. One minute you'll see him commenting on the latest YouTube beef, the next reacting to hilarious compilations on TikTok, a short-form video sharing app. At other times he will stand in front of a microphone and watch funny videos while trying not to laugh, or interact with multiple virtual reality versions of himself in a video game.

PewDiePie's background in the teenage-rich arena of gaming, his constant evolutions and fast-paced videos tell us something about what works on the platform. A rebellion of his, too, threw light on a secretive but crucial aspect of YouTube's success as a platform. In December 2016, PewDiePie posted a video in which he told viewers: 'YouTube is trying to kill my channel'. He complained that YouTube was unsubscribing his followers, not sending videos to those who remained, and directing his subscribers to 'recommended content' ('random-ass videos you don't give a shit about') rather than his videos. It meant YouTube was being clogged up with 'click-bait' and, according to PewDie-Pie, YouTube 'won't explain what happened properly to anyone; it's not just me, a lot of YouTubers are noting it.'

As gentle piano music started playing, PewDiePie warned darkly:

'This is all a conspiracy. YouTube wants to kill my channel. It's because I'm always complaining to them. I don't have family-friendly content. I click-bait too much, huh? Is that it? It all makes sense...'

In short, he was complaining about YouTube's algorithm. YouTube's algorithm is its secret formula – the equivalent of KFC's blend of 13 herbs and spices and Coca-Cola's recipe. Algorithms are sets of rules that are followed by cold, hard computer logic. They are designed by human computer engineers, usually with commercial profit in mind. But they are then programmed into and run automatically by computers, which come up with recommendations. From the nagging adverts that chase consumers around the internet to Instagram serving up the most envy-inducing photographs of our friends flaunting their toned bodies on beaches, such decisions shape our lives.

YouTube's algorithm determines what is presented for your viewing pleasure when you load up the front page of the website. Google Brain, an artificial intelligence research team within the company, powers those recommendations, based on people's prior viewing. The system is very smart, accounting for variations in the way people watch their videos.

It is also, like many aspects of Google, notoriously opaque. Though occasionally the curtain is lifted a little, as it was in 2016 in a paper by three Google employees. They revealed the deep neural networks behind YouTube's recommended videos. Deep neural networks rifle through every video we've previously watched, alongside information described as 'the user's YouTube activity history' which includes our YouTube search history, where we live, our gender, and on what kind of device we're watching. It then uses that information to select a few hundred videos we might like to view from the billions on the site, which are then winnowed down to dozens.

Each video is assigned a score based on how closely the video's characteristics match those thrown up by the viewer's watch history. Think of it like a Venn diagram: YouTube categorises each video and does the same for the end user. Those videos that most closely overlap with the user are then presented – ranked by their score.

Though YouTube's recommendation system is constantly evolving, the same basic principles apply today. One day, I was sat on my couch watching 10-minute-plus vlogs about Video-Days, a German YouTube conference-cum-concert where creators perform in front of tens of thousands of fans. The next time

I returned to the home screen, YouTube suggested I watch two American college students trying to say some German tongue twisters. The algorithm guessed I liked the German content in the first video, so suggested 10-minute long videos on German tongue twisters. Had I been on my mobile phone, it would probably have suggested shorter, snackable videos.

It worked: I sat through the German tongue twister video, then another one on the 10 hardest German words to pronounce, recommended by the algorithm. I'd been hooked. I'm not alone. In the three years since Google Brain began making smart recommendations, watch time from the YouTube homepage has grown 20-fold. More than 70% of the time people spend watching videos on YouTube, they spend watching videos suggested by Google Brain.

This suits Google: it doesn't want viewers to stay in their silos and watch only one or two creators. There are plenty of others they could watch. The more videos that are watched, the more adverts that are seen, and the more money Google makes. YouTube wants to inflate its bank balance by not just serving up the things you want to see, but things you might want to see. As well as helping people find what they are looking for, Jim McFadden, YouTube's technical lead for recommendations, told tech site The Verge: 'We also wanted to serve the needs of people when they didn't necessarily know what they wanted to look for.'

More than 200 million videos a day are recommended through YouTube's homepage – plus hundreds of millions more via 'Up next' autoplay boxes which start automatically after one video has finished.

But, as we've come to learn with YouTube, what seems like a sensible decision to the algorithm can be a terrible misstep to a human. And it can all go hideously wrong. In February 2015, YouTube in the United States launched a child-centric version, YouTube Kids, an app whose group manager Shimrit Ben-Yair described as 'the first Google product built from the ground up with the little ones in mind.' Ostensibly, YouTube Kids was a way to ensure that children could find videos without being able to accidentally click onto other, less family-friendly content. It also increased child viewing figures, which might be seen as a second motivation for its introduction. Even so, unofficial videos of trademarked characters accidentally showed up in YouTube Kids' 'Now playing' feeds. Using cheap, widely available technology, animators created original video content featuring some of Hollywood's best-loved characters. And whereas an official Disney Mickey Mouse would never swear or act violently, in these videos Mickey and other children's characters can do whatever they want. And often what they do is disturbing: sexual or violent. Generally speaking, the people creating these videos aren't trying to wean children off the official, sanitised, friendly content: they are making content that they find funny for fellow adults. They don't necessarily want their adult content to be served to children. But unlike adults who can distinguish between parody and mischief and the real thing, the algorithm can't yet tell the difference between the X-rated pastiche and the legitimate content.

It's not a problem that has been fixed. Nearly two years after 'Elsagate', as the issue with unsuitable content was dubbed, the problem still persists. In 2019, researchers at Cyprus University of Technology analysed 130,000 videos targeted at toddlers aged between one and five featuring characters popular with kids. They also tracked how YouTube recommended subsequent videos – and found that there's a 45% chance of a child coming across inappropriate footage within 10 clicks of a child-friendly video. They found children stand a one-in-20 chance of being recommended problematic videos after watching any video.

That's particularly concerning because of data analysed for this book by The Insights People, who survey 20,000 children and their parents about their media usage. Just four in 10 parents always monitor their child's YouTube usage – and one in 20 children aged 4-12 say their parents never check what they're watching.

Unsavoury content is a problem that YouTube has been slow to acknowledge – and even slower to deal with. For years it has placed its trust in the algorithm to select the site's best videos for users. In almost exclusively outsourcing to computers, rather than humans, what thrives and what barely survives on the site (though it does have a team of moderators, as we will see in the next chapter) YouTube has alienated creators. 'It's a point of frustration,' explains Matt Gielen of Little Monster Media Co, a video agency that tracks audience development on YouTube and Facebook. He says that uploading videos to YouTube is like being a manufacturer of widgets when the regulations governing their production are vague and when every aspect of the widget supply chain is totally variable. The widget producer doesn't know whether the roads they use to deliver their widgets are going to be open, or whether tolls will be charged for using them; and retailers can stop selling widgets altogether when they feel like it – while refusing to reply to your emails. YouTubers, he says, are 'trying to run a business on something that is essentially quicksand' – and it's all down to the dominance of the algorithm, seemingly above and beyond all human common sense.

While opinion among the creator community is split as to whether YouTube's algorithm is a convenient excuse or a genuine bad actor, it is the source of deep anxiety among many creators. Some feel that it encourages people to create the same type of content in the hope of replicating the same viral successes that shot them up the YouTube career ladder.

'The way the website values its metrics can definitely have an impact on the kinds of content that needs to be made to get popular,' explains Charlie McDonnell, a British YouTuber, now based in Canada, who has been uploading to the site since 2007 under the username Charlieissocoollike. 'It also results in a homogenisation of content as well. Maybe people are worried about taking risks as much and so a lot of the content feels quite similar.'

In his rebellious video in 2016, PewDiePie darkly suggested that YouTube wanted someone else on top – 'someone extremely cancerous, like [rapper and comedian] Lilly Singh.' He went on: 'I'm white – can I make that comment? But I do think that's a problem.' (It may not have been a throwaway line: PewDiePie has since been criticised for recommending a channel promoting white supremacist theories.)

He threatened to delete his channel when it hit 50 million subscribers. He was 200,000 subscribers short when he made his stand. That he felt able to make it spoke to the strength of his position.

But others are comparatively powerless to speak out. In their early years, Google's advertising income may be the only return YouTubers get from their hard work — and that is controlled by

Google which can 'demonetise' videos, as it did with the offending videos in Elsagate.

However, once a creator has established an audience large enough, for long enough, brands start paying them to promote their products in videos. At that stage, the crude number of views don't matter quite so much, because the proportion of money coming to a creator from ad money becomes minimal. Instead the creator transcends the platform. At that point the power balance shifts: a YouTuber is no longer a cog in the YouTube machine. They are a name in their own stead, able to independently produce revenue-generating adverts off the platform, in the mass media or on rival social media outlets.

After PewDiePie's outburst, he tweeted: 'YouTube has responded and are digging into the issues.' Whether or not YouTube changed its algorithm (it said it hadn't), PewDewPie didn't carry out his threat to delete his channel. At the time of writing, he has reached a staggering 90 million subscribers.

However, he's up against tough competition – India's *T-Series* is matching PewDiePie subscriber for subscriber. The battle between the two for supremacy at the top of the YouTube hierarchy is a microcosm of the battle for YouTube as it becomes more like the media it's trying to replace.

YouTube viewers who have grown up with PewDiePie in the nine years he's been posting on YouTube see him as the last bastion of the independent, 'broadcast yourself' platform that they grew up with. In *T-Series* – a big company in a vast country of eager, new internet consumers – they see the enemy. *T-Series* represents the shunting aside of creativity by cold, hard commerce. If PewDiePie loses his mantle to *T-Series*, his fans reckon, then the future of YouTube is lost to listless companies churning out content.

Certainly, *T-Series'* output is prodigious: it feeds the algorithm with regular, high-quality content. And it's been richly rewarded: on 1 January 2018, *T-Series* had 31 million subscribers, compared to PewDiePie's 58 million. A year to the day later, they were almost equal. That has some viewers up in arms. 'We are not the evil side of YouTube,' says Neeraj Kalyan, T-Series' president. Indeed, Kalyan sees little difference between his company – which has eight staff solely dedicated to uploading and optimising the content for T-Series' social media channels – and established creators. He says: 'If you look at any of your YouTubers who are really big, they have a staff of people who will shoot, who will edit, who will do some backgrounding or animation.'

PewDiePie's protest against the algorithm, it turned out, was misguided. YouTube wasn't trying to replace him with Lilly Singh. *T-Series* was waiting in the wings. But his outburst did show creators' genuine concern at the impact of YouTube's power to arbitrarily change its algorithm without consulting them.

Almost all video-makers take out their frustration on YouTube's algorithm in volleys of tweets and videos, some of which don't surface because – of course – the algorithm hates them. Then one sunny day in April 2018, one person took her anger into the physical world.

At 1.38am on 3 April 2018, two police officers pulled up to a parked car at a Walmart in Mountain View, California. The video, shot from the officers' body-worn camera, shows a woman asleep in the car. Nasim Aghdam, a 38-year-old Iranian, had emigrated to the United States in her late teens. Though she wasn't well known to the officers, she had a small but dedicated following online in Iran as Green Nasim, a

YouTube star known for her vegan activism and rants against western society – both of which played well back home in Iran. She was not arrested.

Ten hours later and 25 miles away, Aghdam walked through the door of a garage with a Smith & Wesson nine millimetre semi-automatic handgun and began firing at employees sat outdoors in a section of the YouTube campus eating lunch. She hit three of them with bullets, wounding them, before turning the gun on herself.

Media reports initially suggested that Aghdam had attacked the YouTube campus in revenge for being scorned by a past lover. But quickly, the real motive became apparent: she was venting her frustration at YouTube's algorithm. 'I'm being discriminated and filtered on YouTube and I'm not the only one,' she claimed in a YouTube video posted in January 2018 that was quickly taken offline when she was identified as the perpetrator of the attack. Her particular complaint that day was around a workout video of hers showing how to tone your abs – 'a video that has nothing bad in it.'

Almost a year later, in January 2019, YouTube said it had made hundreds of tweaks to the algorithm to improve the standard of videos recommended to users. It also said it would train its algorithm not to promote 'borderline' content that skirts close to violating the site's rules about violence and conspiracies, and can often radicalise users. The change would affect less than 1% of videos on YouTube – probably about 10 million videos. And pay attention to the terminology: 'promote'. The content still lives on YouTube, just a simple search away.

Nasim Aghdam might have been the first to take her grudge with YouTube offline to the site's offices, but she wasn't the last.

In March 2019, 33-year-old Kyle Long stepped into his car in Waterville, Maine and set his satnav for Mountain View. After vandalising the bathroom of a gas station in Iowa, halfway through his 3,300-mile journey, Long told police officers he was making a trip to California to discuss why his YouTube channel had been shut down. If it didn't go well, he told officers, he couldn't be held accountable for his actions. Three miles from YouTube headquarters, police stopped Long and found three baseball bats in his car. He was arrested for making criminal threats. A few days later, the Santa Clara County District Attorney's Office decided not to charge him. A spokesman said: 'Mr Long's behaviour was disturbing but did not meet the elements of a chargeable crime.'

8.

POLICING THE PLATFORM: EXTREMISM AND THE ADPOCALYPSE

US President George HW Bush did not die of old age but was executed. So, too, was US Senator John McCain. US presidential challenger Hillary Clinton, meanwhile, died in 2016. Welcome to the alternative facts about American politics as presented by YouTuber David Zublick. Revealing President Bush's supposed execution, Zublick gave his viewers a stark fact: 'No one else is reporting this. We have it exclusively here on Truth Unsealed.' The *David Zublick Channel* has more than 150,000 subscribers.

Millions of people watch conspiracy theories on YouTube. Many revolve around key moments in US politics and suggest politicians are plotting against US President Donald Trump – part of a wider internet conspiracy called QAnon, which claims there is a deep state movement against him. Such far-fetched, nonsensical or untrue videos are not restricted to America: log on to YouTube and you will learn that 5G spreads cancer, that Jack the Ripper was a plot by the Freemasons, that China found a UFO in the Gobi Desert back in 2011 and is planning to invade Australia.

Conspiracy videos are tolerated, if no longer actively encouraged, by YouTube. But the platform has become more active recently in removing Islamic extremism, paedophile comments and other hateful content. This has followed pressure from advertisers, who have rebelled over the placement of their carefully nurtured brands against extreme and unpleasant messages.

YouTube polices its own platform through a team of 10,000 paid community moderators and automated monitoring of videos which it says represents the collective brainpower of another 180,000 people. Their job is to ensure that users follow community guidelines and policies about copyright, as well as overarching terms of service. The guidelines set out what kind of video is allowed and the rules on spam content, harassment and interactions. They outlaw pornography, graphic violence, hate speech and dangerous content that could be mimicked. YouTube also has strict rules on impersonation, harassment and bullying. Breach the community guidelines and a creator could find their content demonetised, deleted or – in extreme cases – their entire channel blocked. Fall foul of the guidelines once and a creator will get a slap on the wrist. Do it again and they receive a strike, which stops uploading for a week. Get three strikes and the channel is terminated.

The guidelines are constantly evolving as YouTube faces up to issues on its site raised by the media. But it seems to be reluctant to take down conspiracy theories, which it describes as 'borderline' content. Until recently, such conspiracy theories and extremist content were even promoted by YouTube's auto-play algorithm. Left unchecked, a viewer can rapidly spiral into a crazy menagerie of lunatic theories that lend legitimacy to far-right groups, fake news and alternative facts. People are sent ever deeper down into the rabbit hole, where the videos get curiouser and curiouser.

An hour-long documentary-style film by 18-year-old film-maker Dylan Avery, *Loose Change*, for instance, alleges that the attacks on America on 11 September 2001 were an inside job. Avery, now in his 30s, estimates that since it was uploaded to Google Video in 2005 and found its way onto YouTube in various re-cut and remastered forms, *Loose Change* has been seen at least 100 million times.

Conspiracy theories on YouTube often take the form of 'red pill' videos. 'Red pill' is a reference to a scene in the film *The Matrix* where a character sees things as they really are after taking a red pill. Adopted by the digital 'manosphere', where angry, often right-wing men congregate in odd sub-communities, it now defines what a man (supposedly) stands for: male supremacy, a fear of established authority, and a healthy dose of scepticism about the way of the world.

YouTube has become the major method of 'red pilling' online, according to those who self-identify as fascists, surveyed by open source online investigative website Bellingcat. Of 75 different people who say they have 'taken the red pill' thanks to information they found online, YouTube was the website most frequently cited as helping facilitate that transition to extreme beliefs.

A British father of two from Swindon, approaching his 40th birthday, Carl Benjamin, is sometimes mentioned by those who say they have been 'red pilled'. Better known as *Sargon of Akkad*, Benjamin has nearly 900,000 subscribers. Another video-maker is Alex Jones, who shared his views that a 'Jewish mafia' runs the world. He had more than 2.4 million subscribers before YouTube shut his channel in August 2018 for repeatedly violating its guidelines.

Such content may be seen as harmless entertainment, but anecdotal evidence suggests that some people radically change their view of society after viewing 'red pill' videos. One user who lost her relative to the dark side of YouTube tweeted: 'The change in his attitude was like switching the light from bright to dark.'

People have always held fringe or extreme views and indulged in conspiracy theories, such as over the assassination of US President John F Kennedy or the moon landings. Extremists have also always acted on their strange impulses after viewing propaganda. Take the case of David Copeland, a 22-year-old English neo-Nazi who wanted to incite a racial war in his home country. He detonated three nail bombs in London over successive weekends in 1999, killing three and injuring 140. When police raided his bedroom in Farnborough, Hampshire, they found a Nazi flag hanging over the head of his bed, racist and antisemitic books on his shelves, and a collage of news coverage of his bombings on the walls. While Copeland changed many lives, his wider impact was lessened by the fact he was a loner, and that his demeanour changed once he stepped outside his home.

All this happened six years before YouTube launched. Now imagine David Copeland had a camera in his bedroom, allowing him to broadcast to the world. Imagine that his message was being spread by the best artificial intelligence in the world, coded by the highest-paid, highest-performing programmers in the world. And imagine that like-minded people, also broadcasting hate-filled videos, were just a click away.

Social media has allowed such sowers of unreliable or hateful material to connect with previously isolated disgruntled individuals. Until recently, YouTube was vital viewing for jihadists, says Rita Katz of SITE Intelligence Group, a terrorism monitoring organisation based in Bethesda, Maryland. Over a 10-day period in 2017, Rita Katz analysed the number of URLs shared by one major ISIS-tied media agency. Of the 515 links shared over that period, 328 (or six in every 10) directed people to YouTube. A year later, however, Katz analysed the same group's links. Just 15 of 258 total links – or one in every 20 – were to YouTube.

'I was once the biggest critic of YouTube and publicly stated that it wasn't doing enough to prevent jihadists from using its platform,' Katz says. 'Eventually, though, YouTube made major efforts to keep the propaganda off of their platform.' She says that al-Qaeda and Isis now use Dailymotion, Vimeo and Dropbox more than YouTube to expound their views.

But extreme content still exists on the platform. Around 1,000 channels a month are removed from YouTube for 'promotion of violence and violent extremism', according to YouTube's own figures. Around 31,000 videos every month are taken down for being too violent or graphic – one in every 33 videos removed from YouTube.

In February 2017, British newspaper *The Times* uncovered that banner adverts for holiday resorts appeared on top of speeches from guerilla terrorists who swore allegiance to al-Shabaab, an east African terrorist collective. Massive brands including Mercedes-Benz, Honda and Verizon appeared on videos starring a rogues' gallery of neo-Nazis, Islamist terrorists and hate preachers. Pepsi, Walmart and Johnson & Johnson were among the multinational firms who pulled their advertising from YouTube until it cleaned up its act.

This was called the 'adpocalypse' because of the damage it did to the incomes of legitimate creators who were caught up in the widespread loss of ad revenue. Its withdrawal prompted many creators to think afresh about their future on the site, as we will see later.

Separate concerns about unsavoury content being presented to children through their favourite characters came to a head in 2017. 'Elsagate' – named after Elsa, the star of Disney's animated movie *Frozen* – gained traction in newspapers. Compelled to act, YouTube purged 150,000 videos and 270 accounts in a single week. At the same time it stop serving adverts to two million videos and locked comments on 625,000 videos that it said had been 'targeted by child predators'.

And a second adpocalypse reared its head in 2019 as the likes of Nestle and Epic Games – makers of Fortnite – pulled their adverts from the site when paedophilic comments were found on many videos featuring young children. It was just the latest controversy for a platform that has lurched from problem to problem for the past two years.

Still, YouTube is taking some action. To combat the problem of predatory comments in children's videos, YouTube said it would ban comments on almost all videos featuring children – a blunt instrument that damages creators at the expense of keeping advertisers sweet. And in January 2019, the site finally announced in a 485-word blogpost that it would make conspiracy videos (which it termed 'borderline content') harder to find. It was not wiping such videos, however. It was reducing the likelihood that they would appear as recommendations.

YouTube still hosts videos that are manifestly and incontrovertibly untrue. Along with telling people that President HW Bush was executed, videos deny that the Earth is round. Plenty of intelligent people have protested about this on social media. Jill Walker Rettberg, professor of digital culture at the University of Bergen, was asked by her 10-year-old daughter about the theory that you can fall off the end of the world after she had watched videos about it on YouTube. When software engineer Keziyah Lewis dines with her family in Central Florida she debates with relatives who believe the flat earth theory because of YouTube videos.

Like Frankenstein disavowing his monster, Guillaume Chaslot, a former YouTube engineer, now feels intense remorse for the algorithm, which he and 14 others optimised for watch time in 2011. Since he left YouTube in 2013, Chaslot has spent his time and effort trying to raise awareness of the problems. His website AlgoTransparency scrapes the recommended videos of more than 1,000 major YouTube channels from across the political spectrum.

One video, *Christmas in GITMO*, was recommended by 16 of those channels. A creation of the 'corruption detector' channel *RedPill78*, which has 126,000 subscribers, *Christmas in GITMO* runs through some of the biggest tropes and bugbears of the alt-right: 'deep state war machines', 'establishment politicians' and 'predictive programming by the establishment', and links to a series of alt-right websites. It casually declares that 'witchcraft is real' and 'science is not an exact science'. Hundreds of thousands of people watched the video before it was removed from YouTube.

Chaslot says that in pursuit of extending watch time, YouTube promoted extreme conspiracy theories, because it worked. If someone tells a viewer there was a second shooter at the 2017 Las Vegas shooting, where gunman Stephen Paddock killed 58 and injured more than 850 by firing more than 1,000 rounds from the 32nd floor of the Mandalay Bay hotel, the viewer is likely to pay attention. If they are shown a few pixels – a reflection of something – in a window that might be a second gunman, a viewer is likely to delve deeper. If a viewer becomes convinced by that video, and believes there was a second shooter, they're likely to go further down the rabbit hole. The result is that the viewer watches more and more extreme videos and trusts the mainstream media less and less. 'It's trained to maximise that,' Chaslot says. 'That's the crazy part.'

According to Chaslot's research, flat earth videos have been recommended hundreds of millions of times by YouTube's own algorithm. Red pill videos are still available. What you or I may deem 'false', YouTube calls 'borderline'.

Chaslot believes the problem is partly that YouTube's engineers don't know who is popular on the site and why. And they underestimate the power of their platform. Algorithm engineers are highly intelligent, well-educated people. They are scientists. When they watch the flat earth videos, they laugh. How stupid is this video? They don't take such messages seriously. But not every one of YouTube's near-two billion monthly users has a PhD in computer science (or politics). Some people watch what the people on the TV are saying and wonder what else the authorities are hiding.

9.

SPONSORED CONTENT:
THE TALE OF DODIE CLARK
AND HEINZ BEANS

Dodie Clark, a mellifluously-voiced English singer who is a favourite of many teenage girls for her gently acoustic songs about complicated life issues, came out as bisexual to her followers in a six-minute vlog on her music channel in May 2016. It was viewed 1.1 million times in its first 15 months.

Just over a year later, Clark, from Epping in Essex, uploaded a two-minute song called 'I'm bisexual – a coming out song!' It was an advert for Skittles, featuring a packet of the normally colourful sweets stripped of their hues in a demonstration of the brand's support for LGBTQ+ Pride. In the first month, its popularity eclipsed that of Clark's original coming out video, which had been online longer.

Clark uploaded another two-minute video in September

2016. In it she walks into her kitchen wearing a white dress and white and purple flowers in her hair. She leans back on the kitchen counter and picks up an empty can of Heinz baked beans – the contents of which are presumably warming in a pan on her cooker. She starts to play percussion on the metal can, singing an a capella song where several versions of herself harmonise with each other. After a minute or so, the song ends and cuts to Clark, empty can of beans in hand. 'Hello! Hope you enjoyed that,' she begins, thanking Heinz for sponsoring the video, and pointing to its famous blue-green can. The name of the video? 'BEANZ | ad'. More than a million people have watched that video.

Such branded videos show the odd way in which pure creator-driven content and advertising can mix. That the Skittles video – a personal ditty outlining a major moment in the YouTuber's life – is tied to a sponsor isn't troubling, questionable or bad (it was clearly labelled as an ad), but does show that even the most personal moments can be commoditised on the new ultra-commercial YouTube.

Branded or 'sponsored content' has become a major and growing source of income for YouTubers. Put simply, businesses pay YouTubers to discuss, showcase and generally endorse their products in exchange for payment. In return brands receive cheap and effective promotion that is often better value than traditional TV advertising. Sponsored content is also seen as preferable to the advertising that runs before or during a YouTube video – 'pre-roll' or 'mid-roll' ads – in large part because, barring the correct labelling of it as such, it's not obviously advertising.

Viewers thought better of brands that were personally endorsed by YouTubers, a process the authors call 'covert advertising', according to a study in 2016 by German academics, Fabian Göbel, Anton Meyer, Ram Ramaseshan, and Silke Bartsch, published in *Marketing Intelligence & Planning*. They found that such sponsored content, whether labelled as such or not, had a long list of benefits, including 'higher communicator credibility, higher ad credibility, more favourable attitude toward the advertisement, more favourable attitude toward the brand, and higher intention to share than when presented through a brand channel.'

A study for YouTube by Nielsen and Carat Global, an international multimedia network, found that – compared to traditional celebrity endorsements – collaborations with a YouTuber led to four times as many viewers becoming familiar with a brand. 'Whereas celebrities need to be trendy and stylish, consumers expect creators to be friendly, funny, and sometimes irreverent,' said Carat Global's chief strategy officer, Sanjay Nazerali.

He added: 'If I take one thing from this study, it's this: there's a huge cultural shift in the nature of celebrity, authenticity, and community – all topics we marketers care about. And this shift is being driven by a new class of diverse, authentic voices we call creators.'

It's happening on all social media platforms, from Instagram to TikTok to Facebook and Snapchat, but YouTubers also benefit from this shift. By arranging their own promotional deals influencers have more financial independence. Their income from adverts served alongside their videos is dependent on the advertising rules that YouTube draws up. If YouTube's owner Google pulls all advertising from the site tomorrow... well, tough luck.

As influencers saw during the 2017 adpocalypse (where major advertisers pulled their funding from the site because their adverts were being shown alongside contentious videos), there's no guarantee that the ad money will continue as a steady stream. Coupled with YouTube's past and ongoing fickleness when dealing with creators and their livelihoods, YouTubers who rely solely on ad revenue are taking a risk.

So, much like most of us in the modern-day economy, You-Tubers need a side hustle. Beckii Flint, a British YouTuber, has hedged her bets by starting her own fashion business. 'I think it's naïve for a lot of creators to think that YouTube is always going to be the same, and that they're going to be earning the same amount of money from YouTube and don't need to pursue anything else.'

The adpocalypse was a wake-up call, she says. 'People who were paying rent on expensive properties couldn't afford that rent anymore. It's not so much about having a backup plan but acknowledging that pop culture, social media and media more generally is going to change and adapt and evolve. You can't keep doing the same thing.'

As we will see later, astute YouTubers are diversifying into these sorts of brand deals, merchandise and books as well as live appearances. In 2017, Hannah Hart, a 32-year-old comedic YouTuber from Palo Alto, California, struck a TV deal with the *Food Network*. The show, a travelogue called *I Hart Food*, didn't last long: its single series was just six episodes. But it's just one of many side gigs that Hart, who first won fans in 2011 when she recorded a drunken, late-night webcam conversation with a friend while trying hopelessly to make a grilled cheese sandwich, has got away from YouTube. She now has 2.4 million subscribers on the platform.

In all, the Vlogbrothers now make less than a fifth of their total revenue from advertising against their videos. With Hank Green having followed in the footsteps of his brother, John, by publishing his first novel in September 2018, the proportion of their income generated by ad revenue is likely to fall further. Even merchandise sales make them more money than ads on their YouTube videos.

Likewise, views alone account for just 30% of the income of Jordi van den Bussche, a gamer and one of the biggest Dutch You-Tubers. However, Van den Bussche, better known as Kwebbelkop, can't just stop producing videos. He told a Dutch TV documentary: 'Everything is still based on those views. If I lose my views, I'll lose my brand deals and partnerships as well.' He just doesn't need to chase new viewers as desperately as before, freeing him from the need to anticipate the algorithm so slavishly.

The volume of sponsored content on YouTube looks likely to increase in coming years. Boston Consulting Group, one of the 'big four' consulting firms, forecasts that spending on branded content will hit $25 billion in 2019. Facebook's product marketing manager Kate Orseth told a gathering of businesses and developers in 2017: 'Brands are partnering with publishers that build loyal audiences, and can speak to specific audiences they want to reach with authenticity and authority.'

Just 4% of British PR and marketing professionals wouldn't pencil in any money to spend on social media influencers nowadays, according to a survey by influencer marketing agency Takumi. Yet such influencer marketing is in its early stages. In August 2017, Ruxandra Maria, Chupa Chups product manager, said: 'We don't expect influencer activity to convert into sales directly at this early stage; we are looking at the activity in terms of its wider influence on the campaign'. The sweet-maker is running tests with YouTubers, rather than mainstream celebrities. Among the first 15 YouTubers it worked with in its first three years was Dodie Clark. She promoted its sugar-free lollipops.

Jan-Frederik Gräve, from the University of Hamburg, who wrote an academic paper on the perception of influencers compared to traditional celebrities, concluded: 'One of the most popular, and presumed, advantages of influencers is a higher credibility and trustworthiness, because they are seen as a user like anyone else in social media.'

It's a position of trust respected by influencers of all stripes, on all platforms. 'No one wins if the advert isn't declared properly,' Amelia Liana, an Instagrammer with half a million followers, told me. 'While the brand and I can get into trouble, my audience are very switched on and would know instantly.' That would be awful, says Liana. 'The last thing I would ever want to do would be to deceive my audience.'

Nonetheless, melding advertising and editorial in a video represents a risk to viewers. Are they really aware that influencers are being paid to promote products? Perhaps not, judging by the low level of awareness of conventional advertising on YouTube. In one study, just 44% of British adults knew that the main source of funding for YouTube was advertising. Even among avowed users of the site, who were probably younger, only 55% knew. Perhaps more surprisingly in a separate survey, 61% of Generation Z – those born after 1995 – said that they didn't actually care whether a celebrity who marketed a brand in a video didn't declare it as an advert.

Aware of the potential PR problem of undeclared promotional content, as well as acting in the best interests of its viewers, YouTube now advises creators how to brand sponsored content and regularly updates that advice. Creators must flag up paid promotions by ticking a box confirming the video contains promotional material paid for by an advertiser. However, YouTube ultimately points out that 'creators and brands are responsible for understanding and complying with their legal obligations to disclose Paid Promotion in their content.'

Exactly what creators must disclose depends on the country in which they are operating. Britain first tightened the rules on branded content in 2014 after its Advertising Standards Authority found the snack manufacturer Mondelez had breached advertising regulations. Mondelez had asked five creators – Dan Howell and Phil Lester, better known as Dan and Phil, Tom 'TomSka' Ridgewell, Emma Blackery and PF Liguori (who together have tens of millions of subscribers), to film videos of a 'lick race', where they had to eat the filling from Oreo biscuits. The company asked the vloggers to make clear that they were working with Mondelez and Oreo. The ASA ruled that merely saying 'Thanks to Oreo for making this video possible' did not make it obvious that the video was an advertisement. The ASA introduced new, exhaustive advice for vloggers to ensure they don't fall foul of the law, which it regularly updates. At the same time, Britain's Competition and Markets Authority (CMA) has censured a dozen or so influencers for breaching the rules, and in late 2018 began an investigation into the world of influencer marketing.

Similar guidance was issued by the United States Federal Trade Commission (FTC) in 2017 after it claimed two YouTubers, Trevor 'TmarTn' Martin and Thomas 'Syndicate' Cassell, who have a total of 13 million subscribers, failed to properly flag up their interests in a company in their videos and tweets. In one of the videos, posted in 2015, TmarTn appears to take the role of someone who chances upon CSGO Lotto, a website where players of a popular game could gamble using 'skins' their characters wear in game, rather than someone who owned a 42.5% share in the business. The YouTube duo settled with the consumer body. The FTC also wrote to 21 influencers, reminding them of the importance of prominently highlighting that they had been paid for posts. 'Consumers need to know when social media influencers are being paid or have any other material connection to the brands endorsed in their posts,' said FTC acting chairman Maureen Ohlhausen.

A UK industry body set up in December 2018 to educate and advise on how to run social campaigns, the Business of Influencers, wants to codify the rules on how influencers promote products following the practices uncovered by the British and American regulators. On its board are some key industry figures, including Harry Hugo of the GOAT Agency, Ben Jeffries of Influencer, and Liam Chivers of OP Talent, which represents the big British YouTuber KSI.

Today, although pieces of undeclared sponsored content still slip out unnoticed, the once wild west of advertising in online video is slowly becoming better policed. The sheriffs are in town now and the cowboys are misbehaving less. Nonetheless, even when the rules are being followed, the scope for confusion remains. When quizzed by the British media regulator Ofcom in 2017, three in 10 adult internet users didn't know that vloggers could be paid by a company to endorse a product in their videos. 'Some participants felt it wasn't always easy to tell when a YouTuber or social media celebrity was being paid to endorse products,' the UK media regulator noted.

In part, the problem is the demographics of social media, and especially YouTube. YouTube's own survey of teenagers and millennials found that 40% believed YouTubers understood them better than their friends or their family. And 60% said that a creator had changed their view of the world – or their life. Gullible is too cynical a word to use, but many younger users trust the personalities they follow online. It's a friendship called a parasocial relationship, which we'll come back to in a later chapter.

Ian Danskin, a YouTuber who uploads video essays around new media, film and video games under the name *Innuendo Studios*, is wary about branded advertising content. 'The people who use these things the most are teenagers with their first smartphone, or older people who have signed up for the first time,' he says. And for a good number of YouTubers, thinking of their fans as consumers is a profitable way to go about their lives on the site. He takes on the persona of the YouTube celebrity-cum-brand selling a product on the site: '"We're your friends, but also we're not your friends; we just want to present the feeling of being your friends because that makes us money".'

In YouTubers' defence, blurring the line between editorial and advertorial content is common in new media. BuzzFeed, the news and entertainment website that is among the most visited websites for millennial (younger) media consumers, has regularly faced brickbats from legacy competitors for juxtaposing content created by its news and editorial staff and that produced by its 'creative' (advertising) staff.

Besides, this ostensibly new form of advertising actually has its roots at the dawn of commercial television and radio in the mid-20th century. In exchange for getting their name into the title of the show, such as the *Texaco Star Theatre* or the *Camel News Caravan*, which ran from 1948 to 1956, companies would fund the production.

Other brands went further: an *NBC* radio variety programme inspired by the Kern and Hammerstein musical *Show Boat* was named after an instant coffee brand. Uniquely, the audience for the *Maxwell House Show Boat*, which ran from 1932 to 1937, was let into all aspects of the production. When a performer finished their set, the microphones would follow them 'backstage', where they would chat with fellow stars over a cup of Maxwell House. The scripted dialogue praised Maxwell House, blurring the line between showbusiness and plain business. (Plenty of modern creators adopt that behind-the-scenes shtick in their YouTube videos today.)

But YouTube is different to traditional media. Its primary, direct vlogging is far more immediate to viewers. It tends to most interest youngsters. And it's unprecedented in scale: in 2017 an academic survey of German YouTubers by Claudia Gerhards of the Hochschule Düsseldorf University of Applied Sciences found that two-thirds of creators had taken advantage of product placement. And when they did so, they did so frequently – half more than 10 times a year. Most were paid for mentioning products in their videos, and 57% of the creators said it was a 'necessary and indispensable source of finance.'

Indeed, Brooke Erin Duffy of Cornell University's Department of Communication and Jefferson Pooley of Muhlenberg College call these modern-day celebrity-entrepreneurs 'Idols of Promotion'. They are responding logically to a world of part-time, independent contractor, freelance, zero-hours work, where employment can be precarious and fleeting. Only self-employed self-starters enjoy security. So commoditising your personal life for personal gain is simply the best way to get ahead in a world that might not exist tomorrow. Duffy and Pooley wrote: 'The message to the new precariat is that they better identify their distinctive strengths, engage in brazen self-promotion, and spearhead "personal visibility" campaigns. Or else.'

And boy are these people visible. In 2016, 1,000 YouTube channels hit the one million subscriber mark.

PART III

CHARTING THE STARS

10.

KNOW YOUR YOUTUBE: ELITE, MACRO-INFLUENCER AND MICRO-INFLUENCER

Until the early 2000s, there was 'us' – the viewers who would pay our money for cinema tickets and popcorn – and 'them': the Hollywood celebrities who lived the launch parties, premieres and red carpet walks. Every ticket we bought to see their latest hit only widened the gulf between us and them. But with YouTube, it was possible to create our own champions – and they looked like us. Ordinary people were offered a brave new, democratic platform from which to project their thoughts. It was a meritocracy: work hard and you could benefit. Under the giant play button, all people were created equal. Baristas and bar workers could be thrust into the limelight off the back of a viral video. Eventually, they could make enough money from the advertising revenue placed against their videos to do it full-time.

In the first years, regardless of their riches, these new stars created by YouTube stayed humble. They were careful never to appear above those they entertained. In fact, they shied away from calling them fans altogether. New terminology was coined – 'creator' and 'viewer' – so as not to alienate the people who paid the bills. That's not the case today. As we've seen with Jake Paul's mansion, bank account and bevy of cars, YouTube has started looking more and more like the old system it sought to upend. The reason why is simple: money. As advertisers have recognised the importance of YouTubers and the hypnotic pull they have over their viewers, they have started investing large sums of money. According to an industry insider, Jake Paul can command $250,000 for plugging a product in his videos.

When YouTube became big business, it changed. No longer were all video makers created equal; they needed to be graded, classed, and ultimately valued. Brands needed to know which YouTubers to back and how much to pay them. Companies had to be able to distinguish the biggest YouTube celebrities from their less valuable rivals. For years the number of subscribers was the metric. Now that is less useful. As YouTube matures into its terrible teens, the 18-year-olds who started watching as university students become 30-somethings with jobs and kids who are too busy to fritter away their time enjoying themselves. Older YouTubers have a lot of dormant subscribers that can inflate their worth. (YouTube has also deprioritised the importance of being a subscriber by reducing the efficacy of notifications – the method that let all those people know Casey Neistat had uploaded a video mentioning me.)

Instead, the main thing most advertising executives look for when assessing the worth of a YouTuber is the average number of views they get per video. Everyone has different definitions, but an easy way to think about the influencer space is to chunk it up into four categories of influencer: nano, micro, macro and elite. Advertising agencies, brands and influencer representatives argue over whether someone should be called a nano-influencer, micro-influencer, or just a plain old influencer. For the individuals involved, such definitions can be a big deal: a YouTuber may want to shed the 'nano-' or 'micro-' from their title so they're perceived as a higher rank of celebrity.

Ironically, brands are increasingly keen to broker deals with smaller influencers who they believe hold more sway over their fans. This is because although they have smaller fanbases, those who follow them are way more dedicated than 'traditional' YouTubers – who have become too big to acknowledge and interact with all their fans at the level required to, say, travel cross-country to see them in concert.

Take a trending YouTuber who is on an upward trajectory to fame. As they burst through the undergrowth, they may have comparatively few subscribers but their videos are being watched by more people. Are they more or less valuable to a brand than a veteran who accrued millions of subscribers a decade ago, but whose active fanbase – those who take the time to watch their videos – only reaches the low tens of thousands? A local teenager and her counterparts may actually prove better value to advertisers than a twenty-something 'star' feted by the mass media.

So where do you draw the lines for who goes into what box? As we'll see, YouTube has become a hugely hierarchical space, with terminology like 'community', 'creators' and 'featured creators' bandied about at industry meet-ups, each of which marks you out for your size or importance. But for the purposes of our nano, micro and regular influencer (plus A-list elite influencer) divisions, let's sketch out the following boxes.

Get less than 1,000 views on an average video and you're an ordinary Joe, struggling to make it out of the vast sea of content creators trying to strike it rich on YouTube. You're not even a nano-influencer, according to influencer marketing agency MediaKix. Don't be disheartened, though: competition is tough. The last time the average YouTube video got more than 1,000 views in its lifetime was in 2011. Videos uploaded in 2016 (the last year for which reliable data is available) averaged just 89 views before sputtering out of momentum and being cast off into the ether.

Do better than the average and break through the 1,000 view mark and you are a nano-influencer.

You are a micro-influencer if you get between 10,000 and 25,000 views per video, though you probably wouldn't raise a flicker of recognition in a conversation among strangers.

Above that and, in the eyes of marketing agencies, you're considered a bona fide influencer without the need to prefix your status (we will distinguish between what we call macro-influencers and elite influencers).

Let's look at the elite first.

11.

ELITE INFLUENCERS:
FIGHTING THEIR WAY
TO THE TOP

In the drizzle on 3 February 2018, hordes of screaming teenagers have packed out the Copper Box Arena in London where British super heavyweight boxer Anthony Joshua saw off Roberto Cammarelle to take gold at the 2012 Olympics.

The venue is home today to another historic boxing bout, but with a difference. The opponents are not regulars on the boxing circuit, but white-collar entertainers who broadcast from their homes. This is the world's first ever boxing match between big YouTubers.

In the red corner is KSI, a 25-year-old YouTuber best known for playing FIFA from a comfortable leather chair in his bedroom, a semi-iterant rap career and a low-budget movie flop called *Laid in America*. In the blue corner is Joe Weller, a fellow

British YouTuber known for his personality and pranks.

For months the pair have baited each other on YouTube and on Twitter. They have also been training and display muscle-bulging torsos as they shimmy off their bedazzled and bejewelled robes. As they walk to the ring, smooth-skinned, slick-suited YouTubers alternate between leaping out of their seats to get the perfect selfie and playing to the crowd. Young fans are excited. Parents are exasperated and bemused. Dean Piper set off from the Welsh steel town of Port Talbot seven hours before to drive down to London with his children. 'It's a long journey and has been a nightmare,' he told me, recounting endless traffic jams and moaning passengers. 'But the kids got the tickets for Christmas. They love the YouTubers.'

All 7,000 seats sold out.

Thirteen-year-old Maya Pollock was attending her first boxing match. Visiting with her father and a friend, she said: 'I'm not really here for the boxing. I watch both Joe and KSI on YouTube and it's been really hyped up. Everyone's going to be watching it and talking about it.' Her less excited father, standing the teenager-mandated regulation distance away from the group, admitted: 'It doesn't appeal to me.'

Hundreds of thousands of pounds had changed hands on the betting market. Hundreds of thousands of pounds more had been spent on tickets and trains to get to London. Special fight merchandise on sale at tables dotted around the arena was shifting so fast that one person manning a stall said they couldn't keep count of the value. An estimated 1.6 million were watching on a free YouTube live stream.

Yet I was one of only a handful of reporters there. The event confirmed in my mind a long-held theory: that YouTube was the biggest, best-kept secret in the media world. For years I had been following the gossip and drama on the site, and a globally-followed spectacle was happening before my eyes – yet few media people knew about it.

Stuart Jones, the promoter from Upload Events, understood the confusion: you have to seek out YouTubers. 'If you don't know about them, you don't realise just how big they are.' They aren't appearing on daytime TV sofas to talk about their lives with perma-tanned television presenters – at least not yet.

After three rounds, the match was stopped due to a technical knockout. Weller had been rocked by KSI, who was the fitter, taller and faster fighter. As the studs on a slightly plain-looking boxing belt were snapped into place around KSI's waist, he lifted his arms aloft in triumph. It was the latest twist in an extraordinary story. Born Olajide William Olatunji in Watford, just north of London, KSI attended a £15,000-a-year private school, Berkhamsted. Such a gilded education would normally lead to a degree at one of England's top universities, but KSI flunked his A-Levels. Finding out about his grades while on a family holiday, he locked himself in the toilet until he could steel himself to tell his furious parents. It didn't matter. For two years the teenager had been attracting vast, lucrative audiences by uploading YouTube videos of him playing FIFA, a football game. People liked his easy banter and sense of being a big brother. (Coincidentally, his younger brother Deji is also a YouTuber with his own line of merchandise, who has followed KSI into the fight game.) He didn't need his A-Levels.

Acutely aware of the need to diversify his audience, though, he began exploring other avenues than video games. In 2011, he started making music, easing into the genre with a novelty rap about footballer Emile Heskey that would appeal to his existing audience while potentially making him new fans. The song was a moderate success but paved the way for more work. He released his first proper album in 2016, the same year as his first feature film, *Laid in America*, a schlocky coming-of-age movie akin to *American Pie*, in which he starred alongside fellow You-Tuber Caspar Lee. It bombed – in part, KSI believes, because his fanbase preferred to pirate rather than buy the production. However, he kept adapting, bringing the YouTube football experience offline in sold-out matches that see an all-star team of YouTubers play a glorified Sunday league kickabout in top-flight stadiums.

Then he stepped into the ring.

Like his American peers, KSI has learnt to stay one step ahead of the competition. 'Whenever something changes, I'm able to adapt and change into the next thing that's popular,' he told me, sat on a barber's chair in the cramped basement of a photographer's studio in Soho on a spring day in 2018. 'I always take inspiration from Donald Glover and Will Smith and all these people who don't just do one entertainment thing,' he said, also mentioning wrestler-turned-actor Dwayne 'The Rock' Johnson.

KSI's committed fanbase means he can make more money from merchandise than any other British YouTuber. According to industry sources, he earns around £75,000 for endorsing a product on social media. He still can't compete with the American merch-shifting YouTubers like Jake Paul.

Which is perhaps why in August 2018, immediately after the London bout, KSI grabbed the microphone and challenged Jake Paul, Logan Paul or their father, Greg, to a boxing match. When KSI next entered the boxing ring six months later he faced

Logan Paul, Jake's older brother. Logan Paul had become the pantomime villain everyone loved to hate by uploading a tasteless video from Japan's Aokigahara 'suicide' forest. The boxing match was an astute move from Team Paul: it was the first act of a redemption narrative that Logan Paul is still trying to weave. But it was also a boon for KSI and the event's promoters: Paul was on a different level to the mild-mannered Joe Weller, and offered a bit of transatlantic razzmatazz.

This time tickets costs between £30 and £495.

'Everything is bigger this time round,' KSI told me before the bout as he leant against a basement bar in Manchester's Hotel Football, in between press junkets with the BBC and media from around the world. 'I feel like for years, old media has always neglected YouTube, pushed back and felt like YouTube wasn't a real media outlet. Now, it's getting to the point where it's so big you can't ignore it.'

On 26 August 2018, almost 20,000 people filled Manchester Arena. While there still weren't many reporters, their ranks had swelled. But at least they were there, taking notice. In the arena's cavernous halls, 18-year-old cousins Nitasha Sandhu and Shania Kaur had each spent £100 on tickets. Sandhu, who had splashed out $1,300 to fly in from Vancouver, British Columbia, told me: 'Shania came to Vancouver for summer two months ago and we just happened to connect over YouTubers and the fight. When we found out it was happening, I decided to come over for it.'

Some 865,000 people watched the event live, with at least a million more following along on pirated streams. Two of the three judges scored it evenly and one narrowly gave the bout to KSI, meaning the event ended in a draw – a handy set-up to a follow-up match due to be held later in 2019.

The following morning I took a taxi from my city centre Airbnb to Salford Quays, home of *BBC Breakfast*, Britain's biggest breakfast-time TV show. 'There's a lot of people watching this that might not know who these two are,' one of the presenters remarked. The discussion revolved around how the boxing match was a test case for shifting YouTubers' fanbase offline. After the programme ended, we briefly continued discussing how a supposedly fringe event had been so newsworthy. One presenter understood how keen his children were on YouTube. Off-camera, he lamented: 'Nobody watches TV anymore.'

In a way, he was right. We'd just appeared on a nationally broadcast television programme watched by an average of 1.5 million people. More than a million people watched pirate streams alongside the nearly 800,000 people who paid $10 or £7.50 to watch the bout live on YouTube. We were explaining the event that morning to a different audience, yes, but a smaller one than had seen it live.

The bouts dispelled the myth that YouTube fandom is a fleeting, flippant trend. The media had finally grasped that YouTube, with its trillions of views, was a big thing. Elite influencers like KSI and PewDiePie can count tens of millions of subscribers and millions of dollars of income. According to Forbes, the top 10 earning YouTube stars pulled in $180 million in 2018, a rise of 42% on the previous year. At the end of 2018, more than 330 separate YouTube channels had more than 10 million subscribers. At least 4,000 had more than two million fans. Some of these stars have even managed to pass through the generational barrier into the lives of people who don't watch YouTube.

Not that many, though. YouTube's biggest name, PewDiePie, is only recognised by a quarter of British adults, according to exclusive polling conducted for this book by YouGov. Zoella is recognised by a third. Ask those aged 18-24, though, and things change: 70% know PewDiePie, and three-quarters know Zoella. Recognition drops by around half beyond that – proving that while it's expanding, YouTube still is a relatively young people's platform.

Five of the top 10 earners on YouTube are men who play video games for a living, like KSI and PewDiePie did or still do. The fact they are gamers is not coincidental. Gamers speak directly to boys and young men, who are not especially interested in watching TV with their parents and who consequently form a big chunk of YouTube's audience. Since 2012, gaming has had the second highest number of channels on the platform (behind People & Blogs – a catch-all category), and received one in every six views in 2016. For comparison, one in 10 views goes to vloggers.

Gaming's domination makes sense: since 2010, the gaming industry has been bigger than both Hollywood and the music industry combined. While YouTube faces competition from Amazon-owned Twitch, a live streaming website where gamers congregate for this audience, in absolute numbers YouTube's gamers blow their competition out of the water.

PewDiePie and KSI aren't necessarily the best in the world at playing those games. Viewers aren't watching them for tips on how to break down an opponent or to conquer a particularly tricky level. They want companionship and a sense of connection – an invitation into someone else's life, and the ability to make a remote friend, albeit one mediated through a camera. What gamers do away from the keyboard matters as much as their dexterity with a gamepad.

PewDiePie's videos are rammed full of in-jokes, and viewers spend much time staring in baffled bemusement before cracking a smile. It's easy to see why he became YouTube's best-known name. He's a hard-worker who will labour a joke over and over – until you laugh from the sheer absurdity of it all. But at the end of each video, which rarely lasts more than 15 minutes, unless it's a recorded and edited version of a gaming session, there is a feeling of exhaustion. So much stuff happens; so much is said; so many silly voices are used.

PewDiePie earns a fortune – $15.5 million in 2018, by one estimate. His videos regularly rack up millions of views. Like KSI, he has diversified, making himself less dependent on YouTube. He makes money from several tie-in products, including one iPhone and Android game on YouTube. On its release in 2016, PewDiePie's Tuber Simulator, produced by Outerminds Inc, reached number seven overall in the US iPhone charts (in the UK, it was the top-ranking game).

'Let's make a video. First you need a camera,' PewDie-Pie's avatar explains, before taking you to the in-game shop. Everything in the shop is too expensive for a first-time player, but PewDiePie's avatar is happy to step in and offer a rudimentary webcam for free. 'I don't mind paying for you this time, bro,' he wryly explains. 'Got all this Tuber money, y'know?'

Much as gaming tends to attract boys, the beauty industry exerts a similar pull on teenaged girls and young women. After gamers, beauty influencers are top of YouTube's charts. Watch time on beauty videos increased by more than 60% year-on-year between 2015 and 2016, according to YouTube's own analysis.

Many of those beauty followers will watch Huda Kattan. Born in Oklahoma to Iraqi immigrants, Kattan – who used to ask her classmates to call her Heidi to hide her otherness – did a business degree and worked in finance at an international consulting firm. Bored with spreadsheets, she started work as a makeup artist, making up mainstream celebrities like Nicole Richie and Eva Longoria for red carpet premieres and photo shoots. She set up a blog – as well as a YouTube channel – and thanks to her entrepreneurship and the support of her dedicated fans, she's now a star in her own right. Known to many as Huda Beauty, Kattan has three million subscribers (she's massively popular on other social media sites such as Instagram), but her outsized influence on YouTube – and the broader beauty industry – is irrefutable.

She has her own line of beauty products stocked in 1,500 stores worldwide, and turnover at her company is around $300 million. Kattan's big enough of a deal to get other influencers flustered by simply being near her. Eniyah Rana, a Birmingham-based micro-influencer we will meet in a coming chapter, was 'starstruck' when she was invited to have breakfast with Kattan alongside 20 other influencers at a London department store.

Huda Beauty sends review products from Kattan's latest beauty ranges to Rana and other beauty influencers a couple of weeks before their release. 'It's a benefit and an advantage to the brand because you're showcasing it to hundreds and thousands of people who will go and buy it when you say, "Oh wow, I like this",' Rana explains. It's also an advantage to the influencers and micro-influencers: validation.

While PewDiePie is the best-known personality on YouTube and others such as KSI and Kattan are known to millions, the highest-earning influencer is a child. Eight-year-old Ryan, of the eponymous Ryan ToysReview channel, gets to play for a living. He unboxes toys and plays with them. (Unboxing videos show someone literally unpacking a product from the post or a shopping trip.) Ryan also has a branded line of merchandise sold through the US supermarket Walmart, and his own line of toys available on Amazon.

When he grows up, Ryan will have a fortune saved up for his 2028 college fund. According to Forbes, he earned $22 million in 2018 from his YouTube uploads and toy ranges. Ryan isn't the only child to benefit big from YouTube. 11-year-old British YouTuber Tiana has a range of licensed products called Hearts by Tiana. The products, which include duvet covers, bath and beauty products, trading cards and toys, will be stocked in Asda's 400 stores from summer 2019.

Just like Tiana in the UK – YouTube's most popular girl, according to the team behind her success – and Ryan ToysReview in the United States, Australia has CKN Toys, a family from Melbourne, who unbox and play with toys from all the major franchises. Particularly popular in Indonesia, according to data from influencer marketing platform Paladin, the channel is similar to many others. Two young brothers with striking mohican haircuts frolic around the comfort of their parents' home while playing with more toys than any child could possibly want in a lifetime. CKN Toys has 11.6 million subscribers, who watch the videos 460 million times in a month. In 2019 the channel signed a deal with Haven Global, a marketing agency, to help promote it across the world. At the time Ray Nguyen, the father of the two boys who star in CKN Toys' videos, told reporters that 'what started as fun and games in the family living room has grown beyond our wildest dreams.'

Elite YouTubers tend to be young creators whose interests – toys, gaming and makeup – mirror those of their fans. And it pays to start young.

12.

CHILD STARS:

MEET MATTYB, WHO GETS TWO

MILLION VIEWS A DAY

In 2007, a proud mother uploaded a video to YouTube of her 12-year-old son singing so that family members and friends could watch his performance. A decade later, that 12-year-old is doing alright for himself. His name is Justin Bieber, he's worth $200 million, and he has an army of adoring fans worldwide. Bieber found a following in YouTube's infancy. But in the time since he left it for a world of bodyguards, paparazzi photographs and international tours, many young singers have followed in his footsteps, recording covers of pop songs and accruing a fanbase of their own. But if you want to make it to pop stardom, you probably need to start your journey young. The pop stars Troye Sivan and Dua Lipa started on YouTube at the age of 12 and 14 respectively.

Others start earlier: Mini Jake Paul, the pint-sized version of the petulant star so popular with children, started at the age of four. Ben Hampton, another member of Paul's Team 10 entourage, joined YouTube when he was six. He'd been watching since he was two or three, says his father Branden, who runs a social media agency that has worked with Paul. Branden has a video of Ben that he plans to show him when he's a little older. Unbeknownst to his parents, Hampton had grabbed his iPad and began babbling into the camera, giving a review of a toy. 'He was probably three-and-half, maybe close to four.'

The daily exploits of Russian-born brother and sister Mister Max, and Miss Katy, are seen by 25 million subscribers across four separate channels. Their videos involve them playing around their grand home in a sleepy English residential street, just yards from a church, and participating in various skits for their young viewers. They are eight and six respectively.

The American Matthew David Morris was just 11 when he surpassed one billion views for his covers of pop songs in 2014. Now 16, 'MattyB's' videos rack up around two million views a day; his first officially released single, *Friend Zone*, has been watched 87 million times since mid-April 2016; and in June 2016 his memoir became an Amazon bestseller. With understatement, Morris says: 'We realised it was getting big after we sold out my first concert.' He was 10 years old.

From there, Morris has become even more popular. The fans who first spotted him when he was younger are growing up alongside him, while a new generation of children are discovering him now as a cool teenager. But he may ease himself into adulthood more gently than Justin Bieber, whose spoiled and sometimes petulant adulthood as a mainstream celebrity singer came complete with cancelled world tours and peeing in buckets in hotel kitchens. Certainly Morris's parents are eager to keep his head on straight.

'At a very young age, Matthew is learning he is part of a music label; he's becoming an entrepreneur as well as an artist,' explains Blake Morris, a serial entrepreneur and father of Matthew. That said, Blake is quick to establish where the line is between Matthew as a young person who enjoys singing, and wants to share that passion online, and how much of it is him recognising that he is a brand at the centre of a business. 'I've been a father first,' Morris insists. 'If you got to know me, you'd meet all my children and see they're all very special. I've got three kids who have nothing to do with the entertainment business; the two little ones do.'

Each year, Morris asks Matthew several questions: Is this something you enjoy doing? How do you feel about being MattyB? Do you want to continue being MattyB? According to Morris, if Matthew said at any time he didn't, then the YouTube career would stop. He hasn't yet. 'It seems to be he is made for this.'

In 2016, Matthew was navigating his first teenage year, having turned 13 that January. His voice was deepening, explained Blake; like every teenager, his mannerisms, attitude and the way he held himself was changing from the childlike to the adult. 'He's able to have a lot more mature conversations with me and his big cousin and say: "Dad, what can I do to put more into this?" I have to say as a father: "I'll let you take two steps forward but you're not going to run forward".'

But people like MattyB hold plenty of sway. A survey in 2014 asking US teenagers aged 13-18 to name influential figures demonstrated the pulling power of the video streaming website:

the top five most recognisable names were all YouTubers. But why do their names trip off the tongue of sons and daughters, while parents have never heard of them? With his 11 million subscribers, MattyB has an inkling: 'Because adults watch TV and we watch YouTube and the internet.'

Social media is the lifeblood of this connection, with tween pop stars tweeting their every move and engaging with their followers. This gives a sense of intimacy absent from long-lens photographs or staged tell-all interviews. 16-year-old social media star Jacob Sartorius tweets superficially profound statements like 'I'm into you' and 'YOU'RE IMPORTANT'. His three million subscribers on YouTube, nine million followers on Instagram and 1.6 million followers on Twitter may think he's talking to each of them, when in fact he's talking to all of them.

Blake Morris says he will keep his family grounded. 'We're not going to Hollywood,' he says. 'We're not going out on the road for 40 dates a year because we can make money. We're going to continue to do a concert every couple of months, maybe five or six in the summer.'

For now, though, his children can go about their everyday lives with little interruption. Children may gawp in amazement that their favourite YouTuber is wandering the cereal aisle, but adults don't – yet. Though everyone should know about these stars. Not only are they the people children and grandchildren spend most of their time with, separated by a laptop screen, but with nearly two billion users watching YouTube every day, they're already mainstream stars. Just like Donny Osmond brings in a greying audience that first encountered him in their teens, today's YouTube stars are likely to remain popular because of the fanbase they've built up.

Blake Morris sees a future where YouTube is the mainstream. 'When Matt was seven, was eight, was nine, everyone asked me: "Why aren't you getting a TV deal for him, why aren't you signing a record deal for him? What's your next move after covers?"' says Morris. His answer is simple: he doesn't need to. He believes his son will have a 20- or 30-year career.

He mentions YouTubers who rush out to get a record deal. 'I've seen younger kids – and young in this case being 15 or 16 – go and get a record deal, and they don't get the same traction because they abandoned their audience. Their audience all of a sudden isn't going to automatically put half a million dollars into a single to make sure it gets the traction they would want. Then the young artist wonders: "What happened to my audience? Why aren't they watching my videos like they were when I was on YouTube?"'

Morris seems to know exactly what he and his son are aiming for. The company, MattyB LLC, he set up to help manage his son and ensuing profits won't limit itself to promoting Matthew's music. It also has its own mini-network of YouTube channels, including one called *funniflix* where children perform comedy sketches. 'It takes a while to introduce new artists but we're creating a small Mickey Mouse Club,' Morris says. 'We eventually want to open that to a broader base on the internet.' The obvious follow-up question is whether Blake Morris envisages MattyB LLC becoming a modern-day Disney. His immediate response is: 'We would love that.'

MattyB LLC's first major attempt to promote YouTubers outside the Morris family is the Haschak Sisters. Four sisters each separated by two years, they were introduced to the world in a video with MattyB, covering Kanye West's song *Clique* in

April 2015. In the video each sister is given their own small introduction, complete with their names emblazoned in large font on the screen. It was a calculated decision. 'When we put them out there in front of Matt's fans with a very similar product but different at the same time, the fans immediately said we will consume this and we want more,' says Blake. 'What we learned is that the amount of content this audience can consume is endless. They can consume more than we can produce.'

Blake Morris was right. The Haschak Sisters are still going strong, even as the oldest turns 18. They're still posting cover songs alongside quirky videos including dance tutorials and testing coloured contact lenses. Each and every one is seen by hundreds of thousands of viewers. The Haschak Sisters now have six million subscribers.

13.

MACRO-INFLUENCERS:

BEAUTY, CRIME AND DIY

British YouTuber Eleanor Neale buys lots of beauty products because she's worth it. She has 500,000 subscribers. Thousands of viewers watch her try out new products and dispense advice on the best way to frame a female face. But they don't just watch her try on makeup. They watch her buy it. The shopping haul – a YouTuber buying a lot of products and trying them out at home (in front of a camera) – is a staple of the lifestyle element of YouTube. Watch time on 'shop with me' videos, where viewers are taken along for the ride as their favourite creators walk the aisles, grew 10 times on mobile in the last two years alone.

Neale, whose fanbase puts her firmly in the macro-influencer bracket, spent £1,000 on blushers, mascara and other products for one video in June 2018. 'I have bought a crap-ton of makeup,' she told viewers. For the next 40 minutes, she talked almost non-stop about bronzers and foundation, lipsticks and moisturiser. Neale claimed that her makeup haul was potentially the biggest on YouTube in 2018. The outlay, however, was justified as an investment. Neale's beauty video uploads tend to average only 10,000 or 20,000 views. Her mega-haul, however, topped 100,000 views. The viewers have helped her profile as a beauty influencer. But in any case, Neale charges brands vastly more than £1,000 to mention their products in a video. According to her media kit posted on the website of Social Circle, a Manchester-based influencer marketing network that connects brands with suitable creators from a database of thousands of influencers, it costs £23,000 to get Neale to plug your product to her audience. Of these, 94% are women, and 65% under the age of 24. One in every eight viewers is aged between 13 and 17, according to the media kit.

Neale's beauty videos are almost a sideline to the main driver of viewers to her channel – her real crime reports, where she recounts the circumstances of gruesome murders and missing persons cases. Her crime videos generally hit hundreds of thousands of views. Neale, then, is another example of a determined and agile YouTuber who is reaping the benefits of being flexible.

Beauty was Neale's original plan for YouTube. Her first two dozen videos were almost exclusively about looking good. There were guidelines on getting winged eye-liner, tips on everyday makeup routines, and testing cheap, lurid lipsticks. They were moderately successful, with the odd breakaway hit. Nearly two million tuned in when she swapped her makeup bag with her 12-year-old cousin.

But when she uploaded the odd real crime video she tapped a torrent of interest. From that point, the composition of Neale's channel changed: for the following few months, she would almost alternate a beauty video with a crime vlog. Eventually, crime became the core component of Neale's channel, with beauty taking a back seat.

Other creators, though, have managed to build their reputations off beauty and fashion alone, creating videos that tap into the voracious appetite of young women for them. Lucy Moon is a 24-year-old English YouTuber who chanced upon a career on YouTube after graduating from university. She gave herself three months while hunting for jobs to see if she could convert her moderate success on YouTube into something more sustainable, and struck gold. She started gaining subscribers and with it, momentum. She has grown from 3,000-odd subscribers to 310,000, and her videos are seen by anywhere between 25,000 and 250,000 people. A video or Instagram post from Moon is more affordable than one from Neale, priced at £12,000 by Social Circle.

Moon, though, isn't an enormous fan of brand deals. In a video in early 2019, she admitted that she really only feels comfortable endorsing a product that she already loves. She also acknowledged the risk inherent in YouTubers rushing to make money: too many so-called sponcon (sponsored content) posts can do damage to your reputation. 'It's a dangerous game,' she says. 'You can do a lot of brand deals and your audience will gradually lose trust, or you can do a couple and your audience will respect that more.'

People keep coming back to Moon for her fashion tips and beauty advice. In keeping with the attitude of many YouTubers who reach a certain level of fame, she acts like an older sister, doling out support and kindness to her fans. 'I have to give answers,' she tells me over a webcam after finishing up her morning admin, including sifting through a stack of emails. 'You're in a constant dialogue with the audience, which is my favourite part of the platform. You're held accountable for everything.'

Not every big influencer is focused on fashion or the latest lip shades, though. The beauty of YouTube lies not in its flawless-complexioned makeup creators but in the multiplicity of people and their interests. Take Chez Rossi, a 47-year-old living in Darwen, a market town in Lancashire, England. He was initially puzzled why I wanted to talk to him, asking if I was sure – really sure – I had the right person.

I did. Rossi had built a following of 300,000 subscribers on YouTube for his DIY videos, posted under the name *Ultimate Handyman*. But, as he explained to me late one evening after working as a maintenance engineer at a chemical plant, he's not actually a handyman – and his YouTube channel has its roots elsewhere on the internet.

In 2004, a year before Jawed Karim stood in front of his San Diego elephants, Rossi started a website advising novices how to put up shelves, re-plaster walls and build wardrobes. The written guides were augmented by a primitive discussion forum, where visitors could ask him questions. Among the most frequently asked questions were about lighting: people would take down their existing light fitting to replace it, then realise they didn't know how to connect the nine wires they were left with. Rossi wanted to post videos explaining these quandaries to his site, but it was difficult. A friend recommended a newish website that hosted videos for you: YouTube.

Rossi set up his *Ultimate Handyman* channel on 22 January 2008. He uploaded a smattering of videos to test the water. He would post a video, leave YouTube and focus on his own website.

When he came back, he saw the YouTube posts had piled on the views. So he started making more, and found that he drew in more subscribers. By 2011, he was spending more time working on his YouTube channel than his own website and forum.

Now, years later, and having all but abandoned his own site, he struggles to devote time even to the YouTube channel. He'll scrape together a few hours in the evening after work and on weekends, filming odd jobs he's carrying out on his home for the benefit of others. He initially aimed to upload two videos per week, but for the last two years has been restricted to one because of time constraints.

'I've got terabytes of footage on my computer I haven't had time to edit,' he says. Much of his time is spent answering queries posted under his videos and building engagement. And Rossi's 300,000 subscribers are just scratching the surface: only around 4% of his total views come from those who have actually asked YouTube to serve them up his videos.

That's because YouTube is like a video encyclopaedia, the sum of human knowledge in easily digestible form. Learning videos are watched hundreds of millions of times every day, with 70% of millennials saying they log onto the site to learn how to do something new, or learn more about an interest they have. In 2017, videos that had 'how-to' in their titles were watched for more than a billion hours – up 75% from 2015. It can be footage of Rossi replacing a radiator, or someone fixing a washing machine. It can be Tim Blais, who posts videos explaining complicated scientific concepts to the tune of major pop hits to his channel, *A Capella Science*. (His video on evolutional development to the tune of Justin Bieber's 'Despacito' is a favourite.) Or it can be Laci Green talking about how to have anal sex safely (two million views) or explaining what to do if you have herpes (one million views).

As a result of the power of viewers' desire to learn, Rossi is earning well from the adverts YouTube places against his videos – as much as he earns at the chemical plant. A video published back in September 2018 showing how to remove a broken bolt from a deep hole racked up five million views, potentially earning him an average annual salary from a single video. He won't be retiring any time soon, though. In 2011, rich from the income from his website, he moved to Cyprus, but had to come back after three months. Google had changed its search algorithm, and his website, which relied on traffic from people typing DIY questions into their search bar, was affected. 'You never know,' he says. 'The same thing could happen with YouTube. It's always good to have a couple of revenue streams, really.'

Some 225,000 people subscribe to another unlikely YouTube star – 74-year-old American Peggy Glenn. As the character *Granny Potty Mouth*, she sweetly dispenses life advice in videos peppered with swearing. (Around 400,000 people follow her on Facebook too.) 'The values and the language, that's all me,' she says in an expletive-filled conversation. 'But I use the character as a vehicle to try and make the world a better place.'

A decade or so ago Glenn uploaded her first YouTube video, sliding down a hill on an inner tube, but it wasn't until 2016 that the retired secretary began uploading videos under the *Granny Potty Mouth* character. She shoots her videos in a computer room in front of three shower curtains of different colours, depending on the mood of the video, and edits them herself in Windows Movie Maker, a simplistic program a world away from the high-end software that most online video creators use.

Shooting the videos was a hobby she took up after moving to California to live with the man she fell in love with (who takes no interest in her digital exploits). But YouTube has become much more than a hobby. It's now a responsibility. She made a public commitment at a YouTube conference that she would upload a video every Thursday morning. And when I speak to her a few days before Thanksgiving 2018, Glenn's commitment was being tested almost to breaking point.

Just days before we talk, Glenn's partner had gone to bed at 11pm on Wednesday. The pensioner had no video ready to upload at 6am the following day. She didn't even have an idea. But beholden to the algorithm and her fans, Glenn took herself to her home office and wrote the outline for a script: a Thanksgiving message, addressing the fact that she often receives 20 or 25 requests a week from fans to publicise their fundraising for various causes.

The message was simple: if you don't have money, you have time. You're watching this video. So use that time for good by publicising good causes. She spent an hour honing the script, carefully choosing her words. This was from the heart, delivered just days after large parts of California dangerously close to her own home had been consumed by wildfires. By midnight, she was happy enough to set up the lighting, don her Granny Potty Mouth outfit, and hit record.

By 4.15am the following morning, fully two hours before the sun would begin to peek over the horizon, Glenn had finished. She'd recorded her video, edited it, designed the thumbnail, uploaded it and written the captions for her deaf and hard-of-hearing viewers. 'Let's lift each other up,' she concluded in her Thanksgiving video. 'We are all human beings. That's what we do at our best. We help each other; we support each other; we do not throw insults or turn away.'

A day after the video was uploaded, it had been viewed by just 1,100 people. Past videos were seen by far more. 'Part of that is YouTube has become PrudeTube,' she says. 'I lay most of that blame on Logan Paul and his contemporaries for being such stupid idiots, and having no respect for themselves or anybody else, living or dead.' The backlash to Logan Paul's extreme videos has caused an overcautious YouTube to suppress her own foul-mouthed videos, even though they contain a wholesome message. Her viewing figures have halved.

'What really pisses me off and pushes me to the point of, "You know, fuck it, I don't want to do this anymore," is that I do this midnight to 4am run and nobody sees the video,' she explains. 'It's like you're spitting into the wind to get it right back in your face.'

She had hoped to land a job presenting a cookery and advice show on conventional TV, but that now looks unlikely. 'YouTube got Will Smith so they don't give a fuck about us little guys, not at all,' she says. 'You wait for the big guys to fuck up and the rest of us end up paying the price for that.'

YouTube is hard work and constantly evolving. It's difficult for anyone to rise up, and when you get there, there are plenty of hopefuls snapping at your heels: micro-influencers.

14.

MICRO-INFLUENCERS:

SPEAKING TO A

DEVOTED AUDIENCE

In February 2014, Eniyah Rana was at a loose end. When at school in Birmingham, England, in the early 2000s, she had told her Indian Gujarati dad and Kenyan mum that she wanted to be a flight attendant. Her dream fell through when she was told at a school careers day that flight attendants needed to swim, and she couldn't. Back then, at the age of 13, she didn't consider that she could take swimming lessons.

By her own description Rana was 'a typical bored Asian housewife, struggling to wear the hijab' – the headscarf dictated by her religion. She felt frumpy and constrained wearing it, but one day managed to make it work for her. She felt amazing; beautiful. She thought: 'I'm going to film this and put it up on YouTube.'

The seven-minute video, uploaded under her married name of Aisha Rahman, was filmed as she sat on a dining room chair in front of a radiator in her house. As she demonstrated how to tie the £15 scarf she'd bought from Next around her head, Rana chatted to the people she hoped would watch. Some did.

Rana woke up the following morning to two people subscribing to her channel. The following day a third did. 'And it just went from that,' she says. A small business selling headscarves on Instagram contacted her to promote its wares. 'One thing led to another,' she adds. Four years later, she is an accomplished micro-influencer. She has also been through an acrimonious split from her Bengali husband.

Scroll through Rana's YouTube feed and you won't find much evidence of the divorce she secured in October 2018. Like many creators who try to keep their public personas on YouTube pristine by diverting dedicated fans to other platforms to find out about apologies or scandals, she decided instead to broadcast that part of her life on Snapchat, though the multiple-part Snapchat Story was uploaded by third parties to other social networks.

Sat in the passenger seat of a car, wearing a green headscarf and illuminated by the autumn sun, she bared her soul. 'I fought tooth and nail for this divorce,' she told her Snapchat followers. She explained the difficulties for a woman obtaining a divorce in strict Muslim society: 'Youse lot made it so hard for women, made them cry from end to end – they have to keep travelling to your flipping council.'

To hear her tell it, Rana's divorce was made all the more difficult by her digital persona. Fiercely outspoken, outgoing and brash, she's a natural in front of the camera, but that is not to everyone's liking. She says her husband showed videos of her dancing on Instagram as mitigation to the imam overseeing her religious divorce. 'This is haram,' the imam said, according to Rana. 'I said to the imam, "I ain't going to change. I'm going to keep on doing it, even more, 10 times worser".'

And so she does. YouTube, and being a micro-influencer, is her full-time job. Now 33, with five children, she's a YouTube entrepreneur – a micro-influencer whose 48,000 subscribers on YouTube and 110,000 followers on Instagram provide her with a full-time income for her family.

Rana's divorce was a blessing and a curse. Through heart-ache and pain, and a good deal of shame being a divorced You-Tuber in a still-conservative digital Muslim world, she gained a broader following. Mostly, she was scared. 'I thought I would lose my career over it, because I was so vocal about the divorce and being a survivor of domestic violence,' she says. 'It can be make or break when you drop these controversies.'

But it was more make than break. 'So many more women said they were going to be vocal about what they're going through,' she says. 'It gave a lot of women empowerment and encouraged them to speak about what they're going through.'

She is an example of the niches that can exist on a site as vast and sprawling as YouTube: Rana is highly recognisable in 'modest YouTube', a Muslim sub-community for women wanting to look fashionable.

She has bought a PO box near her home in Birmingham – something she says every influencer does – to receive samples and packages from her fans, and got a good deal on an office where she films her videos (taking care to avoid getting the radiator in shot).

She's still on the small end of the influencer scale, so Rana's packages only appear twice a month – around three sacks that she lugs from the PO box to her office, filming videos in which she carefully unboxes the packages she receives and thanks the senders. It can take all day to meticulously film all the packages being opened, and then chronicling them on her Instagram and Snapchat accounts too. 'It's a bit overwhelming at times,' she admits – 'you run out of space. What are you going to do with everything?' But as a makeup artist, the packages she receives helps keep her kit stocked up.

Overall, YouTube has been a boon for Rana. She is planning to launch her own make-up range in the near future. She's earning a healthy living, and has marketing deals with brands. She has also gained more confidence as a result of broadcasting her life on the platform.

Rana is typical of the raft of micro-influencers that are upending the world of marketing. Unique in their own ways, and with passionate followings who will support them through thick and thin, they foster a closer personal connection with consumers than YouTube's bigger names – some of whom can't spend the time to personally thank people for each and every care package they send to an impersonal PO box.

For a business looking to target a certain demographic, micro-influencers like Rana provide a ready-made group of avid buyers waiting to purchase their products. 'We're a lot more honest with our opinions of products,' she says. 'We don't have a certain loyalty or relationship to build with bigger brands. If we like something, we like something. If we don't, we don't.'

Rana's relatively small fanbase isn't a barrier to success or recognition from big companies looking to broadcast their wares. Across the Atlantic, an even smaller creator – a nano-influencer, manages to woo big brands. Like many, Rincey Abraham found YouTube an escape from her job. She majored in journalism at Marquette University in Milwaukee, Wisconsin, in 2009 and began working part-time as a copywriter. By day she wrote marketing copy for clients of a marketing firm. At night she watched her favourite YouTubers, including Charlie McDonnell and Kristina Horner. She didn't like her job and worked alongside people she had little in common with. But she really liked YouTube. 'I missed talking to people who had similar interests to me,' she recalls. 'I remember watching people like them and thinking – "Oh man, this is so much fun. I'd love to do that".'

Abraham was shy and didn't really want to talk about her life, bearing all to the tiny red dot above the lens. Then she came across a video featuring John Green giving a reading of his book *The Fault in Our Stars* in Amsterdam. The reading was compered by Sanne Vliegenthart, a fellow YouTuber who ran another channel, *Books and Quills*, focusing on the joy of reading. YouTube's algorithm recommended more of Vliegenthart's videos to Abraham. She fell down a rabbit hole and realised: people could talk about books on the internet. 'Booktube' is the name given to the corner of YouTube devoted to books.

Abraham's first video came out in 2012. Poorly framed in front of a rainbow-coloured set of bookshelves, with her inky eyebrows bobbing up and off screen, Abraham introduced her channel and held up a well-thumbed copy of *To Kill a Mockingbird* – her favourite book. Seven years on, 32-year-old Abraham posts one video a week for her 23,000 subscribers. She prefers to review a broad range of books targeted at a more grown-up audience than many YouTubers, who tend to cater for readers of young adult fiction. She also produces a further two videos for *Book Riot*, an independent book website, and helps manage its YouTube channel (creating the all-important thumbnail pictures for other booktube creators the other days of the week).

For now YouTube remains a hobby. During the week she works at an online hardware store in Illinois between 7.30am and 4.30pm, allowing her to spend a couple of hours every night – and one day a weekend – working on her YouTube channel. Although it doesn't currently pay a full-time wage, YouTube has changed Abraham's life in several ways. 'I used to spend so much money on books, and now I don't have to spend quite as much money,' she says. As a micro-influencer, publishers are keen to get her to review or include books in the occasional haul videos she posts on her channel – so she's peppered with galleys and review copies on a regular basis. 'That is the best perk – besides getting paid, I guess.'

Most of her viewers are in their mid-20s, 30s or 40s, and like the rest of booktube, more than half are women. How does it feel to be the arbiter of taste for a small town's-worth of readers who rely on her opinions for their purchases? She laughs: 'Oh man, that's a big responsibility!'

In many ways, these micro- and nano-influencers are the soul of YouTube; its good conscience in a body of cold commerce. But even they are of interest to brands: Rana deals with beauty influencer Huda Kattan, while Abraham has the ear of agents looking to promote their book. So why are brands turning to micro-influencers rather than the traditional endorsements of celebrities that have powered their marketing for decades? Olivia Allan, an independent talent agent who used to work for Social Circle, has a simple answer: 'Because their audiences are so engaged.'

While YouTube's biggest stars, the PewDiePies and Huda Kattans, are mass media; the advertisers are beginning to appreciate that lesser-known, niche creators are better value, dollar for dollar. The smaller an audience, the more loyal they are – 'because the chances are it's your family and friends following you,' says Allan. 'They're more likely to listen to you.' Some of the larger influencers on YouTube who have millions of followers have proportionately lower individual view counts. The reason? On social media platforms, you rarely unfollow or unsubscribe from content creators, unless they've produced content that offends you. Deadweight followers count towards subscriber totals.

Allan explains: 'It's also finding influencers that really fit the brand. Often I'll hear about startups pumping £20,000 or £30,000 into videos with [British YouTubers] Tanya Burr and Zoella because they're the ones they've heard of because they read about them in *The Daily Mail*. It's such a waste of money: if you split that budget working with seven or eight smaller You-Tubers or Instagrammers, you're actually going to get a much greater influence over that audience, casting your net much wider and have a lot less wastage.'

As Mats Stigzelius, co-founder and chief executive of social media marketing firm Takumi, has said: 'Many people still wrongly prefer macro influencers with hundreds of thousands of followers, but the reality is that you now reach the same audience with micro influencers, while also benefitting from higher engagement.'

Brands brokering a big money deal with a celebrity might receive a single social media post in return. Working with micro influencers, a company can generate the same reach and 100 pieces of social content with exactly the same budget. Stigzelius says: 'From our experience, we're seeing more and more brands realise that celebrity isn't everything and ditching big names in favour of micro-influencers.'

PART VI

BEHIND THE SCENES:

SNAPSHOTS

15.

SUMMER IN THE CITY:
A GATHERING OF
INFLUENCERS

At 11am sharp, thousands stream into the exhibition centre, holding their arms in the air to show off their coloured wristbands, as demanded by the shouts of bored-looking security staff. Those at the back of the queue, who file in after minutes of shuffling forward, are significantly less enthusiastic at showing their wrists. The odd parent waves at the security staff when exhorted to raise their hands.

Summer in the City at the ExCeL exhibition centre in London's Docklands is a three-day summer jamboree for fans and creators. 'The UK's online video festival' has become the biggest fixture on the British YouTube calendar. Held in early August, business here ranges from panel discussions to merchandise and meet-and-greets.

Around 1,200 people already attended the first day of the 2017 event, 'Creator Day', for industry figures, where YouTubers, creators and content networks gather to discuss the state of the online video world. The second and third days are for the fans, with panel discussions, the chance to meet your favourite You-Tuber, YouTube-themed shopping and gaming.

Around 8,000 people are expected on the second day and slightly fewer on the closing Sunday. At 10.45am, 15 minutes before doors officially open, the queue for entry is several hundred metres long. It snakes past cafes and Subway outlets, blocking access to toilets and car parks. Gaggles of teenagers clutch Summer in the City-branded plastic bags containing a 30-page pamphlet about the panels, an advert for an upcoming movie, and a handful of Chupa Chups lollies. Some have flowers in their hair and carry pompoms. Many drape themselves in the rainbow colours of the pride flag. Typically British, those in line queue sensibly and quietly, a ramrod-straight line, with only the odd scream when requested by passing news crews or camera-men filming promotional videos.

Two men in fluorescent jackets and with spotted dogs, 'Dog Handler' written on their backs, mingle around the entrance. It takes 12 minutes for the last stragglers to stream through the door of the exhibition centre. The excitement and volume of fans speak to the incredible growth of YouTube. So too do their wristbands. In the first years of YouTube, the small band of creators and fans were equal. Creators often knew each other personally when they met at small functions. A decade later, YouTube events are hosted at some of the biggest convention centres in the world. VidCon attracts more than 20,000 fans annually in California, and 7,500 to its European outing in Amsterdam. A new event formed by creators including Zoella and Alfie Deyes, HelloWorld!, was hosted in the UK's second-biggest city, Birmingham, in October 2017, but proved a flop due to poor organisation and a massive backlash from unhappy children and their parents who felt they were oversold on the promise of the event.

Whether it's Summer in the City, VidCon or HelloWorld!, all have to distinguish between stars and fans. At Summer in the City, component parts of the YouTube system have been isolated and colour-coded. The 150 members of the press are given a pink paper wristband. Ordinary visitors are given an orange fabric wristband. The most important members of staff have candy cane-striped paper wristbands in different colours. Guests of YouTube receive red-and-white which allow backstage access to a plush green room away from the action. Green-and-white bands give access to all areas. (A similar system operates at VidCon: yellow speaker/featured creator lanyards get you almost everywhere bar the exclusive YouTube Creators' Lounge backstage, for which you need a fabric band that a YouTube employee checking your name off a list will slip round your wrist.)

The event is an assault on the senses. Walking into the main exhibition space, you're first confronted with ExCeL London security staff shouting at you to move on through and let the next wave of individuals in. At the front of the room is a vast wall adorned with a YouTube logo, red, black and white drawings of bearded men, cupcakes, basketball courts and fidget spinners along its length. In one corner sits an intricate drawing of a man wearing a unicorn head, holding a sign reading 'Free Hugs.' Behind it, a gaming stage, where video game streamers and personalities perform live for the audience at regular intervals. To the left, a vast booth for McDonalds, where visitors take selfies and post them online in exchange for a free McFlurry. To the right, a queue is already forming for fairground rides including dodgems and a seated ride that raises periodic screams from its riders, and ahead, a maze of stalls selling everything from T-shirts adorned with cats and witty slogans to subscriptions to the Dogs Trust.

Along the length of the 77-foot far wall are merchandise tables for creators. Metal guard rails separate the queues for the stalls, which are already building up. The most popular appears to be the stand selling clothes for Thomas 'TomSka' Ridgewell, who produces animated videos and vlogs.

Truthfully, the main exhibition space looks and feels like a soulless convention centre, rather than the epicentre of a mass media movement teeming with teenage enterprise. But it proves popular with fans who have saved up for their Summer in the City tickets. The aisles between the stalls throng with people, with big queues forming for the most popular parts, including an Instagram photo backdrop decked with hundreds of balloons.

People mill around the dodgems as a queue forms for a fair-ground ride. Friends use their iPhones to snap photos of each other lounging about on giant letters spelling out 'SITC 2017'. People peruse the stalls, pulling out their purses and wallets. A young woman hares past in a Pikachu costume.

A woman is nursing a large coffee in a takeaway cup in the seating area outside the main hall. Two of her three daughters (a 13- and 14-year-old) are attending the convention from their home in Melton Mowbray – the second time they have come. She, however, has decided to sit it out, despite the orange band tied to her wrist. 'I went in with them last year and stood and queued to see whoever they were seeing,' she says. 'At the end of it, I said: "I can't believe how long we've just stood to get a photograph".' This year, she's taken a different approach. 'I said I'm going to go and sit in Costa and I'll have a coffee. I've got all their coats and bags.'

Her daughters mostly wanted to return to the event for the meet-and-greets, which are decided by a ballot. She says: 'They put in for the top eight, and they've got their first choices. They're quite pleased. There's three lads, Joe and Jamie and somebody else. I've got no idea. It goes over my head. No interest in it whatsoever.' That extends to her third, oldest daughter, who at 16 'knows about it but isn't into it as much.' She sips her coffee. At £25 per child for an early bird ticket plus the travel down to London, it isn't a cheap weekend. But she's content, if bemused, to let her daughters attend. 'You don't get people like Zoella coming to Summer in the City,' she explains. 'They're like, really big. These are the ones that they know about but want to expand their fanbase a little bit.'

Everyone here is a viewer, but a fair number of those walking round the floor of Summer in the City are also content creators in their own right. It's a hot-button issue, discussed at many of the panels: just what separates the creator-celebrities from their creator-fans in the strange new world of YouTube? Who – or what – dictates where the line is drawn between creators and audience? What differentiates those who get candy cane wristbands, and those who get the generic orange fabric ones?

At 2.30pm at the Bridge Burgers & Dogs, two young women and a man, each no older than 20, sit at a table with burgers and fries. Before tucking into their meals, each one of them picks up a camera they placed on the table in turn and points the lens towards themselves.

'We're here at lunch and I've got to say, the customer service at this burger and hot dog place is awful. But I got a cheeseburger, some chips and a Coke,' the first says. Her friend passes sarcastic comments on the service too, while the third expounds on why she chose a hotdog. As they put their cameras down and tuck into their meal, at another table a young girl, perhaps 12 or 13, gesticulates into her own camera. Sat across the table, her father scrolls through his phone disinterestedly.

The headline panel of the day stars the singer Dodie Clark. The panel moderator, Taha Khan, asks the audience to raise their hands if they too make YouTube videos. Around half the gathering throw up their arms. Khan remarked later: 'It's places like this where you can really see how the creator/viewer divide has really manifested itself.'

Tom Burns is all too keenly aware of how things have changed. Wearing a blue Oxford shirt and a green-and-white wristband, Burns is youthful and lanky, with a sweep of hair covering his forehead. He founded Summer in the City aged 16 in 2009 as a gathering of 200 YouTubers in Hyde Park in central London. Now the creators have their own backstage area. Burns added one in 2012, partly by accident. At Summer in the City 2012, the venue, The Brewery in central London, had a room where the organisers could dump their bags and boxes. The storage room had to be made a safe room, because 'there were crowds, and there were mobbing and capacity issues. From then on it became the norm.'

Burns explains: 'Even then we weren't anticipating YouTube to have boomed up the way it did back then, but it did. People we'd had coming for years and years, like Dan and Phil and Charlieissocoollike, suddenly had queues forming for them. It was interesting because VidCon had happened the year before, and they'd had meet-and-greets growing at VidCon, but the culture was completely changing. It caught everyone off guard. It even caught the content creators off-guard.'

In effect, 2012 was when YouTube passed from a democratic community into an entertainment industry that minted its own celebrities. The meet-and-greet culture formed around events like Summer in the City and VidCon, and what had once been a vague divide between creators and viewers was solidifying. That same year also saw a step change in how YouTube marketed itself: the platform's motto, 'Broadcast Yourself', was dropped from the logo when the site underwent a wholesale redesign. It was perhaps an indication of the introduction of commerce onto the platform; the first sign that this was now a business, not just a social network.

All the big conventions draw a firm line between who can enter the luxury lounges and who can't. The problem is that – on YouTube, a modern social media platform where anyone can upload anything and become a celebrity or viral sensation in a matter of minutes – those lines are smudged. And that caused bafflement not to mention consternation. Burns says: 'It was confusing for people. They weren't really sure about the boundaries. They'd watch people, their vlogs, telling their stories, and it's very easy to think you're involved in that person's life, that you're part of it. We'd have a lot of people coming down feeling entitled to meet someone – almost as if they're seeing a friend.'

Of course, fans and creators aren't friends. They are engaged in a creator/viewer relationship; where one side profits from the other, and uses their support in order to build their reputation. When money – from ads, from sponsorship deals, and from merchandise – entered the YouTube equation, the balance changed.

'If you went to a gig, you wouldn't expect to meet Taylor Swift,' reasons Burns. 'You'd appreciate there's a difference there, but back then there were shaky boundaries.' Back then Zoella (who we'll meet later) wasn't branded a celebrity. Now, she drives traffic to *The Daily Mail* website. Her fanbase is so large that she can no longer know every single one of her fans, and can no longer make time for all of them. She's no longer 'one of us'. She's a celebrity.

In the backstage area at ExCeL, some of the biggest British YouTubers are networking and setting up collaborations with each other. Security guards are more numerous here, checking the colour of wristbands. Both YouTube and Facebook have extensive lounges backstage above the busy show floor, where creators can relax with their peers, away from the gaze of the masses.

16.

COLLABORATION:

SAPPHIRE

BUILDS A CAREER

Sapphire has played Wembley two times. She has brand endorsements and is on a retainer with an American sponsor. And she's been flown out to Germany for arena performances at VideoDays.

But the life of a 16-year-old YouTuber is not easy. 'Last year when I came here I was on 280,000 subscribers,' Sapphire says, looking out onto the Thames from the VIP room, a sense of frustration in her voice. 'I was stuck there for a really long time because my content wasn't showing up anywhere. We had rights issues. But at 280,000 I was stuck. Now I'm on 370,000. I've gone up a lot. I only reached 300,000 in February. It's gone up lots since then. So hopefully we'll be at 400,000 at the end of the year, then next year when I come I'll be nearer 500,000.' As of mid-March 2019, she was at 525,000 subscribers.

'That's why I'm trying to collaborate,' she explains. 'If someone has a million subscribers and you have 400,000 that's an extra million people who haven't seen your videos. Also when you do a collaboration, it's so potent – doing things with people your fans don't know gets you in front of other people.'

Sapphire is careening around on the YouTube rollercoaster. It has all happened so fast, though it's also been a lot of hard work and astute management. Sapphire first got the itch for performing when she joined a stage school near London at the age of four. The school had around 80 pupils, and the end of term spectaculars would draw crowds of 3,000 or more. Though she happily performed on stage while the spotlights prevented her from seeing the size of the audience, as soon as they dimmed she would realise how many people were there and get stage fright.

It became too much and Sapphire stopped attending the stage school aged six and had a year off from performing. Nick Upshall, her father and manager, a lean man with his iPhone constantly in his hand, says: 'Then mum discovered this thing called YouTube.'

Aged seven, Sapphire performed a song from the Disney musical *Camp Rock* in her front hall, with Upshall holding a camcorder. 'It was basic, but it worked,' he recalls. They uploaded the video and it got 100 views. A month later, Sapphire uploaded another video. That one got 1,000 views. Another got 2,000; another 5,000. Now her videos are seen by thousands upon thousands, and she's managed to travel the world as a result – all while barely into her teenage years. 'She's always loved doing it,' says Upshall. 'Now she's like, "I want to make this work forever. This is something I want to do as my job, my career. I want to travel the world and do that".'

Most of Sapphire's fans are 13-17-year-olds, and around 70% are girls. However, a significant number fall into the 35-45-year-old demographic – children under 13 (theoretically barred from accessing YouTube) probably using their parents' accounts. 'I can't believe people from all over the world watch my videos,' says Sapphire. 'It's pretty amazing.'

Yet like grown-up celebrity, name (and face) recognition can on occasion have its drawbacks. Sapphire has been followed around a Claire's Accessories by young fans who recognised her. They then ran out the shop and screamed at their mums: 'That girl is famous on YouTube.' Another fan filmed her in Waitrose carrying a box of Rice Krispies. 'That was odd, but it's pretty amazing.'

'It's been pretty surreal,' says Upshall. 'Obviously having any child, you want to give them opportunities – your mum and dad drive you everywhere, to football matches, to athletics, to dances. They go the extra mile for you as parents. It just so happens the girls [Sapphire's sister Skye is also a YouTuber] are into a world of music and they have shown an extraordinary talent for it as well.'

For most parents, that means busy evenings shuttling their sires from football matches to singing practice and friends' houses. For Upshall, it means weekend mornings shooting music videos in parks and shopping malls, and evenings spent in front of an Apple Mac Pro in a converted studio that was once the family's spare bedroom editing footage into slickly packaged videos that go viral.

'It's a huge commitment of time,' he admits. At the time we

spoke, Sapphire was producing around two YouTube videos per week that take around 12 hours to make. She'll spend a couple of hours recording covers of mainstream pop songs into microphones installed in the spare bedroom; she and her parents will take the same amount of time filming; then Upshall clips the footage together. Sapphire has uploaded hundreds of videos online, some of which have more than six million individual views. 'We've got more sophisticated as time goes on,' says Upshall. 'And mum and dad have got slightly better at videoing.'

Parents of YouTubers navigating the early days of online fame have to keep their progeny's feet on the ground. They also have to carefully manage how much of their personal lives are shared online. 'You've got two hats to wear as a parent,' says Upshall. 'You're proud of them on one hand, but on the other, what are they going into? This wild world of music and fame... What does it mean to them and for their future?' So far, says Upshall, the positives outweigh the negatives. 'She's got her own small business that generates income and pays for nice stuff for her but also pays for her musical development.'

Sapphire's first performances on YouTube were relatively low-key; perhaps just singing into a microphone. By 2016, her videos had become complex productions, mimicking mainstream music videos. A year on, they've evolved even further. 'Every video we're trying to get a dance in,' she says, rationalising the decision by explaining that 'the more boring the video the less people watch it.' In 2019, she's started testing out medleys, cramming 12 songs into a three-minute video.

'My fans are not people who want to watch someone singing by a mic anymore,' she says. 'We do put the odd one up, acoustic stuff, behind the scenes type things. We're kind of testing how my new audience respond to it. You grow an audience, they get older as you get older.'

The challenge for cover artists like Sapphire is retaining viewers – which explains why she's tried to incorporate elaborate dance routines into her videos. Viewers already know what they're listening to, she reckons, compared to vlogging, where the content is completely original and often off the cuff. 'People have no clue what's coming up, but with a song, they've already heard it on the radio, they've heard it on Spotify already, they've downloaded it. So that's why we're making it different, because then they really don't know what's coming.'

Viewers can be finickity, though. They only want certain types of original content. Original music is always a hard sell on YouTube. 'Fans say they want original songs but it's really hard because songs are searchable, whereas original songs aren't,' she explains. 'People are always searching the latest chart hits, but people aren't going to search your original song names, unless you're being searched as an artist. You've got to get your name searched, then your songs get searched.'

It's a complex situation for anyone to be in, never mind a 16-year-old, juggling her career online with studies at school.

At Summer in the City she and her father want to make contact with fellow creators, networking and getting the opportunity to expand their audience by combining fanbases. 'We're more interested in picking up contacts with other creators,' shouts Nick, over the din of the fairground attractions in the convention hall.

Collaborations with fellow vloggers offer several advantages. They will extend Sapphire's reach into other fanbases, preferably larger ones. They will offer increased exposure on social media, through sharing by her collaborator's fans. They will vary her material. And they are generally a way of keeping up with the fast evolving nature of YouTube, where the most successful creators are dynamic.

'It's a funny thing, because there are some super-creators like Zoella, then there are the micro-ones,' Nick Upshall says, barely audible above the shouts and screams. 'Sapphire's really a micro-one, and there's quite a leap between the two. Pooling resources, collaborations are the way forward. You meet someone in one area, you meet someone else in another area, and it cross-pollinates. Look at Zoella's friends: all of her friends are famous YouTubers. That's not a coincidence: she didn't make friends with famous people. It's more that they've all become famous.'

We are walking through the convention hall alongside Sapphire, who is on the lookout for a similarly aged Musical.ly (which has since merged with the all-encompassing super short-form video app, TikTok) creator called Becky she arranged to meet to discuss a collaboration. 'Becky's got half a million followers on Musical.ly,' explains Upshall, craning his neck around me, casting his gaze around the room to try and find the star. 'It's perfect for Sapphire.' After a minute or so of wandering through the stalls, Sapphire spots Becky by the Instagram installation, and the two chat animatedly. Her father explains what they're spending their weekend doing while the attendees shop until they drop, on the lookout for their favourite micro-celebrities.

'You're running round, and a lot of what's happening is off the show floor,' he says. 'We've got meetings set up. There's a whole thing happening behind the scenes.'

An ad hoc meeting occurs at the stand of Zoomin' TV, a video production company founded in 2000 by two Dutch entrepreneurs in Amsterdam, where Upshall chats animatedly with Jayden Rodrigues, an Australian dancer with a million subscribers on YouTube who cut short a holiday in Europe to attend the event. (Sapphire and Jayden collaborated on a Christmas charity video and have since kept in touch.) 'We should try and do something while we're here,' says Upshall to Rodrigues, who nods as they exchange phone numbers.

As they do so, a pair of teenage boys approaches Sapphire and asks her for a photo. They're two of her biggest fans, Upshall later explains, who send her packages from Germany. After wrapping up the conversation with Rodrigues, Sapphire and the two boys head to a wall adorned with a YouTube play button logo, where they take a quick photograph. From there, we rush off the show floor, past the merchandise stands and into the backstage area.

17.
MANAGEMENT:
SARAH WEICHEL,
STAR AGENT

Sarah Weichel initially wanted to be a talent manager in the music industry, figuring it was the quickest and easiest way for her to get free tickets to her favourite bands. But when she applied to The Collective (now known as Studio 71), a talent management company in Beverly Hills, it wasn't hiring people to work in the music department. It did have vacancies in its digital arm, though. 'That was back in 2011,' Weichel says. 'I thought: "Shoot, I'll just take this job in digital and transfer to the other department when something opens up".' She became one of five people in the digital department in 2011 just as YouTube's popularity was beginning to surge: 'It was a good time and a great opportunity to immerse myself in everything YouTube.'

Now Weichel, a glamorous blonde with a preppy American accent, is a serious powerbroker, representing some of the world's biggest YouTubers, including Lilly Singh, the Canadian creator who goes by the nickname IISuperwomanII (who PewDiePie was worried YouTube wanted to usurp him). Singh earned an estimated $10.5 million in 2017, has 14 million subscribers, and in March 2019 said she'd be replacing Carson Daly as a late-night TV talkshow host on NBC. Weichel also represents Jon Cozart (who has 4.5 million subscribers) and *Smosh* co-founder Anthony Padilla (who has three million).

Weichel is not alone. YouTubers are taking on mini-empires of support staff to handle all aspects of being a big name influencer, including hiring social media managers and merchandise experts to help broker the countless brand and interview requests they receive daily.

British beauty and lifestyle blogger Zoe Sugg, aka Zoella, and her boyfriend, Alfie Deyes, have a company, A to Z Creatives, to look after their burgeoning business interests. Sugg has 11 million subscribers who watch her beauty hauls and makeup tips. A to Z Creatives employs a creative manager to 'keep an eye on the wide range of Zoe's exciting projects, from beauty products, books & websites to many other fun secret things'; a manager 'to build a robust and diverse 360 strategy for Zoe'; a merchandise manager 'turning ideas and designs into products, getting the products to viewers and everything in between'; a creative producer creating 'imagery for @Zoella including product shots and any other photography needed for various projects including graphics and designs for social feeds'; a business advisor to 'make sure we are thinking to the future about what is important and fulfilling for us'; a social media manager and an office manager. (Alfie, who has 3.9 million subscribers, has his own staff, too.)

Such a large staff is necessary for the biggest YouTubers to keep all the plates spinning. KSI laughs when I ask him what he thinks of the perception that YouTubers stay up too late, lie in too long, and simply switch on the camera and hit record. 'I wish it was that easy,' he says. 'It's way more than just that. Whenever I think of a video, I need to write scripts of what I'm going to say and make sure I know my selling points, then make sure the lighting and everything looks good visually, and then obviously talking in front of the camera, you've got to do that.' And that's before he even thinks about editing it, posting it, and then considering how best to market it so it gets the most clicks. Once you add on the idea of running a startup business and brokering brand deals, vetting merchandise and organising personal appearances, the need for support is obvious.

If anyone wanted to see in person the way in which YouTube has become a business, and its stars celebrities with staff like any other, they needed only to poke their head around the door of the ICC Capital Suite rooms 3-4 at the 2019 VidCon held at London's ExCeL conference centre.

Holding forth was Patrick Starrr, resplendent in a sequinned blue bodysuit, criss-crossed from collarbone to crotch with the Union flag. Starrr (real name Patrick Simondac), a makeup wearing 29-year-old proudly gay Filipino, was surrounded by five other people wearing a rainbow-full of colourful outfits. The YouTuber, who previously worked at US sandwich chain Panera Bread and on the makeup counter of MAC cosmetics in Orlando, has turned his outlandish character into major success, with more than four million subscribers and collaborations with supermodels and Hollywood royalty. He's walked the red carpet at big mainstream awards ceremonies. But Patrick Starrr the brand isn't the work of one person. Team Patrick (or to give it its formal, legal name, PatrickStarrr Inc) is far more.

Christina Jones, Starrr's manager, who had taken him across different talent agencies she has worked at, was there, along with Megan Smith, his publicity manager, who arranges for him to appear on red carpets for film premieres. Sat at Starrr's left shoulder was his business manager and younger brother, Peter Simondac. Then there was Fabian Quinonez, Starrr's director of operations, and Dez Mandl, his video editor. Two others stayed at home in the United States to keep Patrick Starrr the brand going while he was in London for the week, while occasional freelance staff are brought in to do odd jobs when required.

'Did you guys ever think that I would have this many people?' he asked the audience. 'Boy is this expensive,' Starrr joked. 'I gotta feed these hoes. With my day-to-day, it's so busy. I had to realise what my weaknesses were and what were my strengths.' As Starrr explained, he still oversees everything that goes out under his name, providing notes and feedback to his video editor before they're published online. 'When it comes to working with editors, it sounds great and sounds fun,' he said. 'But the hard part is you start to lose your voice.'

For her part, Sarah Weichel is often asked what the difference is between traditional celebrity and this new group of pop culture figures, who also have their own entourages. 'I think the answer is pretty simple,' she says: 'for the most part, nothing.' The job of the talent manager hasn't evolved much either. Her job is to build a strategy that will allow her client to maximise their opportunities.

Like many creators who are the contemporaries of those she represents, Weichel feels that some of YouTube's innocence and cultural importance have been lost. 'We've gone so far in the direction of asking what does the algorithm say, what does the audience want, what do the numbers say. I think that's not a long-term solution for entertainment in general, and creative people specifically.'

A few weeks before we spoke in 2018, Weichel attended a panel discussion involving contemporary YouTubers: those who had set up their channels since she started representing talent on the site, and had enjoyed the first few moments of success. 'They were very strategic in their approach to content,' Weichel laments. 'There was almost no creativity rooted into it. It was simply a strategy of how to identify an audience and how to find attention.'

That can be difficult for the talent she represents (and has represented), who first came onto the site for creative fulfilment and found themselves – almost by accident – thrust into the spotlight. 'Right now there's a common misconception that all YouTubers are created equal and their value is the same,' she says. 'I don't think that's the case.'

Part of her job is to dissuade talent from grabbing all they can in the YouTube goldrush at the risk of undermining their credibility. 'Not all YouTubers should write a book,' she says. 'Not all YouTubers should go on tour. Not all YouTubers should create a T-shirt line. My role in this is to help actually figure out the right business opportunities for proactive talent.'

Months after we spoke, Weichel crossed back over into traditional media, taking her charges with her. In July 2018, she joined Anonymous Content, an entertainment firm behind TV shows like *Mr Robot* and *True Detective*, to head up their 'emerging platforms' division. It was yet another example of YouTube joining the respected media firmament, and the lines blurring between YouTube and traditional entertainment firms.

Weichel denies she's down on YouTube as a platform, though it's hard to see how such a demoralising forecast for the future is exactly a ringing endorsement of the site. 'I think my concern with YouTube,' she hesitates, 'is where they're placing value. I can tell you a story.'

Back in 2013, Weichel was representing Hannah Hart, who was enjoying serious success. At the time Hart had just won a Streamy award for best female performance in comedy for her YouTube series, *My Drunk Kitchen*. A two-year veteran of the site, she had begun the year posting a video mooting the idea of undertaking a world tour she was calling Hello Harto. To do so, she was asking her fans to crowdfund the trip, aiming to raise $50,000 within a month. Within hours her fans had met the target and more, and would go on to raise more than $220,000 in a month. She was one of the biggest creators on the platform, and with her friends and fellow YouTubers Grace Helbig and Mamrie Hart (no relation), was an inspiration and idol to millions of fans.

She was also flirting with opportunities outside of YouTube. She, Helbig and Mamrie Hart had been approached by Michael Goldfine, a film producer, who wanted to make a movie starring the trio as counsellors at a summer camp. The group agreed to be part of the film, called *Camp Takota*. Around the time pre-production began, Hart was invited to speak at a global YouTube meeting in San Francisco, where the site's employees and executives were gathering to brainstorm ideas. 'There was a little direction on what she should and shouldn't talk about,' recalls Weichel, 'but there was a massive opportunity for her to say something.

Before the meeting, in Hart's hotel room, the YouTuber and her manager were deep in thought. Hart brought up *Camp Takota*. 'She said: "Do I tell them I'm working on a film off YouTube?" At the time it was almost "Let's not tell YouTube what we're doing off YouTube": I don't want them to think I'm not a valuable creator or that I shouldn't be involved or that I'm going to potentially leave them. Maybe I shouldn't talk about this at all.'

The duo agonised over whether to hint to YouTube that Hart was able to find success (or at least was exploring life) outside the platform. In the end, they decided to bring up the film in Hart's keynote speech; to explain how the site had helped Hart grow an audience, and how it could help keep her audience in tandem with success away from YouTube.

Shortly after, YouTube launched YouTube Red (since renamed YouTube Premium) and YouTube Originals: two initiatives that supported creators on the site to make bigger-budget, paid-for programmes that were more expansive (and more creatively rewarding) than blurting out your thoughts to a camera.

Though Weichel isn't suggesting that Hart's speech catalysed the decision to launch the initiatives, she does think it may have nudged YouTube towards making the decision to invest in its creators. 'It was a great example of YouTube leaning in, listening to creators and wanting to work arm-in-arm.' The reasoning seemed smart: 'At the end of the day, the press headline – for the most part – doesn't read 'Actress Hannah Hart' or 'Comedian Hannah Hart': it reads 'YouTuber Hannah Hart'. And I think it's good for everybody to be able to grow and evolve together.'

18.

TRAINING CAMP:

WITH THE 11-YEAR-OLD

YOUTUBERS

In a villa 20 miles from Madrid, scores of teenage YouTubers are in bikinis and swimming shorts, excitedly chattering over the sound of summer pop hits and Disney songs. Some paddle around in the blue pool filled with inflatable plastic doughnuts, while others race round the garden carrying Super Soakers, firing off the occasional spurt of water. The acrid smell of hot dogs wafts over the evening air. Those old enough to drink can duck into the villa, where they are served bottles of Desperados beer from an ice-filled tub in an anteroom used during the week as a child's playroom, if the discarded toys left strewn behind a hastily put-up curtain are any indication. The younger ones swig from bottles of Coke.

It's June 2016 and the event looks like an ordinary pool party, except that all the teenaged partygoers are carrying cameras and smartphones. Barely audibly over the thumps and whomps of the music blaring out of the PA system, Bastian Manintveld, a long-haired Dutch entrepreneur, says admiringly: 'They're little one-person enterprises. They're their own scriptwriters, directors, editors and social media managers.'

All the partygoers look like they're having the time of their lives, but underlying the fun there's a sense of performance to the proceedings, a calculated check that they are accruing enough footage for their YouTube channels. Teenagers and young adults who are having perfectly pleasant conversations make sure to mug for the camera and strike a pose when they know they're in its viewfinder. People stop scooping up condiments for their freshly-grilled burgers to make sure they capture the branded products they're eating. At one point, a partygoer absents himself from the action and stands on the villa's balcony performing a monologue to the camera in his outstretched hand, his back to all the fun and entertainment going on without him.

Yet it makes sense: all of the fresh-faced performers here are ruthlessly good at what they do. They've built up an audience from nothing in a highly competitive world which daily throws up more rivals to dilute their prospects. The supply of potential young YouTubers is vast. Being a YouTuber was the main career ambition of British youngsters surveyed by holiday firm First Choice in 2017. Of 1,000 six to 17-year-olds, a third wanted to be a YouTuber – six times the number who wanted to be a lawyer and three times those who wanted to be a doctor or nurse. Tellingly, becoming a professional YouTuber was three times more popular than being a TV presenter. Given that YouTube viewing is growing among continental Europeans at a greater rate than in the UK, the figures may be even higher there. A survey in Japan in 2017 found that being a YouTuber was the third most popular choice for boys, and the tenth most popular one for girls. Alice Marwick of the University of North Carolina, Chapel Hill, who has researched online celebrity, says: 'Fame in American and British culture is held up as this ideal: if you become famous, it's a goal you've achieved.'

2btube will help children to achieve that dream. It is a multi-channel network (MCN): part talent scout, part production company and part-ad agency. The 100 youngsters preening and pouting for the camera are some of the 150 influencers Manintveld's operation had on its books in 2016 (500 today).

Manintveld, whose straggly hair and goatee make him look like a lion, bridges the gap between the old, anarchic YouTube and its new sleek business incarnation. He's a TV man at heart, a former executive who made the jump from linear schedules and bunny ear aerials to streaming channels and brand deals. He leapt into new media in 2014 because of his children. In the old days he couldn't sit down on the sofa to watch TV after a day at the office because his kids were slouched there controlling the remote. But slowly and surely, Manintveld found his viewing less and less interrupted. Eventually, his two teenage daughters were nowhere to be seen.

'One day they're monopolising my living room and I can't watch television because they're always there watching the Disney Channel,' Manintveld recalls. 'The next, all of a sudden they're not in the living room any more. I thought: "What the hell's going on?"'

Manintveld went to investigate and found his daughters watching YouTube videos on his iPad. It was a moment of revelation. Puzzled by what had grabbed their attention so quickly, he explored further: 'I started to dig deeper and I saw this is a revolution that's going on. Young kids are starting to shift away to this, and then I started to look into the numbers.'

His Googling revealed that Disney had just bought a company specialising in YouTube videos, Maker Studios, for $675 million in 2014. Maker Studios had only been founded five years earlier by a number of early YouTubers including Lisa Donovan, Kassem 'Kassem G' Gharaibeh (a Jordanian-born YouTuber who became famous for his rambling videos where he would wander the streets of California asking scantily clad tourists invasive questions), and Phil DeFranco, whose monologues on current affairs lit up the early days of the site.

'I saw it wasn't just my daughters doing it. It was an entire generation,' Manintveld says. 'I thought: "Fucking hell, this is massive." This is really big business, and nobody in Spain or in the Spanish language part of the world is really doing anything about it.' Manintveld set up 2btube later in 2014.

As 2btube's executive chairman, he is happy to joke around with his young clients, but it's clear that he's in charge. As the pool party winds down, he heads for the balcony, guitar in hand, to lead his clients in a rendition of *Feliz Cumpleaños* (*Happy Birthday*) before giving out awards to the best-performing creators poolside, posing for photographs in front of a 2btube backdrop with the winners. He can share a laugh, but there's a competitive edge among the polite applause. The party is a way of celebrating and thanking his youngsters and staff. But it's also an advert for 2btube, and for YouTube in general. It's good content for the hundreds of millions of people who subscribe to 2btube talent: glistening, sun-kissed glamour that fuels the YouTube dream.

But as Manintveld is at pains to point out in the days I spend with him, before you reach the pool party, the free doughnuts and the chilled Coke, you have to put in the hard work. The following day, a half-hour tear along the highway in Manintveld's BMW, just how early that starts becomes abundantly clear.

Francisco de Vitoria University was thrown up quickly in the 1990s and it shows. Tap the sharp, square-edged fascias in the corridors and you realise they're not marble, but plastic. In the late afternoon heat, the corridors are dingy and sticky. The campus is hosting a YouTuber training camp for children, run in collaboration with 2btube.

According to Manintveld, 100 or more enquired about the camp, held in the summer of 2016. Ten are attending, all aged under 14. Their parents have paid between €650 (daytime classes; around $730 at the time) and €1,705 (full-board; nearly $2,000) for intense tuition in how to triumph on YouTube. The set-up seems to jar with the age range. But lessons on how to 'grow your audience' and 'monetising videos uploaded to your channel' are all-important weapons for a YouTuber and hence of interest to pre-teenaged children plotting out their path to fame.

Nine of the small superstars of the future sit in rows in an airless, silent classroom with a couple of 'teachers' flicking through their phones at the front. A cheap plaster depiction of Christ on the cross hangs on the front wall by the whiteboard. Each child stares intently at a video editing programme on an old flatscreen monitor in front of them, deep in concentration and cut off from the outside world by black can headphones. They are editing clips they have shot of themselves to put into the final footage they will post onto YouTube: the grand culmination of two weeks' worth of work. Whether it's the stress of the project, the concentration needed for the edit, fatigue from being separated from their parents on the penultimate day, or all three, there's a strange feeling of deflation in the room. A summer camp evokes colour and fun in the outdoors, health, freedom, vitality, but this one is very much a working holiday.

Hunched over the monitors, 11-year-old Alex Bortnyk and 12-year-old Julien Seny are watching a metallic-shaded cylinder worm its way across a screen; footage of themselves playing the game slither.io. When I can drag them away from splicing together the most exciting scenes, Seny takes me to the back of the classroom where he shows me a sheet of A4 paper daubed with felt-tip pen. On one sheet of paper is a stick figure wearing a black top hat. Written underneath are the words 'Mr Chapeau', Seny's proposed YouTube username. Seny, a cherubic Belgian boy, has decided to use this branding to make him stand out in YouTube's ultra-competitive ecosystem – one of the main lessons he's learned. 'I have four hats, and that's going to be my thing,' he explains, eyes wide open and attentive. 'You need a "thing" on YouTube.'

Before Seny joined the camp and transmogrified into Mr Chapeau, he had already set up two YouTube channels, which focused on Minecraft videos. He's here on the camp partly because his parents needed somewhere to send him, and on a long list of camps, the YouTube one stood out. But also because he wants to learn more about how to turn his hobby into a lifestyle – like the increasingly large percentage of youngsters who envisage filling out 'YouTuber' when they're asked for their job title on forms. But to get there, Seny knows he'll have to graft. 'There's a whole world out there,' he says, 'and all of them want to be on YouTube. They're professionals; it's like a job for them. And for me.'

Francisco Javier Zurita, a small 13-year-old with an easy smile and a deep tan, spends around two hours each day watching YouTube. 'They make me feel happy,' he says in a voice that makes him seem older than he is. 'And they motivate me. I think, "What if I create my own channel?" If you keep on doing videos, you can get a channel big time, with 100,000 subscribers. But I do it because I enjoy it, not for the fame.'

Exchanging a summer with its ripe promise of freedom from teachers and playing outside in the sun for a screen-based pro-gramme mixing the creative arts with MBA-style case studies is becoming much more common. Manintveld's summer camp is, in fact, one of several new courses around the world offer-ing tips to wannabe YouTubers. As well as 2btube's operation in Europe, there are a range of other YouTube schools aimed at children dotted around the globe. In the UK, Tubers Academy, a collection of classrooms, studios and computer labs in Exeter, operating since 2017, offers lessons in all things YouTube all year round, from £30 per session.

American parents can choose from more than 20 schools to send their starstruck kids. For thousands of dollars Camp17, which began in 2016, provides 'one-of-a-kind camp experiences where fans interact with their favourite digital influencers' in California, Connecticut and Illinois. iD Tech Camps holds special courses for 13- to 17-year-olds wanting to learn 'digital movie production for YouTube' in 15 US states. At another summer school, SocialStar Creator Camp, which launched in 2017, industry expertise comes from Michael 'WhatTheBuck' Buckley.

In Japan, a YouTuber Academy run by a company called Fulma teaches children the tips and tricks of becoming a successful content creator over the course of two-hour classes, each costing around 3,240 yen, or $30.

The growth of the YouTube education sector emphasizes the platform's increasing professionalisation. In a world where early movers win, children are increasingly seeing the need to sign up for camps as soon as they go to secondary school. And for good reason.

Jonathan Saccone-Joly, a father of four children and a family YouTuber with 1.9 million subscribers says that if he were starting out on YouTube now, 'I think it'd be silly not to' go to training programmes on how to become a better YouTuber. But he'd take his new career slowly, making a realistic plan rather than expecting to dominate the viral video charts. 'That's where a lot of people make their mistake,' he says.

'They think they've got to get the big cameras, they've got to get the lighting and microphones. Dude, go back and look at my early videos,' he exclaims. When he first started on the website, much of his content was in grainy 260p resolution, with poor-quality audio and video. 'It was disgusting. It didn't matter. It was about getting content up.'

That said, today's YouTube is different. It is infinitely vaster and more competitive. Bastian Manintveld, who runs his empire from a glass-walled office in a former car garage in the centre of Madrid, acknowledges that globalisation has altered children's lives. 'When I was young and a kid in the playground, your universe was pretty much limited to that playground,' he says. 'It was really small. Now the universe for these kids is a lot bigger.'

19.

YOUTUBE SCHOOL:

WITH THE ADULT

ENTREPRENEURS

Mi Elfverson is a tall Swedish blonde woman with close-cropped hair who has lived in New York and London. As a commercial photographer and video director, she spent much of her working life labouring over videos that cost hundreds of thousands of pounds to make. Until YouTube disrupted her industry.

Ultimately, she decided that if she couldn't beat YouTube, she would join it. 'All of a sudden there was this opportunity for anyone to have their own little commercial, which was fantastic,' she explains to 15 small business owners gathered in a glass-windowed conference room on the sixth floor of the Hilton Metropole hotel in Brighton, 60 miles south of London.

So she started a new career training people how to YouTube

in soulless conference rooms on seafront hotels, where the pastries and sandwiches slowly ossify under the air conditioning. Which is why we are here on 24 June 2016 at a half-day course called Vlog on the Beach: to teach businessmen and women who don't know their Bruce Lee from Caspar Lee the basics of YouTubing.

It's one of a number of such schools trying to unlock the secrets of YouTube for adults, as well as children. And one of the highest-profile shares a homeland with Elfverson. The Folkhögskola in Kalix, a northern town in Sweden, began classes to teach students how to make YouTube videos in October 2017. 'There are a lot of people who dream of becoming YouTubers, and there will be more in the future,' the school's principal told Sweden's SVT television channel.

As Elfverson stands in front of a temperamental projector whose images are washed out by the late morning sun, she tells her converts: 'We believe we can help and support businesses with videos and video blogging. We've come from me giving small group sessions in how to do your own video blogging to implementing a bold video strategy for companies. I love seeing people develop and blossom in front of the camera, and people sharing their passion.' Before people can embrace and share their passion, though, they have to sit through some PowerPoint slides.

'What's the bonus for getting out there with a video blog?' Elfverson asks. 'Well, first of all, you're presenting yourself in a much more powerful way than you would in a written document. This... will show your clients who you really are and open up a different connection with them.' As the seagulls bravely battle, then eventually give up in the face of a bracing seaside wind outside the window, she explains the importance of brevity. 'If videos are short and snappy, people click on it. We go watch TED talks or go to seminars – we don't read lists.'

She tells the story of a client, Kathy, who is an interior designer. 'Her market is in London – and you can imagine, if you tap in "interior designer London" into Google, how many hits you're going to have.' Kathy separates herself from the competition online by producing videos. 'She's done a presentation about herself, so people can see and feel who she is. When they bring her into their home, they know they kind of already met her and have a different connection with her.'

The talk is peppered with statistics and soundbites about the power of video: Amazon statistics show that companies who connect videos to their account get 30% more sales on their products; people are 10 times more likely to share a video online than anything else; establishing yourself as an expert by uploading videos is simple; building up your online presence is crucial.

She tells her students: 'We want to be more visible, we want to get online, we want to build up an online audience, and video is the quickest way to do that. The written word is slow. We have an aversion to reading documents. We put it in our read-later bin. Videos, if they're short and snappy, people click on it much quicker. You work on all the different levels, work with all the senses,' she says, before quickly correcting herself. 'Almost all the senses. Not the smell or taste.' She makes a half-apology for the 'all the senses' claim.

She digresses into a long explanation of how companies are changing their branding to accommodate the new, post-YouTube world. 'Everybody is talking about telling their stories,' she explains. Previously, big brands were just that – nameless, faceless business behemoths. Now, they are shunning the corporate and embracing the personal. 'A lot of people are standing out there and giving their honest story,' she says, because personal stories have a 'secret power'. They've done MRI scans – 'proper ones', she adds – of people listening to a compelling story. When a person is telling a compelling story, major parts of their brain start triggering.

She does not explain which parts of the brain, and what the firing of the synapses of the cerebral cortex mean, but it's compelling, and after all, she's telling a personal story, so something must be working. Then she brings the room to a halt with a flourish of rhetoric. 'We want to be very careful, though.' She lets the pause linger. With great power comes great responsibility, and the knowledge of how to make compelling video content must be used carefully. Elfverson tells the wide-eyed audience: 'What we want to do as business video bloggers is we want to tell not just our story. We want to tell our clients' story, we want to talk about the good things we're doing, and preferably let them tell the good story about us. The whole history of YouTube has been kids having fun and not selling things.' But that has now changed. YouTube has entered the mainstream; the fun Elfverson spoke about remains, but hard-nosed commerce is muscling in.

Participants have paid £45 each to attend Elfverson's Vlog on the Beach, though a surprising number of the people mingling around before the event admit they are her personal friends. They are a generation away from both the photogenic 20-somethings profiting from the wave of online video, and the aspirant teenagers watching them on their laptops. They are baby boomers: people for whom the internet is an invention and a confection, rather than a permanent, ever-present utility. It's something to be wrestled with and tamed, rather than innate and vital. Importantly, they realise there's a potential profit to be made from YouTube.

Heather Barrie is one person looking to take advantage. A short bundle of energy enthusiastically working the room in a panama hat, Barrie runs a Chichester-based coffee company. A former accountant who has also been a personal trainer, sports nutritionist and shiatsu practitioner, she has been running her business for eight years from a mobile Mercedes outside Arundel train station. In 2011, she launched her own coffee blend. She doesn't just want to sell single-shot Americanos to commuters trying to shake off their sleepiness. She wants to install large coffee-making machines into companies. 'I'm trying to get into a different aspect of it,' she says. 'It's the same product, same brand, it's me, but it's a total change of focus, I'm trying to get people to spend some money – not just £2 or £3 on a latte.'

She explains her pitch: 'Don't spend all your money on instant coffee. We supply the beans; and the amount people can save compared to going to high-street chains is amazing, and they get my coffee, which is gorgeous. I want you to invest £1,500 in something but you get that back in three months.' I tell her I am a journalist who doesn't drink coffee.

In looks and demeanour, she comes across as a brunette version of the TV presenter Sandi Toksvig – fizzing with joy, but with a sharp tongue and a quick wit. 'It's a very crowded space, so how can I stand out?' she asks. 'I'm a bit of a gobby shite, so YouTube makes sense.'

She's dabbled in online video before, asking a friend to help her with a couple of videos, and getting 'a young lad at uni' to help film them and upload them to her YouTube channel. 'I've done little bits,' she admits. 'Now I need to start vlogging and getting them out there.' She'd read a story in the paper about a YouTuber with 25 million views. She thought that was a market she should get into.

During the session Elfverson introduces a friend, a tall actress with immaculately preened hair and a full face of make-up, who speaks with a deep, Scottish accent. She's there to teach the class how best to present themselves on camera – to learn how to ease the understandable confusion and nervousness that older generations have when having to talk about themselves into a lens.

'People don't want the hard sell,' she explains, 'and we don't want to give them the hard sell,' she says, before correcting herself. 'Actually, it's become a marketing tool as a sideline, almost. Something that just developed. But the medium itself didn't start out as that. It was about people sharing their passions and interests and connecting with their friends.'

It's a simple explanation, but gets to the heart of what separates the new media world of YouTube from the traditional broadcast media that most of her attendees grew up with.

She goes on: 'When people sit down in front of the camera, they might have this image of a lot of people sitting in the room, like you guys are right now, but actually if you think about how people are receiving their video, it's much more intimate than that. They are probably on a train with their laptop, or on their bed with their laptop, cooking dinner and watching you chat to them. They are watching you and having a one-to-one relationship with you. You're not actually talking to a lot of people; you're talking to one person who is actually in quite an intimate situation in their home.'

As the class winds down, Elfverson sets the participants a final task: go out and record a video, and report back in 20 minutes. I tag along with Barrie and a couple of others who bowl out of the dark lobby of the hotel into the bright midday sunshine streaming down. After a brief discussion, the others dash off towards the beach to find a quiet spot to record their video. Barrie has another plan: she's eyed up a 360-degree viewing platform, undergoing final testing before its public opening, rising 161 metres into the air on a thin silver needle. The viewing platform, flat and curved like a flying saucer, has yo-yoed up and down all afternoon.

'I'm going to have that in the background,' she says, opening up the camera on her iPhone. It takes a couple of takes and the strength of the wind may have affected the video, but she's happy enough with what she's shot. As we dash across the road, avoiding the cars as they speed along the shoreline, I ask Barrie a question: 'That celebrity vlogger who had 25 million views: do you get it? Do you understand why he's famous or popular?' Half-distracted by typing in the hashtag #vlogonthebeach2016 into the description of her video, her response is unequivocal and flippant: 'No. I thought, "Who the hell are you? I don't know who you are." They just talk shit all day.'

PART V

CAUGHT IN THE MACHINE

20.

PRANKS FOR VIEWS:
WHY MONALISA PEREZ
SHOT HER BOYFRIEND

With a wild look in his wide eyes, a glistening stud in each ear, and a camera in his right hand, Pedro Ruiz III stood on a scrub of green space behind the garage of his family home in the town of Halstad (population: 597), Minnesota. In the background was his car, a white Toyota Celica. On the right side of its tail fin was a GoPro camera. On its roof sat a cheap red cushion. And on that red cushion was a gold .50-calibre Desert Eagle pistol.

Aged 22, Ruiz was going to make a special video that he hoped would secure the future for his childhood sweetheart, Monalisa Perez, and their three-year-old daughter Aleah. Ruiz and Perez, three years younger, had grown up with YouTube. They knew all too well that YouTube could make a somebody out of a nobody. But Perez's YouTube presence, a parenting and family channel called *LaMonaLisa*, hadn't taken off. She and her boyfriend aimed to make it big on the site by filming increasingly daredevil stunts. Starting in March 2017, her channel contained videos in which they had pranked each other, with titles such as 'WORLDS HOTTEST PEPPER PRANK!! GONE MAJORLY GONE!!' [sic] and 'SHE TOOK IT TO [sic] FAR...'

Despite the couple's inventiveness, the channel hadn't taken off: its 18 videos had been viewed a total of 8,460 times, averaging just 470 views per video. But the time was ripe for optimists. In one video, Perez said to her boyfriend: 'Imagine when we have 300,000 subscribers.' They were not the kind of couple to give up on the dream and Ruiz had a plan. He aimed to set up his own channel, calling himself Dammit Boy, because that's what everybody would say when they watched one of his stunts. And to kickstart his channel, he planned to undertake a wow-worthy stunt that couldn't help but get people's attention. Perez was reluctant: it sounded dangerous. But Ruiz had been thinking about it for weeks, begging his girlfriend to help him, and eventually she had given in. She would do it. She would shoot him.

Naturally, Dammit Boy realised he needed to be more than a one-hit wonder, so he protected himself against the bullet. Sort of. He test fired his pistol at an abandoned house three or four miles away, at one of several books he found there. The book – particularly thick – blocked a bullet. So he found another, similar book. With a black marker pen he drew a target in the centre of the hardback cover, and an arrow pointing to it, then wrote 'Plz Hit Here'.

Ruiz had just come home from work at BNSF Railways in nearby Hillsboro at 4pm on 26 June 2017 when he decided the time was right. Two video cameras would record the stunt, for the benefit of millions of YouTube viewers (hopefully). 'Me and Pedro are probably going to shoot one of the most dangerous videos ever,' Perez tweeted hours beforehand. 'HIS idea not MINE'. She had previously re-tweeted a motivational tweet reading 'Every vlogger on YouTube starts at 0 subscribers. Believe in what you do!'

Ruiz started his video with supreme confidence. 'What's up everybody, it's Dammit Boy,' he said speaking with boundless enthusiasm. 'My channel is going to consist of a lot of crazy stuff,' he continued. 'Entertainment just for you guys. My thing is crazy.'

After 38 seconds, he started to struggle. 'I just love the adrenaline, the pumping, the near-death experiences...' He paused as his mind flickered. He regained his composure. 'With this being my first video, I hope to capture all my audience' – he clicked his fingers – 'like that.'

He held up the inch-and-a-half-thick, hardback encyclopaedia. His heavily pregnant girlfriend was reluctant. She said: 'I can't do this babe, I am so scared. My heart is beating...' She added: 'Babe, if I kill you what's going to happen to my life? Like, no this isn't okay... I don't want to be responsible'. But Ruiz reassured her that she would not hurt him as long as she hit the book.

She fired into the book. Ruiz recoiled backwards as the bullet passed through it. He stumbled back, fell to the floor, and said 'Oh shit' as he looked down at a hole in his chest. His girlfriend rushed indoors to ring 911. As his body turned blue, all she could do was wait for the emergency services to arrive.

Ruiz was merely the latest of a series of risk-taking creators hoping to make a living off the site. It can seem – especially for a journalist who has set up a Google alert to trigger whenever a news story mentions YouTube – that the pursuit of views is creating more and more chaos.

Attempting to break into the White House is a bad idea at any point, but to do so simply to try and create good video content seems particularly troublesome. Yet that's what police believe happened in October 2017 when Curtis Combs, a 36-year-old former US Marine from Kentucky, attempted to scale the outer fence of America's most highly guarded home – dressed as cuddly yellow Pokémon protagonist Pikachu. The arrest affidavit, filed by the police in the District of Columbia, said that Combs 'wanted to become famous and thought jumping the White House fence and posting it to YouTube would make him famous.' (Combs told a Kentucky radio station that 'YouTube' was just a simple answer he gave to Secret Service agents, and that he had actually been protesting about the poor rights of blue collar workers.)

In March 2017, five pranksters snuck into the BBC's New Broadcasting House in London, in a vain attempt to interrupt live broadcasts. The group accidentally chose a time when none of the studios were on air, but managed to get into the television studios which film the national news. A video of the group running amok, uploaded by one of the YouTubers nicknamed Carnage, gained just 184,000 views in its first seven months.

Two of his fellow pranksters, Trikkstar and Harris, then 'invaded' Facebook's London headquarters. Trikkstar, a fresh-faced youngster with a half-shaved right eyebrow, explained in the ensuing video: 'We're going to do this stunt because everybody loved when we invaded the BBC headquarters.'

Despite the fast-paced music soundtrack, the seven-minute video is mundane. More than 40 seconds is the duo walking up and down stairs. At one point one of them says: 'Maybe see if there's a café?'

In September 2014, British YouTuber Sam Pepper uploaded a more notorious video called *Fake Hand Ass Pinch Prank*, in which he groped five separate women on the street after distracting them with a fake hand. Sex vlogger Laci Green (who came to fame for her videos promoting the idea of people embracing their sexuality) wrote Pepper an open letter, which was co-signed by 63 other YouTubers including Tyler Oakley, Hannah Witton, Hank and John Green and Michael Buckley. The You-Tubers said: 'We are deeply disturbed by this trend and would like to ask you, from one creator to another, to please stop. They added:

> 'While it may seem like harmless fun, a simple prank, or a 'social experiment', these videos encourage millions of young men and women to see this violation as a normal way to interact with women. 1 in 6 young women (real life ones, just like the ones in your video) are sexually assaulted, and sadly, videos like these will only further increase those numbers.'

The Vlogbrothers banned Pepper from appearing at VidCon, and Pepper later claimed his video was a 'social experiment' so 'I could watch you guys go crazy in the comments'. Pepper paused his YouTube videos in early 2017, but he is now uploading again.

The pursuit of subscribers can also harm children. Heather and Mike Martin – together known on YouTube as *DaddyOFive* – garnered more than three-quarters of a million subscribers to their videos, where they pranked their children for the benefit of viewers. After a particularly unpleasant video, and a rising acknowledgement and discomfort among viewers about how severely they were mistreating their children, the pair uploaded a strident defence of their actions, before eventually apologising publicly after realising just how strongly public opinion had moved against them.

The family initially seemed unaware of just how much the pursuit of views and subscribers had warped their approach to their children, but eventually reneged. 'It started out as family fun,' Mike, the children's father, told *Good Morning America*. 'It started with me and my kids, but then it was just about making a video and then making the next video more crazier than the next. It was more for shock value.'

The Martins were sentenced in a Maryland county circuit court in September 2017 to five years probation for two counts of child neglect, and lost custody of their children. (The sentence was reduced in January 2019, though the judge retained a probation condition preventing the couple from uploading new videos.) YouTube finally deactivated their ability to upload in 2018.

Another way in which YouTube can encourage extreme behaviour comes courtesy of Jay Swingler and Romell Henry, two YouTubers from Wolverhampton in England who together run the *TGFBro* channel. As part of an *Extreme Christmas Calendar* series of videos on the channel, Swingler and Henry were undertaking ever more ridiculous tasks. On 7 December 2017, they uploaded a video called *I cemented my head in a microwave and emergency services came.. (nearly died)*.

In a preamble to the scene recorded after the event, Swingler, then aged 22, said: 'I would give you a good intro, but in this video I nearly fucking died. The following footage isn't a joke and I really wish it was click-bait, but this is as serious as it can get on this channel.'

The video showed what they had done. In a bucket, Swingler and Henry had mixed up four boxes of Polyfilla, a cement-like substance that fills holes in walls. They tipped the contents into a disconnected microwave without a door. Swingler wrapped his head in a plastic shopping bag with some thin plastic tubing as a breathing mechanism. He then dipped his head into the Polyfilla-filled microwave and waited for it to set. Henry left to buy a hair dryer to make the Polyfilla set quicker.

Then Swingler realised he couldn't get his head out. As a caption on the video claimed, 'thr [sic] air tube got blocked'. 'I'm going to die,' a panicked Swingler shouted. The couple of friends watching on and filming tried freeing him using a spoon and an electric drill to chisel away the plaster, before one called the emergency services asking for the fire brigade and an ambulance.

Swingler's friend Jake told the 999 dispatcher: 'He has a microwave stuck to his head. I know this sounds like a prank call, but he was trying to film a YouTube video. My friend was trying to do a stunt with a microwave where he basically put plaster inside the microwave and stuck his head in there, and now we can't get it off.'

Five firefighters, with the help of paramedics, spent an hour freeing Swingler from the microwave. All the while the pranksters kept the cameras rolling. While the emergency services' workers stood cross-armed, Swingler and Henry embraced and laughed with relief being freed. The West Midlands Fire Service tweeted: 'We're seriously unimpressed.'

YouTube viewers were interested, though. Within 13 hours of being uploaded, the video was viewed 850,000 times. Within two days, two million people had seen it, with 25,000 leaving comments. *TGFBro*'s gamble may have resulted in public disapproval, but it probably paid off. It earned up to $8,000 from the video in its first two days online, according to estimates by Social Blade. Another 17,247 people subscribed in its first day online – three times the channel's daily average (though the most successful single day for the pranksters was in June 2016, when the group featured in two videos with KSI, who called them 'fucking retarded', before joining in with them by running over plastic sheeting slicked with washing-up liquid and covered with mouse traps, and jumping into fields of nettles. They gained nearly 90,000 subscribers that day).

Swingler was unapologetic for wasting the emergency services' time. 'I think this shit's hilarious,' he said in a video uploaded the day after the prank.

How often do YouTube pranks go wrong? Using freedom of information laws in Britain, I asked each police force in the UK how many times they had been called out to deal with incidents where YouTube was mentioned in the notes made by the emergency call operator. 90% of police forces responded to my request. Every year between 2013 and 2017 the number of YouTube incidents increased, rocketing from 1,887 in 2013 to 3,172 in 2017– nearly nine every day. As this book was going to press, police data for 2018 was still coming in – but many forces had recorded even more calls about the video sharing website. West Yorkshire Police had 406 incidents in 2018. In about half those cases it sent an officer to investigate.

Pranks are an important part of YouTube – 'a genre of content that is largely designed to the platform's algorithmic preference for click-baity and shocking content,' says Zoë Glatt, a PhD researcher at the London School of Economics. 'In some corners of YouTube there is a race-to-the-bottom mentality. If the appeal of your content is that it is shocking or risqué, then the competitive nature of YouTube means that people have to post increasingly shocking and risqué content in order to be seen.' They're also global: The Crazy Sumit, an Indian YouTuber, has 612,000 subscribers who watch his cringe-inducing videos where he pranks young women.

That doesn't mean that they're respected by everyone, though. And YouTube's pranksters and chancers are damaging the platform's perception amongst the public. In an exclusive poll carried out for this book, polling company Poli asked nearly 3,000 British adults whether they thought YouTubers are good role models for children. Half said they aren't. And worse, almost everyone else was uncertain. Just 14% thought that they are. Those same people were asked who is responsible for the content of videos on YouTube. A quarter said YouTube; a fifth said the creator posting the video. Half said both were equally responsible.

Incidents requiring a police response and the Bird Box challenge viral sensation (where participants did everyday tasks like driving a car while blindfolded in homage to the Netflix film) have caused YouTube to crack down significantly on dangerous content. Dangerous challenges and pranks that have a 'perceived danger of serious physical injury' were banned from the platform in January 2019, with a two-month grace period for creators to clean up their act. But informally YouTube has been exerting pressure on extreme content creators for a while.

In the first half of 2018, YouTube started to age-restrict Swingler and Henry's videos, throttling their ability to sell adverts against their content.

Jay Swingler lived to tell his tale after his tussle with a microwave, but Pedro Ruiz III didn't. He bled out through a bullethole. The video he and his girlfriend shot has never been publicly released but a transcript, and clips prior to the shooting itself, were published during the police case against Monalisa Perez, who was charged with second-degree manslaughter, and sentenced to 180 days in jail.

Three months after she shot her boyfriend, her account was stuck at 21,942 subscribers, a fraction of the number they planned. But Perez was not done. On 31 July 2018, after she'd served her time, she removed all the videos from her past life on her YouTube channel from public view and uploaded a new video entitled *Something to say...*

Sporting a new, dyed-blonde haircut and two new tattoos of red flowers over each collarbone, Perez sat on her bed and said: 'I'm sure a lot of people are probably surprised that I'm even here right now making a video. I'm even surprised a little bit but I feel like I'm ready.

'I've always wanted to do YouTube, and I feel like now I'm healed enough.

'This past year has been – hoo – one journey, I tell you,' she confessed. 'A lot of downs. Honestly, now, it's a lot of ups.' She had started weekly counselling. Her son Rayden, born just a few months after her boyfriend's death, was approaching his first birthday. She had found a new boyfriend. And she felt the time was right to start again with YouTube. 'I'll be posting again, probably twice a week or three times a week.'

Perez hasn't just eased back into the YouTube lifestyle, though. In September she posted a vlog titled *THINGS AREN'T JUST EASY*, where she said:

> *The sadness came over me deeply, it feels like. I miss Pedro a lot, guys. I've really learned to, like, not show any of my emotions. I really suppressed all my feelings inside of me because I don't want to feel anything, and it's really hard for me to get emotional now. It's really hard for me to just cry. [...] I think it's maybe because I've seen a car just like his.*

She gets a couple of thousand views a day now.

21.

AUTHENTICITY:
THE FOURTH WALL
FOR YOUTUBERS

One of the first faces of YouTube that appealed to viewers was Bree Avery's. As we saw in Chapter 4, the 16-year-old would complain that her parents had grounded her, she had too much homework and that her friend Daniel had a crush on her. She became the most followed individual on YouTube.

But viewers first started wondering if things were awry when she claimed that she was being targeted by a mysterious group called The Order. Either Avery was crazy – or her fans were for believing her. Eventually, the *Los Angeles Times* revealed that Avery, aka *lonelygirl15*, was not a real person. She was a 19-year-old actress, Jessica Lee Rose, who had been hired by three film-makers working for media company EQAL. Their goal was to show that short-form scripted drama on YouTube could be taken as seriously as normal TV. They did well out of it: they were snapped up by Creative Artists Agency, a major Hollywood talent agency, about a month before *lonelygirl15* was exposed in August 2006.

That Bree Avery turned out to be just as fictional as characters on cinema or TV dramas was difficult for her fans to take – precisely because YouTube was meant to be more authentic than both those mediums.

Authenticity (at least the semblance of it) is the glue that binds YouTubers and fans together more powerfully than the traditional relationship between Hollywood stars and their fans. It's the essential commodity of YouTube, even if imbued by someone very different. As Tyler Oakley, a peppy LGBTQ+ activist with an easy smile, a scattergun mouth and seven million subscribers, told *Time* magazine: 'Authenticity is more important than attempting to seem relatable.'

Researcher Alice Marwick, of the University of North Carolina, says: 'With social media, celebrity in general is much more accessible than what I would call broadcast celebrity, which is what we would think of as more traditional celebrity produced by mass media entertainment. The content is produced by the kids themselves. Some of these people do break through to the mainstream, but for most of them their fame is concentrated on social media. Part of that fame is the feeling of accessibility and the feeling of authenticity,' adding quickly: 'Note that I didn't say accessibility and authenticity.'

In general, we share more of our lives than we did a few decades ago. Structured reality TV programmes like *The Simple Life*, *Jersey* and *Geordie Shore* and *Keeping Up With The Kardashians*, which follow real people (albeit often wealthy or ostentatious ones), have been phenomenally popular. The rise of social media has engendered and normalised sharing, too. The growth of the platforms tell the story starkly. Facebook now has more than 2.3 billion monthly active users, YouTube has topped 1.9 billion monthly logged-in users, and Instagram has more than one billion users. All of these sites survive through their user-generated content, acting as a megaphone through which people can shout the latest updates about their lives at maximum volume. Instant reactions to life-changing events can be captured on camera phones or in a pithy 280-character tweet and blasted out to anyone who cares to pay attention. (At its most tasteless, mourners share funeral selfies on Snapchat or Facebook.)

We've turned 180 degrees from when oversharing was regarded as uncouth. What were once private thoughts, feelings and fears perhaps shared with closest friends in confidence are now broadcast to the world through Facebook, Twitter and YouTube. Now not to share is suspicious, inviting questions about why a person is reticent. We've entered an era of radical transparency, where every fear and foible can make for legitimate content. When the British YouTuber, Lucy Moon, brought the camera with her into the shower as part of a Paris travelogue, which ended with her performing a song hinting at a one-night stand, one fan commented: 'Your honesty is what gives this series and all your videos something that YouTube really needs.'

YouTube viewers won't countenance following creators who are standoffish, and who don't let them into their lives. But how much is shared online is another question altogether. Marwick says: 'They certainly have things they keep to themselves, and a strong sense of what is and isn't appropriate to put online, but they speak quite passionately about maintaining the authentic side to their fans. They understand that's key to their popularity.'

Through its format a YouTube video helps put across that essence of authenticity, the faintest wisp of intimacy. In television shows and films, actors are trained never to look directly into the lens for fear of breaking the fourth wall. ('Spiking the camera' is used occasionally to provide an impactful personal connection – a shot out of the ordinary that makes the audience sit up and pay attention.) On YouTube, creators lock you firmly in their gaze, never breaking eye contact, a ready, beaming, easy smile to hand. It feels almost like a conversation with an old friend – particularly now that apps like FaceTime, Skype and Snapchat encourage us to interact with friends face-to-face, but mediated by a screen.

The location of where most of these videos are filmed – within the YouTuber's home, and often in their bedroom or front room – also fosters that personal connection. 'The traditional form of YouTube address where you have someone in their bedroom talking to their webcam feels very intimate,' says Marwick. 'It feels like you're getting a glimpse literally into their bedroom. Bedrooms are very important to teenagers – sometimes they're their only personal private spaces in their house.'

When delivering monologues to the camera, YouTubers speak in a way that maximises intimacy, according to another researcher. German academic Maximiliane Frobenius of the University of Hildesheim found that YouTubers insert vocal phrases and terms into their monologues in order to cajole viewers into interacting with them, making it seem like they're in a conversational dialogue with their fans rather than simply talking at them. At its most obvious, they'll end a monologue before adding: 'Let me know what you think in the comments below'.

The term for this type of engagement is a parasocial relationship – a definition coined in 1956 by Donald Horton and Richard Wohl, who wrote an essay called *Mass Communication and Para-Social Interaction: Observations on Intimacy at a Distance*, which analysed viewers' reactions to the people they saw on the burgeoning technology of television in the mid-1950s.

Horton and Wohl discovered that, though the viewer and the television personality were separated by a thick pane of glass, cathode rays and often several thousand miles, the viewer often equated the relationship they had with the people in front of the camera with ones they had with real friends in a one-on-one conversation. That's in spite of the fact that in reality, the 'conversation' between the television host or news anchor was almost entirely one-way: the host was doing the talking, the viewer was doing the listening, and the viewer's only right of reply would be a telephone call or letter that might be read out in a subsequent edition of the programme.

Early stars of television became viewers' best friends – even if they had never met, or regardless of whether the viewer even knew that much about them. They often exploited the medium by presenting true monologues that were designed to engage the viewer in what felt like a one-on-one address. Think about Walter Cronkite's small essays at the end of the *CBS Evening News* during Vietnam which bolstered anti-war sentiment across the United States, and the esteem in which news anchors have long been held because of their ability to comfort and explain the complexities of the world when invited into a viewer's front room.

YouTube multiplies that power, making the relationship seem even stronger. And it's become a hot topic in academia. Chih-Ping Chen of Yuan Ze University's College of Management, described YouTube as a 'tool that consumers use to digitally self-construct, self-present, and parasocially develop social relations'. A study of German YouTube viewers by Alexander Rihl and Claudia Wegener at the Konrad Wolf Film University Babelsberg in Potsdam concluded that the bonds between fan and creator were neither deep and emotional nor hierarchical, but 'virtual relationships between equals, in which YouTubers appear to act as reliable, albeit somewhat superficial, friends.'

Many YouTubers combine this intimacy with holding back nothing. And fans lap it up: watch time on videos where creators let viewers into their morning routines has more than trebled between June 2016 and June 2018. Some, though, don't even try to take advantage of people's prurience. They just don't want to. Taha Khan, a British YouTuber, whose unique, witty videos, uploaded to his channel *KhanStopMe*, have an outsized popularity among fellow creators, deliberately doesn't share lots about his life online.

'It's difficult for me, because I feel deeply uncomfortable at times when I'm sharing things with people I don't know,' he says. He describes his perspective on how he presents himself to his followers as 'cynical': 'I don't see the things I put online as me.' Rather, he thinks of the process as creating a product that he places online. 'That product is a reflection of my personality but it's not me,' he says. 'People are vastly complex. YouTube videos are highly edited. Authenticity is something you can play with and think about.'

Khan gives away small parts of himself to his audience, but it's carefully controlled and distributed sparingly. 'In my videos I make it very explicit that this is a constructed piece of entertainment as much as it is my personality,' he says. 'I highlight that to my audience because I feel uncomfortable with the pretext of authenticity.' He also feels uncomfortable with the pretext of YouTube, and the notion that you have to give up parts of yourself to your audience in order to participate. 'It's one of the things that is just taken as a given. It's like, "Okay, you're on YouTube, you share your life." There will be certain YouTubers who will really think about that and say: "I don't want to do this," but the default is you share your life online. It's less of a pressure and more of a kind of... presumption that is already there.' Some creators worry that fans equate their online existence with their physical presence.

Charlie McDonnell, the British YouTuber now living in Canada who has been on YouTube for more than a decade, told me he finds it odd that people comment 'Are you dead?' when he hasn't uploaded a video for a while. 'It seems funny on the surface but when you dig deeper into it, it's uncomfortable to think that maybe people equate the regularity of my YouTube content with my actual physical life,' he says.

Most of the old guard of private celebrities keep themselves to themselves, but the new crop of 'traditional' film and television stars have had to engage with social media in order to build and maintain their audience. Jennifer Lawrence's tell-all, girl-next-door persona borrows heavily from the YouTube playbook, and it pays off. In exclusive polling commissioned for this book from market research company YouGov, 57% of people said they believed Jennifer Lawrence was authentic; just 14% said they thought her inauthentic. (By contrast, 22% of people told the pollsters they thought Zoella was authentic, less than half the number – 48% – who thought her fake. However, that survey was completed just weeks after Zoella released what some saw as a money-grabbing advent calendar, which we'll look at in a subsequent chapter.) In being so frank about her love of pizza and acting as the goofy girl next door, Lawrence and others are borrowing from the confessional style that typified early social media users. Marwick says: 'If you're a starlet going up for a role and there are two starlets, and one has 20,000 fans on social media, and one has one million fans, the girl with the million fans is going to get the job. It's become a part of the celebrity apparatus.'

But rather than traditional celebrities adopting the total openness of early YouTubers, what has happened is that both extremes are meeting in the middle. As traditional stars have learned they need to open up – a little – so the new online celebrities have recognised that they need to hold back a little. 'It will be very rare for us to see someone who looks like Jennifer Lawrence in the future,' says YouTube talent manager Sarah Weichel. 'Her team has done a really excellent job in helping her identify the right material that has crafted her into the next Hollywood A-lister.'

Lots of celebrities will tweet pictures of their dog or post video of them lip-syncing to a song. Will Smith has his YouTube channel, and Jack Black plays games on YouTube. They are purporting to give access to their fans but what they're really doing is presenting an image of themselves that looks more authentic than say, a *Vanity Fair* profile or a staged paparazzi photoshoot. Thus stars, whether the last film franchise starlet or the upcoming YouTuber, have become adept at giving fans that 'feeling of accessibility and the feeling of authenticity'.

Bastian Manintveld, the Dutch entrepreneur behind 2btube, believes that the TV industry hasn't quite appreciated that YouTube is not just 'videos of cats' but a more intimate medium. Viewers don't care whether TV executives did a degree in audio-visual production or carefully draw up their TV schedules, they want to see winning personalities up close and personal. 'If the audience decides they like that girl or that guy that just sits in their bedroom better because their style or personality appeals more to them, the guy without preparation or more closeness and authenticity, that's the winner,' Manintveld says. 'Authenticity is very important to this young audience.'

22.

BURNOUT:

SLAVES TO THE ALGORITHM

Making videos full-time and being in control of your life appeal to many aspiring YouTubers. But the reality is that the two are often difficult to combine – as countless YouTubers have found out. Olga Kay's story tells the rise and fall of a YouTuber. Like many, she burned out on the path of celebrity.

In the mid-2000s, Kay (real name Olga Karavayeva) was discussing how best to break into showbusiness with some of her friends. She was a professional juggler with the Ringling Brothers circus, travelling across the United States. But the itinerant circus lifestyle she'd led for years wasn't enough. She was trying to audition for TV shows or commercials.

Her friends suggested she open a YouTube account. At first she thought they said U2.com, like the band. She went to the site and didn't understand how Bono could help her get fame on TV. It took her a while to pinpoint precisely what her friends had meant. When she did load up the YouTube homepage, she created a throwaway account with the username *OlgaKay* ('I remember thinking I'll probably never visit so what's a word I can use for my screen name I'll remember?' she tells me over Skype in the late summer of 2016), and encountered a young girl pouring her heart out to the camera who was enthralling viewers of YouTube and crossing over onto mainstream news programmes. She, like many others, was watching *lonelygirl15*. Kay also was an early fan of *LisaNova* also known as Lisa Donovan, a popular You-Tuber who we've already met – she eventually founded Maker Studios, a multi-channel network. 'As I was watching these girls I remembered being fascinated. I had this creativity I wanted to express as well,' says Kay. 'I remember thinking I can do it better – if only I knew how.'

Kay didn't have a camera or know how to edit videos. She only had a built-in webcam on her chunky laptop and a copy of Apple's basic movie-making software, iMovie. Her first attempts at vlogging were painful, long experiences, punctuated by awkward silences and long spells spent staring off to the side of the camera. She'd recount her experiences juggling at events and business conferences, occasionally filming videos from smoke-filled airport departure lounges in eastern Europe. 'If you watch my older videos it's very uncomfortable to watch,' she says. 'I really didn't know what I was doing.' Still, she persisted. She spent 10 to 12 hours each day figuring out how to make videos, uploading them, then watching as the view counts remained resolutely static. 'I'd spend all that time making a video, put it up and nobody would watch it,' she recalls. It wasn't long until she began asking how long she could sustain that lifestyle.

Kay was labouring for nothing; at the time there was no apparent way of making much money from the site. She had retreated from her friends and her personal life to pursue a career on YouTube. Friends were shunned, family was ignored, and her boyfriend at one point confronted her and asked her what exactly she was doing wasting her time uploading videos to a poxy little website. 'They were embarrassed at this new path I was taking,' she says. Most people were uploading videos to the website for the hell of it, or to belong to a broader community. Her friends and family didn't know which she was aiming for.

But Kay was determined. By 2008, two years into her time on YouTube, she had managed to build up a following of around 50,000 people – and she hungered for more. By now, the brand deal had become, if not mainstream, a possibility for YouTubers of a certain size and at a certain level. Ever the entrepreneur, always seeking out new opportunities, Kay asked herself a question: 'How can I break into this system?' A self-starter, Kay started contacting some of her favourite brands off her own back, offering to create a piece of content that would represent their product to her growing audience. At one point, she even faked sponsored videos to send to advertisers, to convince them to partner with her (a tactic that Taylor Lorenz of *The Atlantic* has flagged up as an increasingly popular trend for teenagers and children looking to attract the attention of companies offering brand deals on Instagram and YouTube today). Ford was among the first to take the bait, picking Kay as one of 100 YouTube influencers driving its cars across the country, and filming collaborations with each other. 'Back in the day it was very simple,' Kay recalls. 'Brands didn't understand the platform. They didn't really believe in it, but they knew that there was a lot of organic reach and a lot of authenticity among creators, so they wanted to be part of it – but they didn't know how to utilise it.' As a result, those early sponsored videos were led largely by the creators with little oversight from brands or PR agencies. There were no rules about what could or could not be said or done.

It was a happy time. When she brokered her first big brand deals, and the money started rolling in, Kay felt justified for spending so many years building her platform on YouTube. 'YouTube was tough because a lot of people still don't understand being any kind of social media personality you do the job of at least five people,' she explains. 'You have to be creative; you have to be a writer, be a performer, an editor, a director, a marketer. You have to have some kind of a business sense to make it work, and make it sustainable.'

But when she finally made it, it was just too much. A feature in *The New York Times* in 2014 captured how busy her life was at that time. She was producing more than 20 videos a week in return for around $100,000 a year. (The article demonstrated the slightly incredulous tone of early newspaper coverage of YouTube: 'Ms. Kay, 31, is part of an emerging group of entertainers who are trying to make a living by producing content for YouTube'.)

Much like Monalisa Perez being willing to post every aspect of her life to YouTube as she tries to rebuild it, Kay's videos were a warts-and-all insight into her life, with nothing left on the cutting room floor. 'I would film every single step of my life and everything I was going through,' she recalls. 'Did I cry all day? Did I laugh all day? That was all filmed and documented, and posted five times a week.' She had some help managing her channels from one or two other people she had hired as part of her business – something commonplace among the biggest YouTubers today, but relatively unusual then (remember, Hank Green was baffled at VidCon just three years earlier by the idea of hiring staff). The schedule was punishing. She didn't have a life, she admits. When she received an invite to a party, the first question she asked the host: 'Can I film there?' 'If somebody's uncomfortable with me filming I don't think I can go and have fun with you guys because I need content,' she says. It was 'a really unhealthy way of living life'.

'I was really burned out, and it was actually at the peak of my YouTube career where I was getting lots of opportunities and was making so many videos and great opportunities would come in. Instead of seeing it as a fun chance to get money to do something more exciting, I saw it as a burden. I have to make more content, and I'm so exhausted. I was really tired and remember all these great things were happening and I wasn't happy.'

'A lot of people see it as something that would be really fun and cool, to be famous,' explains academic Alice Marwick. 'But in reality, YouTube fame is very precarious. It can be very difficult for the young people who are successful at it.' Marwick is stark about the pitfalls of too much fame, too soon. 'It's something to be the guy who invented Minecraft and end up with a billion dollars. It's another thing to be somebody who doesn't go to college because they're working on their YouTube channel and are spending 16 hours a day responding to fans, creating new content, and feeling a huge amount of pressure.'

Marwick has interviewed social media celebrities as part of her research. She believes that most young people can hack the pace alone for two years before burning out.

A few years after his success with the celebrity gossip channel *WhatTheBuck?*, Michael Buckley, one of the first professional YouTubers, started experiencing emotions that would become common to successors: the feeling that they were making a living out of their soul; that they were not showing themselves fully; that they were living behind a false persona created for their fans. Like many of the site's early stars, he enjoyed the money and recognition, but felt constrained and exhausted by the high workload and the feeling that he wasn't quite himself. Away from his late-night, over-the-top persona, Buckley was shy. He was fascinated by human behaviour and relationships, and hankered to become a life coach.

In the intervening years, Buckley has left YouTube and returned time and again. 'I burned out four or five times. It happens. It is what it is... I always joke I should be a life coach just for YouTubers. Whenever I speak at conferences and see people so burned out and miserable I say: "I can help you, I really can help you feel better about YouTube."' He reflects: 'I think I put too much into it. My relationship with YouTube was too addicting and all-in; I used to see my whole world as YouTube.' (Nonetheless, he is grateful. 'I just got a YouTube tattoo on my wrist to remind me every time I feel stressed, I look down and think YouTube has made my entire life possible.')

Another big star who joined YouTube at the same time, Michelle Phan, has also experienced burnout. Phan, who joined the site in 2007, became the official makeup artist for the French beauty brand Lancôme off the back of her success on the site. L'Oréal released a range of cosmetics under her name. Phan launched a multi-channel network and a make-up subscription box service. She published a book, and raised hundreds of millions of dollars in funding for her businesses.

Eight million subscribers followed her tips and advice on how to apply makeup. But Phan wasn't happy. In July 2016, she posted a video providing advice about hair removal. Then she stopped. The uploads dried up. Her fans were left wondering where she went.

Almost a year later she tried to explain. In an 11-minute video entitled *Why I Left*, Phan admitted she felt like her spirit was broken. 'Once, I was a girl with dreams, who eventually became a product – smiling, selling, and selling,' she said. She moved to Switzerland and cut herself off from social media, business success and the trappings of fame. Her viewers were relieved: they believed that Phan had overcome her troubles and was about to start posting again. They were disappointed. At the time of writing, her last video was that one, uploaded on 1 June 2017.

Lucy Moon, too, has begun to worry what YouTube fame is doing to her. 'Yesterday I received the tweet that every YouTuber will receive at least once when they start uploading regularly,' the British vlogger said in a blog on her website in September 2017. Moon had not uploaded a video for a month and a fan had sent a tweet asking if she had stopped doing YouTube. 'Upload soon please', the tweet ended, punctuated with two hearts.

Moon had assumed that her audience wasn't bothered about the regularity of her videos, but she realised that a gap in the subscription box must be more obvious than she thought. She explained: 'In short, I've been feeling overwhelmed.' In a short period of time, she had become a brand as well as a person – and her social media accounts had come under greater scrutiny.

'Posting on social media is a big part of my personal life, but has also become a big part of my job,' she wrote. 'It becomes hard to draw the boundaries; the lines blur when I'm deciding whether to share my feelings, photos and discussions within my usual posts and on my regular social media platforms.'

This then was the YouTuber's dilemma: the algorithm wanted her to post regularly, and she wanted to be authentic, but making and posting videos so regularly was draining and she felt she was giving up too much of her self. She wrote: 'With all of the shit that we encounter from being on social media, I think that looking after ourselves isn't prioritised nearly as highly as it should be.' A social media detox helped her. Moon told me: 'I don't know a single YouTuber who hasn't had a burnout in some form or another. I know lots of people whose burnout led to them being scared off the platform entirely. You're telling everyone online you've got a perfect life. You're putting out perfect images. You look like you're having an incredible time.'

Just how acutely the stresses and strains of a life lived in the online spotlight can be felt was plain to see under the glare of a few hundred camera-phones and a few thousand watts of professional lights on stage at VidCon London in February 2019. I chaired a mental health panel with four big YouTubers, including Thomas 'TomSka' Ridgewell, Hannah Witton, Gabbie Hanna (a big Vine star turned top YouTuber) and Jaiden Dittfach, who goes by the name Jaiden Animations.

Though she was literally distant, stretched out across a massive black leather chair in tracksuit bottoms at the other end of the expansive stage from me as I asked the questions, 28-year-old Hanna, who has 6.5 million subscribers, was incredibly open in front of the audience.

YouTube had 'poisoned her mental health', Hanna said mat-ter-of-factly, and that her own sense of self-worth was directly tied to the number of views each of her videos attained. She – and the others partaking in the discussion, except for Witton, who Ridgewell jokingly mocked for being the most 'neuro-nor-mative' of the group – said that they found it easier to share their troubles online with strangers via the camera lens rather than talk directly to their friends and family members.

But that caused them trouble: Hanna described how she'd previously shared her difficulties with her audience, forgetting that those closest to her were also watching their videos. She was shocked and embarrassed when they'd call her up and ask if she's okay. 'It's so psycho,' she said.

As we stepped off stage, the four creators, with a combined 18.5 million subscribers on their main channels, continued chatting, handing their microphones back to the stagehand waiting in the wings. 'That was very journalistic,' Hanna told me. I thanked her for sharing – though I wondered if thanking someone for doing something that makes them feel like that is the right thing to do.

Anthony D'Angelo, a video essayist on YouTube who also acts as the site's unofficial historian, says: 'A lot of the time it's kids who weren't trying to get famous and fame is sudden-ly thrown on their lap. People don't know how to maintain privacy. They don't know how to maintain a sense of self.' The rise of youngsters coming to fame at a younger and younger age could be causing problems in the long term, he reckons. 'When you feel a pressure at a very young age to perform, how can you really develop a sense of identity independently from that audience?'

Laura Chernikoff, who helped run VidCon with the Green brothers for several years, says the drive to remain popular on a results-driven website that requires ever-increasing quality and quantity can frustrate creators. Among the creators she met at VidCon 2017 'you could palpably feel a little bit of tiredness and a sense of "I don't really care as much as I used to" among the more established creators.'

Because a person's rank on the website – and the amount of income they can derive from the platform – depends on keeping their audience entertained, creators can sometimes feel trapped into making videos. Almost all of those who upload videos to the website are creatively minded individuals and don't enjoy standing still. Chernikoff says: 'There's the sense that your audience signed up to watch you do a thing and if you try and change what that thing is, they may not like it. It does hold creators in a pattern of feeling like they have to do the same thing they've always been making, and that's going to burn anybody out in any job.'

Take Laci Green, who started making videos at the age of 19, based on her personal experiences about sex, life and body image, while studying for an undergraduate degree in law, social sciences and education at the University of California, Berkeley. When I first interviewed her in 2013, she was running her YouTube channel, hosting videos for the *Discovery Channel* on YouTube, and working with Planned Parenthood. 'I'm just enjoying doing so much awesome work,' she said at the time. 'It is a lot of work, but it's awesome. I'll be putting out videos for quite a while.' Five years later, I caught up with her. She'd undergone a shift in politics, and had burned out on YouTube for a while. She wasn't the person she once was. And she sounded exhausted.

'It feels like you get trapped, and no matter what, you can't win,' she said. 'You have those moments where you sit down and think: "What is my life right now? Is this what I hoped to be by now, at 25, at 30? Is this what I want for my future?" And the answer is no.' She had devised an exit plan to quietly fade away, to slip the gilded cage of online fame. She had a book to promote, and her publisher needed her to maintain her YouTube presence for that.

I watched her YouTube channel in the months since, sworn to secrecy about her plans. In March, she posted a video about her book; in April, she posted a couple of videos. She went silent over the summer, then added a handful of videos in the autumn. Her last upload came in November, around two weeks after her 29th birthday.

She hasn't posted since. She made it out by the age of 30, just as she hoped. Others have been more open: Charlie McDonnell admitted to his fans he had stepped away from YouTube in March 2019. 'I've grown out of my internet persona,' he said. 'I made that mask when I was 16 and it just doesn't fit me anymore.'

Creators' difficulties producing content for the site are backed up by data compiled by Little Monster Media Co. 'One major change has been the frequency at which you need to distribute content,' says Matt Gielen, the company's founder and president. 'You used to have one video a week as a threshold, where you could do perfectly fine. Nowadays, we're seeing a minimum of three videos a week to do any kind of significant viewership on YouTube.'

Those videos also need to be longer, from a maximum time of three to four minutes to 10-12 minutes. The race upwards in volume and length is ultimately driven by viewers, but exacerbated by YouTube's desire to grab every last second of watch time out of viewers. Creators are caught in the middle, trying to placate the site that is trying to sate the seemingly endless appetite of its expanding viewer base. 'Audiences are demanding more content,' says Gielen. 'Who doesn't want more of the thing they love?' He draws an easily digestible comparison. 'Would you rather have one scoop or two scoops of ice cream? Most people would rather have two scoops.'

People want ten tubs – and big ones, too. Stoked by the release of a number of multi-part documentary series, many of them hours long, by popular YouTuber Shane Dawson, the length of videos is increasing. In 2015, the number of videos by individual creators more than 20 minutes long that received more than 1,000 views was 6.3 million. Three years later, it had more than doubled. Viewers want to watch for longer, and creators are creating extra-long videos to meet that demand. A number of creators I've spoken to have planned to produce feature-length documentaries to be released on YouTube in 2019 and 2020. They're doing so partly to meet their fans' needs, but also because they're bored of posting the same old, short videos. They want to slake their creative thirst and to produce something of worth that can last for posterity.

With the reflection that comes from standing aside from the rat race, Olga Kay says: 'YouTube became the fast food restaurant of videos. It became this confusing thing that you had to create more and longer, and more often. So ultimately that resulted – I think – in less quality. It was just too much.'

Kay sometimes runs into her lapsed fans when out shopping. It happened once in a Target store, when an employee in their early 20s engaged her in conversation. 'They said, "We grew up watching your videos." I've started hearing that more in the past few years. I said, "Why don't you watch it now?" They say, "Sorry, I don't have time to watch content; I have to pay my bills".'

Kay used to take these interactions personally: had she done something wrong? Could she have kept her viewers engaged, even as life, kids, work and friends intruded on their ability to watch YouTube? 'But the truth is, whoever brings you to the top of your YouTube career grows up and has to move on.'

23.

FANATICAL FANS:

OBSESSIVE RELATIONSHIPS

Christina Grimmie was a fan of talented Disney starlets like Hannah Montana who parlayed careers in children's television into pop music. Aged 15 in 2009, Grimmie uploaded one of her first tracks to YouTube – a cover of *Party in the USA* by Miley Cyrus (who played Montana in an eponymous TV series). It went viral. In 2011, she released her first EP, then moved to Los Angeles. In 2014, she came third in the US TV talent show *The Voice*, extending her popularity beyond her millions of subscribers. All the while she kept uploading videos, knowing that it was important to maintain that personal, unfiltered connection with her fans. Little did she know the trouble it would bring.

On 10 June 2016, after a concert in Orlando, Florida, Grimmie held a meet-and-greet for her fans. One of them was Kevin James Loibl, a 27-year-old from nearby St Petersburg, who arrived with two handguns and a hunting knife. As Grimmie signed autographs, Loibl shot her four times, then turned the gun on himself. Grimmie was pronounced dead later that evening. She was 22. Local police said that the gunman had shown an 'unrealistic infatuation' with Grimmie.

The desire of obsessive fans to harm famous people is not new (John Lennon was assassinated in 1980 and Gianni Versace in 1997 by fans who felt some kind of ownership or relationship with them), but YouTube can stoke that obsession even further. Firstly, there is the apparent closeness of the relationship between star and fan, with the creator throwing out mentions in their videos and social media posts and staring directly into the lens – and thus the viewer's eyes. Secondly, those stars are expected to be more accessible than conventional celebrities, as shown by the Grimmie meet-and-greet, common to pop stars and YouTubers. More than a quarter of people aged 18-24 told the pollsters asking them for this book that they know KSI well.

Viewers feel that connection intensely: 47% of millennials admitted in an Ipsos Connect survey that YouTube improved their mood or health. Rather than picking up the phone to a friend, people are turning to their favourite YouTuber.

Ian Danskin, a YouTuber who posts essays on new media, film and video games, says: 'Internet fame simultaneously creates the sense that a person is a celebrity but also that that person is your friend. Having those two things happen at the same time (not only is this person famous and getting judged by the rules of famous people, but also you have an intimate access to them and judge them in the way you would if your friend was acting badly) is weird.'

Many viewers want to get close to their YouTube heroes. In January 2019, the centre of Britain's second biggest city was brought to a standstill when the makeup artist and model James Charles appeared at a makeup store in Birmingham's Bullring shopping centre. A three-year veteran of YouTube about to enter his 20s, Charles has more than 14 million subscribers who he calls Sisters. Eight thousand people poured into Birmingham to see him, many driven by their parents. During the worst traffic jams at 2pm on the day, what would normally be a 15-minute bus journey took 75 minutes.

In February 2018, one fan decided that he wanted to get even closer to another big YouTuber, Logan Paul. Twenty-year-old Tahj Deondre Speight decided to break into Paul's $7 million home in the San Fernando Valley in California. When the YouTuber returned home with his father at around 10pm, Speight was asleep on the sofa in the living room, charging up his phone in a power socket under a coffee table. As Paul's father grabbed the intruder, Paul shouted at Speight: 'Yo, who the fuck are you? My boy, we are about to fucking murk [stab] you.' Though the footage was captured on camera and uploaded to Paul's YouTube channel, police confirmed the incident actually happened, saying that Speight told them he wanted to meet the YouTuber. One of the many reasons Logan's brother Jake left his rented home for the McMansion in Calabasas was that the fans who would stake out his front door had tested his neighbours' patience.

Whenever the mass media reports such incidents, it does so in bafflement, but it shouldn't. YouTube has created a new dynamic between fans and stars. Creators involve fans in achieving their triumphs and fans feel a sense of ownership of those successes. This tends to surprise adults who have never been within 100 miles of Tom Cruise or Nicole Kidman.

British newspapers, for instance, mocked the news that vlogger Joe Sugg was a contestant on the high-ratings BBC talent show *Strictly Come Dancing* in August 2018. Four months later, Sugg was in the final. Despite his gangly limbs and awkward demeanour, 27-year-old Sugg's route to the final was smoothed by a growing aptitude for fleet-footed dancing, yes, but also because of a dedicated following who voted for him in the public vote, some 30 or 40 times every week.

Summer in the City organiser Tom Burns points out that Sugg's sister, Zoella, and her boyfriend Alfie Deyes are similarly adulated. 'There was a period when people would make videos and say: "I just went down to Brighton Pier and 200 of you showed up, it was crazy",' Burns says. At face value, that sounds like a compliment to those 200 fans – so 200 more would turn up the next time. Fans would begin tracking the movements of their favourite YouTubers, triangulating their location from social media posts (because this generation of celebrity always has to shine some light on their personal lives to be considered authentic), hoping to catch a glimpse of them.

Burns watched a video uploaded by Deyes of a tour he and Sugg were doing as part of Zoella's book tour in London. He says: 'The taxi is surrounded by fans banging on the window trying to get their attention. He's [Deyes] saying this is crazy, but at the same time not wanting to slam the fans while umming and aahing about how it's gone too far. That's where it happened.' A boundary had been crossed, and new rules about the interactions between creators and viewers (perhaps now better called fans) needed to be drawn up. That is why Summer in the City now has a backstage area. Burns says: 'There was this initial burst of: "This is so cool, I've got this big following, come meet me", and then: "Actually guys, when we're in public we want to be private; don't look over our walls at home." The boundaries got pushed further and further away again.'

Burns is definitive about the change. 'YouTubers have become less accessible,' he says. 'Some people say it's for good, some people say it's for the worse, I think it's one of those things where as it got more popular, it's inevitable.' Almost every year in videos or newspaper interviews, Zoella and Deyes plead with their fans not to visit their home to try and meet them. In 2017, Deyes told *The Telegraph* that he and his girlfriend face daily intrusions into their lives from parents driving their children to their door. 'I'm always polite, but the way I see it, not even my mum turns up uninvited,' he said.

Christina Grimmie was 'a huge wake-up call for a lot of YouTubers', according to the site's unofficial historian Anthony D'Angelo. Major personalities on the site began bumping up their personal protection; VidCon that year made major security changes to keep the talent attending the event safe. 'For a long time YouTube survived on this rhetoric of equity,' D'Angelo said. There was a belief that the playing field had been levelled; media had been democratised, and success could come to anyone. 'In many ways this is true, but it brings problems with it.'

Until Grimmie's untimely death, people knew that the more open, democratic way in which YouTube encouraged connections between creators and viewers might be a problem. After her murder, they realised it was a problem.

PART VI
THE BATTLE
FOR CONTROL

24.

YOUTUBERS

FOUND A UNION

For five years after she signed up with *MyDamnChannel* in 2008, Grace Helbig, the sisterly vlogger we met earlier, uploaded more than 1,500 videos. Her YouTube presence, *DailyGrace*, gained nearly two-and-a-half million subscribers. Ostensibly, things were going brilliantly for Helbig; she had turned a spot of amateur vlogging into a career; she was adored by her fans.

But all was not well: Helbig's contract with *MyDamnChannel* gave her little say over the videos she posted. And besides, she was weary. 'I felt really dry when I came to sit down at the end of the day and make a YouTube video,' she explained to fellow YouTubers Rhett and Link later. 'I was just recycling the same content, repackaged over and over. I felt like a fraud every time I went to VidCon or Playlist [another video conference]: no one really knows I'm owned by a corporation.'

Helbig was on a simple salary to run her channel, meaning that she did not get many of the benefits YouTubers receive from the site, such as an exponentially increasing income from more eyeballs seeing their videos. 'I could have a viral video every single video that went up and nothing in my life would really change,' she said. 'It's really frustrating when something did really well [as] you don't necessarily get the benefit of that.'

So she wanted out. Discussions over how to renegotiate her deal with *MyDamnChannel* to give her more power over the content she could post, and the amount of income that she could get from her booming fanbase, faltered. Then they stalled. In December 2013, she posted a final video to *DailyGrace*, saying she was taking a break from the internet for a while. '*MyDamnChannel*, thank you,' she told her fans. 'They are great. I want to thank them. I've been working for them for five years. They've provided me with a job, which is awesome.'

MyDamnChannel announced that Helbig had elected not to renew her contract, said she had been 'great', and wished her the best of luck for the future. It would, however, keep ownership of her channel – and wouldn't be giving her access to it. Instead, Helbig set up her own channel, called *Grace Helbig*. '*MyDamnChannel* owned *DailyGrace*, but they didn't own Grace Helbig,' Helbig told YouTube double-act Rhett McLaughlin and Link Neal, who go by the name *Rhett and Link* on the site. 'You're just hoping that your personality and the intimacy you've built based on yourself is enough.' A YouTube celebrity with millions of viewers was suddenly left to start back down at the bottom of the pile, with only a handful of subscribers. Helbig's brother Tim posted on Twitter: 'Thanks to the internet, I now have two sisters!! One is real and the other is a corporate entity.' Helbig herself admitted she was 'terrified' by the scale of the challenge.

Luckily, thanks to the help of other creators, the audience did come across to Helbig's new channel with her. Within a month, *Grace Helbig* had more than a million subscribers. Now, she has three million. Meanwhile, her old channel has shed 10% of its 2.2 million viewers since she left.

It was Helbig's experiences – and those of other YouTubers who dove in feet first in the early days of YouTube without much knowledge – that inspired the Green brothers to set up an industry union.

'It just makes sense for there to be an organisation that exists solely to promote the interests of this extremely culturally important group of creators,' Hank Green emailed me in July 2016, just after he'd announced the initiative. 'Every week I see another example of why this organization needs to exist, and that's been happening for years. We're taking a lot of lessons from a lot of places, but this new industry is so new and different that we pretty much have to build from scratch.'

The Internet Creators Guild (ICG) was set up to fill a gap, explains Laura Chernikoff, who moved from her job organising VidCon with Hank and John Green to become executive director of the new internet creators' union. (She's since moved on, replaced by Anthony D'Angelo.) Chernikoff said: 'It's an industry that's functioning as a professional group of creators much like screen actors or writers or producers. Whenever there's a group operating like this that has no way to communicate with each other and are relying on outside industry forces entirely to give them advice – like managers, agents and networks – there's the opportunity for someone to get taken advantage of.' She was worried that creators had signed away the rights to their channel or agreed deals that left them with a miniscule percentage of any profits they made.

Hank Green said: 'Some information is kept intentionally hidden, like standard ad rates. This keeps creators guessing and taking sub-standard deals. Other information is just hard to get at because this is all so new. Creators need these resources and they need connections with each other to help when things go wrong.'

He believes that creators can actually sign more adventurous deals than their Hollywood counterparts: 'I think you can do what you want to do with it, because there isn't so much of a model as there is with traditional celebrity… If you're a movie star, you have to do the movie thing and participate in the movie system. Those things are starting to exist for online creators, but they are very new and a lot more of the control is in the hands of the creator.' John Green says: 'I think one of the benefits of being an online creator is that you have a lot more independence and a lot more freedom, and that includes who you talk to and how you deal with work.'

At the same time, others are trying to help redress the information imbalance between multi-channel networks and content creators.

Sam Mollaei is a Californian lawyer who advises YouTubers looking to navigate the complicated agreements they are offered with multi-channel networks (MCNs) and agents. Around a tenth of his caseload is focused on YouTube. 'From what I've seen, MCNs are taking advantage of individual YouTubers,' he said when we first spoke, in July 2016. 'I see a lot of YouTubers getting locked into a one-sided relationship.'

A traditional business and contract lawyer, Mollaei was contacted by YouTubers who were seeking advice about their contracts. Already a fan of YouTube, he knew the talent well. Like a growing number of people, he has stopped watching traditional TV, relying instead on YouTube for all his media consumption. Yet, until he was approached by creators, he had little idea of the back-end business that increasingly drives the site. By delving into the world of multi-channel networks, and scanning the kinds of deals that were being agreed by young creators with little experience of copyright, trademark ownership and working in a professional environment, he realised that few if any other lawyers were working in the sector. An average YouTuber is more likely to be a teenager shooting videos from their bedroom than a canny observer of the media world aware of their worth – that makes his role so important. 'They're not big businesses or corporations, and there's nobody on their side.'

Lucy Moon, who became a successful vlogger after leaving university, agrees: 'We're walking into rooms with people who are experts in marketing. They understand how to take advantage of you and how much you're worth. That's quite scary. You don't even realise it's happening, and then you look back a year later and think: "I should've been paid a lot more for that".'

Mollaei has a specific bugbear: it's not any one thing that the multi-channel networks do, but their very existence. 'In reality, there's no need for YouTubers to really sign with MCNs unless there's a very specific need,' he believes. Larger content creators, whose days are being filled with demands for them to scan licensing agreements, to book travel to international meet-and-greets, and to continue to create content may need a hand – simply because there aren't enough hours in the day. But for young, new YouTubers, there's no need to sign away their rights to a firm who'll take a cut (based on the contracts he has inspected, an MCN's take can range anywhere from 10-30% of a YouTuber's income for doing some admin).

But if MCNs really are to exist, then the lawyer wants to make sure his clients are getting good value for money. The main thing that MCNs offer in their contracts with YouTubers is 'support' – 'whatever that means', he drily notes. Any time a creator has issues with their channel, or they need marketing or creative support, they should be able to rely on an MCN to help rectify the situation. In reality, Mollaei believes the loose wording in contracts means MCNs do the bare minimum for most people, focusing instead on the bigger names they represent, whose reputation builds them a brand (and most importantly, whose advertising revenue secures their profits). What they promise and what they actually deliver are often two different things. And events like the November 2018 closure of *Defy Media*, an American MCN which left 50 creators among the talent it represented – including one of the biggest channels on early YouTube, *Smosh* – owed a combined $1.7 million, have posed even more questions of the model. (*Smosh* was bought by Mythical Entertainment, the entertainment firm set up by Rhett and Link, in February 2019.)

Mollaei believes that many MCNs are deficient for the majority of their clients after the initial focus and 'over time the MCN doesn't really bring in any more deals for the YouTuber.' He believes that many YouTubers would be better off concentrating on their craft and improving their videos, rather than relying on an outside business to cut deals for them. That's particularly important at a time when YouTube is reaching saturation: the improved business model and administrative support that YouTube offers and the influx of ad money mean that people can now earn a five-figure income from 100,000 subscribers.

Instead, there are several ways that creators can take their destiny into their own hands: by brokering more sponsored content, by selling merchandise and by exploring the opportunities of the crowdfunding platform, Patreon.

25.

PATREON:

SEEKING

INDEPENDENT SUPPORT

Many creators were jolted in spring 2017 when YouTube lost advertising clients because it promoted their brands against extremist and offensive content. Some YouTubers saw their ad revenue drop by 80% for months after the 'adpocalypse', according to Laura Chernikoff, the former head of the Internet Creators Guild.

Chernikoff said: 'The whole advertising situation shook people up a bit and made them realise they can't rely completely on what they have on YouTube. The smart creators are realising that YouTube is not a direct mailing list to my audience. They [YouTube] can turn on and turn off that reach. There's a fear that they could do that arbitrarily or in a way that creators can't understand, so I think they're realising they have to be able to reach that audience – particularly superfans – in a more direct way that they control.'

Smart stars make sure their contact with fans now isn't mediated solely by YouTube. Instead they connect with fans directly on every platform possible – and sign them up to mailing lists – so that if one or more shuts off access, their interactions can still continue unabated.

They are also turning to Patreon – a platform on which supporters (or patrons) pay money to support a particular artist or creator. Patreon was co-founded in May 2013 by Jack Conte of the band Pomplamoose, when they received a YouTube AdSense cheque for the million views they received for a creatively shot music video for one of their tracks. It cost $10,000 to film. The return on investment for Conte and his wife, Nataly Dawn, the other half of the band? Around $150.

'Jack thought: "How on earth can I fill 10 football stadiums with people watching this and I get like $150?"' explains Tyler Sean Palmer, Patreon's vice president of operations and the company's first employee. 'He said: "I'll just turn to my fans".'

Patreon's founding idea was simple: the internet advertising model was broken and creators should instead be paid directly by their fans. Palmer believes that advertising revenue skews creators away from their original artistic leanings. In short, people chase views, because views equals money. 'It seems so weird to me that YouTube can change an algorithm and that changes the content we create and consume,' Palmer says.

He's not the only one who is baffled by YouTube's desire to slavishly follow the algorithm at all costs, and the site's unwillingness to lift the curtain even slightly on how it works to help creators try and produce content that audiences want. 'They program for the lowest common denominator,' says Matt Gielen of research company Little Monster Media Co. 'Their belief is that keeping their super-precious algorithm secret from people who would abuse that knowledge is more important than helping the people who pay their salaries: the creators on the platform. I think it's foolish and shortsighted, and one of the reasons the creator community has such a bad attitude towards them.'

Laura Chernikoff says: 'At their most fed up, when YouTube has pulled something, or adpocalypse has happened, there's this sense that: "Nothing is keeping me here except I have to be here, my audience is here." The only alternative is being very savvy and building up some way of reaching your audience that doesn't depend on YouTube or any one platform. That's the escape route for people. You see something like Patreon: you only need to pull off your superfans or your core supporters. You're not going to get every single one of your subscribers.'

Within a year of Patreon's founding, around half those who had joined the nascent site were YouTubers looking to earn additional funds for their creativity. (Today, that's diversified: when I speak to Palmer at the start of October 2017, he estimates that online video – though still the biggest single area for creators on Patreon – accounts for only one in every three people using the site to make money from their work.) Patreon takes 5% of each pledge made by hardcore fans, who give an average of $12 a month to creators they want to support.

It's big business: the company has successively arranged funding in order to grow, the last round valuing the firm at $450 million. In 2019, 100,000 creators on Patreon are receiving money from more than three million patrons, and the site expects to pay them \$500 million.

Creators like the site, reckons Palmer, because of two main reasons. The first is money: a creator with hundreds of thousands of views every month could only earn a couple of hundred dollars a month through YouTube's AdSense scheme. 'Patreon is proving that if you can get that top few percent of fans that really dig your stuff, and get them to pay, you can continue making the content you want to make for them, and make more of a living,' says Palmer.

The second is that it's more dependable income than YouTube ad revenue, which seems often at the whim of what the site deems acceptable at any given time. 'YouTube controls what can and can't be monetised,' says Palmer. 'We saw hundreds of creators come to Patreon overnight when YouTube said some stuff [such as more extreme or adult-oriented content] can't be monetised anymore.'

It makes sense – particularly given that, as we've seen in previous chapters, YouTubers are often no longer sole traders trying to eke out a living in front of the camera. 'Some of these people have payroll, have employees,' says Palmer. 'I don't mean to bash on YouTube too hard. But their customer is the advertiser, so they're not aligned with creators in the way we are. Our customer is the creator, whereas YouTube, as much as they want to say otherwise, their customer is the advertiser and always will be.'

In a blog post in May 2017, just as YouTubers were feeling the initial losses from the adpocalypse, Sean Baeyens, head of small business growth and management at Patreon, appealed to YouTubers to supplement their ad revenue income with support from fans using its platform. He wrote:

'Professional artists and creators should view themselves as small businesses, and it's risky for any business to be too reliant on one source of revenue or too dependent on one platform. So what's the solution? Diversifying your income streams. This doesn't mean you need to abandon a platform altogether, or that you should compromise your creative projects because they aren't 'ad-friendly.' It simply means exploring alternative ways to generate income using your videos.'

Some of the biggest YouTubers have answered Baeyens' call to diversify their income through Patreon. Among them was Phil DeFranco, one of the closest things YouTube has to a media mogul. DeFranco first uploaded videos a decade ago in the form of the eponymous *Philip DeFranco Show* at university in Carolina. Now 33, he is senior vice president of his own company, Phil DeFranco Networks and Merchandise, and his YouTube channels have more than 7.5 million subscribers.

DeFranco has publicly estimated his annual income over the course of his career as ranging between $100,000 and $250,000. However, in early 2017 he ran into problems with some of his videos. One entitled *People Outraged Over Now-Deleted Video and The Trump 'Witch Hunt' Rabbit Hole* was a 14-minute monologue covering his various thoughts on a contentious McDonald's advert, video game consoles, and footage of Turkish bodyguards kicking protestors in the head. It started with him saying 'What's up you beautiful bastards', his usual greeting.

YouTube marked the video with an age gate (the equivalent of age ratings on films), removing the opportunity to place adverts against it. DeFranco shared the mature demographics of his viewership (a tool accessible to all YouTubers): 95.7% of his viewers are aged 18 or over. But despite the fact that the majority of his viewers were old enough to accept the content of his videos, Google refused to back down. Handily, the financial hit wasn't as great as it could have been: DeFranco had set up his Patreon page a couple of weeks before, on 1 May 2017, asking for between $5 and $10,000 a month so that he could continue making his videos. On the first day, more than 8,000 people pledged him money.

Today, around 10,000 people fund DeFranco on a monthly basis (down from a peak of 15,000), giving him a stipend that allows him to create his videos regardless of whether or not YouTube yanks the adverts from them. He is the 12th most popular Patreon project, and is earning at least $26,000 every month from his fans, according to one estimate.

Patreon's rise has worried YouTube. Fewer than 1% of YouTubers used its own abortive attempt at a Patreon-style monthly subscription service – the ability to support a channel with as little as 99 US cents a month – after its launch in 2013. In September 2017, YouTube announced it was expanding its Sponsorships programme, where viewers pay creators $4.99 a month for additional perks, which had originally been tested with gaming creators. Like Patreon, Sponsorships give creators a more reliable monthly income away from their ad revenue, while also allowing some viewers extra access and benefits for supporting their favourite vloggers.

When I ask Palmer if he's worried that YouTube just ate Patreon's lunch, a few weeks after the Google-owned monolith announced Sponsorships, he seemed sanguine. 'We're not disappointed by that stuff. Of course the big companies are going to follow suit. We've proven the model.' Although he never mentioned YouTube by name, he also drew some stark contrasts between the two sites' approach to creators. 'There's something about the culture we've built here,' he says. 'It's people that are creator-first, giving their blood, sweat and tears to try and get creators paid, and they want to make decisions that are in creators' best interest, and they want to communicate well and don't want to be vague. They want to share data, to earn business and not to hold people captive.' By implication, he thinks YouTube does none of those things.

'Folks are begging to partner with us because we have that trust with creators, and that's not something you can buy, or it's not a feature set you can build. It's four years of treating creators the right way and making creator-first decisions. Our biggest asset right now is the relationship we have with these creators.'

It's an approach that echoes Revver's early attempts to reward creators directly in 2006. However, even Patreon has made missteps. In December 2017, it shifted the responsibility for paying transaction fees from creators onto donors. Creators were unhappy that backers would end up paying more without any consultation. In the end, Patreon backed down.

Perhaps because of Patreon's popularity among YouTube creators, in 2017 YouTube introduced new rules that blocked users who were not part of the YouTube Partner Program (for which creators at the time needed to have at least 10,000 views on their videos) from linking to external sites such as online shops or Patreon pages at the end of their uploads. Creators were up in arms at what they saw as an attempt by YouTube to cap their outside earnings, but the site maintained that it only wanted to determine whether the channel was following its 'community guidelines and advertiser policies'.

Others disagreed. One of the loudest voices speaking out against the action was Ian Danskin, whose video essays about gaming and the internet are seen by 160,000 subscribers. Danskin helps fund his essays on his channel, *Innuendo Studios*, through Patreon, where at the time of writing, 1,236 people give him a total of $3,391 per month.

'Incentivising people to join the Partner Program is supposed to curb abuse... just... how???' he tweeted. 'How does stripping the ability for smaller channels to effectively monetize their work AT ALL curb abuse? I've known many YouTubers who are happy to get 200 views on a video, that 10k threshold is a long way off for them.'

Part of the reason Danskin was so concerned about the change YouTube enacted was that he relies on Patreon in order to create his elaborate, thought-out video essays. 'Ad revenue is so variable,' he explains. 'It's something that can disappear overnight. If the algorithm decides one day that they're demonetising your video and it's your biggest video, that's a whole bunch of money you don't have, and you can't predict it.'

YouTube can decide to demonetise any of them for often inscrutable reasons (including that they contain controversial content, without fully explaining why – the reason why Phil De Franco's videos were delisted from hosting adverts). Even if it doesn't, creators are still at the whims of its opaque algorithms, and the wildly fluctuating rates paid for any advert.

'If the algorithm picks your video that day, you might get a lot of ad revenue,' says Danskin. 'If the algorithm doesn't pick your video that week, then what do you do? It's not even your fault. There are algorithms out there and they just decide, and they don't necessarily have any rational logic behind what they decide.'

Danskin has first-hand experience of the whims of You-Tube's algorithm benefiting him. In December 2015, he published a 22-minute video called *We Don't Talk About Kenny: Telltale's Walking Dead*. For six months it did nothing outstanding, simply ticking up views. But then the third season of the television show ended, and Danskin's months-old video began to be promoted more in YouTube's autoplay algorithm. The number of views shot up. 'I have no control over that,' says Danskin. 'I didn't do anything. I made this video, a year and a half ago, and it went from one of my most popular videos that never went viral, to one of my most viral videos. You can't predict that. You can't plan your life around that.'

For that reason, Danskin turned to Patreon – and reckons that even if he'd turned on adverts for all his YouTube videos, he'd still have earned only around a quarter of the amount of money he's received from Patreon.

In an October 2017 interview with Re/code's Kara Swisher, YouTube's chief executive officer, Susan Wojcicki, described the platform as 'an ecosystem between advertisers and creators and users'. The order is deliberate. To YouTube, advertisers come first; then the creators producing the videos; then the people watching it. Unwittingly, Wojcicki showed where the real power lies in every business: with the people who pay the bills. At Patreon, that's the fans. At YouTube, it's the advertisers.

26.

MERCHANDISE:

FROM BOOKS TO POP SOCKETS

YouTubers are 360-degree brands looking for opportunities and no longer just people playing with cameras. The past few years have seen the rise of YouTube tie-ins: trinkets, T-shirts and books. Plenty of YouTubers are capitalising on their personal connection with their fans to sell additional items, on top of receiving AdSense income and sponsorship money from brands.

Zoella had first shown the immense commercial potential for YouTubers to sell large numbers of books in 2014, when she released her debut novel, *Girl Online*. In its first week in the UK, 78,109 copies were sold, the biggest ever first-week sales figures for a first-time author. It was also a *New York Times* bestseller for young adults.

The novel attracted controversy because Sugg relied on a ghostwriter to write the book. In pre-release publicity, the book's publisher, Penguin, said that *Girl Online* was 'told in Zoe's relatable, fresh and engaging voice.' In reality, Siobhan Curham, an accomplished young adult author, co-wrote the book with Sugg. Contemporary reports suggested that other ghostwriters were approached to pen the novel with Sugg for between £7,000 and £8,000. The controversy around Sugg's use of a ghostwriter to help her with her debut novel was baffling, given it's established practice for many first-time writers, particularly celebrities and sportsmen and women. (Before you ask, no, this book isn't ghostwritten.)

Caroline Sanderson, who previews new non-fiction titles for Britain's *Bookseller* magazine, doesn't see anything wrong with employing ghostwriters. 'Why shouldn't she need help to write a novel? Nobody expects Wayne Rooney to write his own books; that's not his expertise.'

The anger that Sugg faced from the press and from fans seemed to have two causes: one, that this was a new media figure trespassing on a literary preserve. Secondly, that Sugg's book was co-written with someone else seemed to jar with the idea of YouTube as an authentic, personal medium. Not that it made much difference: a second book in the *Girl Online* series was published in October 2015, followed by a third just over a year later. (A subsequent book, *Cordially Invited* – a vapid guide to celebrating Christmas – was published in October 2018.)

Sugg's boyfriend, Alfie Deyes, was a similarly powerful draw for book publishers and arguably a more cynical one. Deyes wrote his first book in 2014, *The Pointless Book* with the subtitle: 'Started by Alfie Deyes, finished by you'. Borrowing from the likes of Keri Smith's *Wreck This Journal*, where readers are cajoled into scribbling over their book in response to prompts, Deyes' *Pointless Book* was thin on content, barely managing to fill its 192 pages. But it sold 30,000 copies in its first two weeks; combined with a similarly sparse follow-up (*The Pointless Book 2*) that *The Guardian* called a 'two volume non-extravaganza' and 'the worst thing you're likely to see in a tin this Christmas, unless someone buys you a can of beans and miniature sausages', the two *Pointless Books* have sold more than 600,000 copies, making nearly £4 million in sales. The first book was on *The Sunday Times* bestseller list for 11 straight weeks, and a London book signing at Waterstones had to be abandoned after thousands more fans than expected turned up to see their idol. Shop staff were worried that the crowds pressing against the door might smash the glass and so called off the signing early. Sales of Deyes' books show no sign of slowing, either. His publisher, Blink, said in February 2017 that the two *Pointless Books* still sell more than a thousand copies per week, years after the first one went on sale.

With YouTubers' books such big business, it's no wonder that the big talent agencies are also looking to cut out the middlemen, creating and selling those products themselves. So it was in July 2017 that Gleam Futures, a major UK talent agency stowed under with big-name YouTubers, announced it was setting up its own book agency, Gleam Titles, poaching staff from established publisher Simon & Schuster.

What is most interesting about the YouTubers' books revolution is that they are bringing a new audience to the literary world. *The Bookseller*'s Caroline Sanderson has two children: 'They're both big consumers of YouTube, particularly my son.' He grew up in a home with lots of books around him, but wasn't a big reader himself. Yet he's bought and read plenty of books by YouTubers. One of the books he was tempted to read because of the authors was *Sidemen: The Book*, the product of seven famous You-Tubers including KSI, the FIFA-playing YouTuber-turned-boxer and rap artist. On its release in October 2016 the Sidemen's book rocketed to the top of the UK non-fiction book charts, selling 26,436 copies in its first three days. What makes those figures so impressive is that the book was released on 'Super Thursday', the most competitive time in the book industry in the run-up to Christmas. In its first week on sale *The Sidemen* had outsold Jamie Oliver's latest cookbook (shifting nearly 20,000 more copies) and the diaries of Alan Bennett.

The Sidemen weren't unique: on Super Thursday 2015, another YouTube tie-in topped the UK book charts on the most important week for the industry. *The Amazing Book is Not on Fire* by Dan Howell and Phil Lester, better known as simply Dan and Phil, sold 26,744 copies, beating Bill Bryson and more than 400 other hardback books released on the same day to reach the top of the charts. Sanderson says: 'Some people are pretty snotty about YouTube books. I think they're fantastic for our business.'

YouTubers, though, still need to ensure that they are giving their fans good value for money. In November 2017 the British chemist chain Boots released the 12 Days of Christmas Advent Calendar – 'the ultimate Christmas calendar from Zoella Life-style'. Behind the doors of the calendar – which lasted 12 days, rather than the standard 25 – were 'amazing and exclusive treats, from beautifully scented candles to stunning accessories, stationery, baking goodies and other special surprises.'

Fans soon realised what they got for their £50: a packet of confetti, two cookie cutters (one of which seemed to cost 77p to buy individually), seven stickers, two candles, a pen, a key ring, a notepad and a room spray, plus a bag. Twitter users discovered that the entire contents of the calendar could be bought separately for under £20. Fans lambasted the product on social media. One review described it as 'literal tat'. Boots apologised and immediately halved the price. Zoella explained that she had worked on the calendar for a year. 'I'm all about the creativity, about getting from a design to a product. Where my input ends is there,' she said. 'The retailer can decide how much they sell that for; that's completely out of my decision making.' She added: 'I don't want people to think I'm sat at home counting £50 every time someone buys this calendar. If you know me, there is not a bone in my body that would think that way.'

YouTuber merchandise has always been overpriced. A branded pop socket has always been a relatively useless mobile phone dongle that can be picked up unbranded for a fraction of the price. While social media was castigating Zoella for her advent calendar, American YouTuber Johnny Orlando was advertising tickets to watch him and his sister Lauren take part in a photoshoot for a teen-focused magazine for $40. And in 2018, PewDiePie launched a clothing line, Tsuki, where a cotton-polyester blend hoodie adorned with a small embroidered logo cost $100.

But on 23 August 2017, Alfie Deyes and Zoella broached a new boundary. They found a way to combine the lure of a personal appearance with the sale of stuff. 'Today is the day,' explained Deyes as he wandered around a rented Airbnb in London, Sugg making breakfast behind him. Deyes was vlogging about the opening of a Sugg Life x PointlessBlog pop-up shop (combining the power couple's two brands). Ahead of its launch, they were anticipating enormous queues and an influx of YouTubers wanting to visit their first real physical retail presence, in Covent Garden, one of London's best-known shopping destinations.

As they and Sugg's brother Joe (the *Strictly Come Dancing* finalist and also a popular YouTuber) opened the doors at 10am, a crowd of several hundred fans who had stood for hours outside the shop off Upper St Martin's Lane began screaming. Hiring the 1,450-square-foot store for 12 days was a gamble: rent cost £1,000 per day before VAT. Still, they needn't have worried. The crowds were almost as massive as the mark-up. Posters, tote bags and phone pop sockets started at £10 (even the store's staff seem to blanch at that, with a sign for the broken staff toilet reading: 'It's free, unlike our pop sockets, which are £10 please'). T-shirts emblazoned with the Sugg Life and Pointless Blog logos cost £15, while a hoodie set buyers back £25.

More than 4,000 people visited the shop on the first day. After six hours spent taking selfies with fans, they had to beat a hasty retreat. 'Guys, remember this pop up isn't a meet & greet,' wrote Deyes on Twitter. 'It's a pop up shop. We've had to leave the shop due to security telling us things.'

Other YouTubers saw their success and followed. Jake Paul announced similar pop-up shops in Los Angeles and New York just in time for the run-up to Christmas 2017. On 1 December, the doors of the Los Angeles shop didn't open when planned for safety reasons: the size of the expected crowd was too great. It switched to another, bigger location. Nine hundred fans attended the first day of a store in New York on 8 December, paying $10 for a ticket before buying any merchandise. And Tiana, the 11-year-old who is one of Britain's biggest child YouTubers, brought 11,000 people to Birmingham's Bullring shopping centre for her own pop-up shop in September 2018.

The trend isn't limited to creators alone, either. YouTube's London Creator Space behind King's Cross station (the site's base in the UK) gave over part of its shop, which has since closed, to Dodie Clark for three weeks in November 2017, setting up a small shrine to the YouTuber, with museum-like exhibits, including original artwork and tableaux including excerpts from her first book, *Secrets for the Mad*. It was perfectly positioned, right next to one of the major hubs for creators – and thus an obvious place for star-spotters with money burning a hole in their pocket to congregate.

Generally kids have been willing to overlook the overpricing of their favourite creators because of a personal connection they feel with them. In an exclusive survey for this book after her advent calendar controversy, a third of adults aged between 18 and 24 who recognised the name Zoella told the pollster YouGov that they felt they knew her well. (Tellingly, half of those who recalled Zoella's name didn't trust her – and 28% distrusted her 'a lot'.) While fans often still consider their favourite creators to be their friends, the creators themselves see things differently. They have changed from being one-man bands to self-sustaining businesses with employees, books to balance, and profits to make.

That shift in the viewer-creator relationship has coincided with fans' parents starting to pay more attention to the people their children are supporting – and paying more attention to the press coverage describing their ever-increasing incomes, too. Though parents may grouse at their offspring spending money on things they could buy more cheaply without branding elsewhere, the likelihood is that many parents make the same judgements in their own shopping. Why do many adults shun the stack-em-high, sell-em-cheap products at chain stores in favour of artisanal products made by named designers? Why do they pick the organic grass-fed beef from their local butcher, rather than a vacuum-packed steak on a supermarket shelf? Because there's a sense of supporting the individual behind the endeavour, and the warm feeling that comes with that. Parents can complain that their children are frittering away their money on their favourite YouTubers, but the reality is that most of us make imperfect spending decisions.

That's not to say that something hasn't gone wrong in the relationship between YouTubers and their fans, though. Both fans and parents are beginning to recognise that, as YouTube matures, the creators they once thought of as friends are in fact just brands – and successful ones at that. People who five years ago may have needed their supporters to buy an overpriced tote bag or hoodie in order to make a living from their few thousand fans suddenly have millions of fans. They have realised they can make a real profit from them, rather than simply living from pay-cheque to pay-cheque.

PART VII

THE FUTURE:

YOUTUBE V TV

27:

INVASION OF THE

HOLLYWOOD STARS

For decades, some of the biggest names in entertainment have prowled Radio City Music Hall in midtown Manhattan. As well as the Rockettes, its famous in-house dance troupe, Madonna performed her infamous rendition of *Like A Virgin* on its 5,376-square-foot stage – and hundreds of films have premiered in the vast auditorium.

But on 3 May 2018 it was home to a more prosaic group of people: a handful of YouTube executives who unveiled their latest round of original, platform-supported programming at Brandcast, an event for the many advertisers who had gently eased away from the site as it stumbled through scandals in the previous 18 months. The shows, called YouTube Originals, were longer in form and bigger budget than the grassroots videos shot by individual YouTubers, and included plenty of familiar names – just not to YouTube's core audience.

British comedian Jack Whitehall would front a show training with the world's best football players in a show executive-produced by James Corden, another mainstream celebrity whose clips from the *Late Late Show* are highly promoted on the site. Kevin Hart was returning for a second series of his comedy show where he works out with celebrity friends while exchanging punchlines and barbs. And Will Smith, YouTube's latest luvvie, would front a programme where he would bungee jump from a helicopter.

Smith, the Hollywood star who holds the record for the most consecutive $100 million-plus-earning films, opened his YouTube channel 10 days before Christmas 2017. 'I cannot believe how much YouTube has awakened me,' he said in a trailer a few months into his vlogging career. 'I'm finding my voice. There's so much stuff I wanted to say.' Smith's series – starring some of traditional media's biggest names – 'will not only engage and entertain,' said Kate Stanford, the site's head of global advertising marketing, 'but also celebrate diverse and authentic voices.'

Some queried how diverse and authentic the voices were given that they had spent the last several decades on television screens and movie posters, but it signalled a change of focus for the site. YouTube had entered the mainstream – and in some ways, what made YouTubers unique in those early days has disappeared. It was the latest example of the site's evolution. But it wasn't the starkest example – nor did it create the most vociferous backlash. That came seven months after YouTube announced its slate of original programming. And it too featured Will Smith.

For an indication of the way mainstream celebrities have infiltrated the video sharing site, stripping it of its 'Broadcast

Yourself' mentality, viewers needn't have looked any further than YouTube's *2018 Rewind* video, a recap of the platform's most momentous moments of the last 12 months. A record-breaker, it notched up more than 10 million dislikes in the first few days after it was uploaded in December 2018 – making it the most hated video in the history of YouTube.

There were several reasons why people so hated *YouTube Rewind 2018*. One of the biggest names featured in the video was Tyler 'Ninja' Blevins, a new media celebrity, who had made his name not on YouTube, but on Twitch, the live streaming video gaming website that could be one of YouTube's major competitors. Blevins qualified for inclusion in *YouTube Rewind* because of his enormous reach – which comes closest to matching PewDiePie, who was conspicuous by his absence in the video – but also on a technicality: he uploads highlights of his Twitch streams to a separate YouTube channel, subscribed to by 21 million people. For YouTube purists, Blevins was an interloper whose success shouldn't be co-opted (or celebrated) by YouTube.

Others disliked the way the video nearly stopped for a preachy, carefully scripted (and awfully acted) segment praising YouTube's corporate social responsibility and diversity, while overlooking the site's many issues and controversies. The discursive chat about how YouTube was so great took place by a campfire.

But the main reason *YouTube Rewind* ignited the ire of 15 million people in total to date can be summed up in the sarcastic words of one commenter: 'Will Smith, my favourite YouTuber.' Grinning ear to ear in both the first frame of the video and the last was the Hollywood actor. It's not that Smith is a bad person, or that he's a bad YouTuber – his videos are actually okay, if a little cringeworthy – but that he is a lightning rod for popular opposition to the way in which YouTube has changed. YouTube viewers love their home-grown stars, and Will Smith is categorically not a home-grown star. It all comes down to the creator-viewer relationship, and the parasocial element behind it. YouTube viewers can feel partly responsible for helping Jake Paul reside in his multi-million-dollar mansion, or chipping in towards KSI's Lamborghini. Their clicks, likes and views have helped contribute to that person's success.

But Will Smith was already a millionaire before joining YouTube. He hasn't, by any definition of the word, been a 'normal' person for the best part of three decades. He's remote and different, a world away from the raw, unvarnished videos that ordinary people post on the site. Any dead bodies in Will Smith's closet, should they exist, would have been unearthed by now. He's polished and pre-vetted. YouTube viewers hate that. YouTube themselves – desperately seeking stability after being buffeted by successive scandals and facing the breakwaters of a second adpocalypse in early 2019 – love it.

Smith, who has 4.6 million subscribers on the site, isn't the only Hollywood superstar to present a different side of themselves on YouTube. Dwayne 'The Rock' Johnson has more than 3.5 million subscribers who watch his regular uploads. At one point these were behind-the-scenes vlogs of the actor's on-set exploits; now they've become more mundane ways to plug his movie projects.

Hollywood leading man Ryan Reynolds' YouTube channel is slightly more low-key, gaining 750,000 subscribers since it was set up at the end of 2015, but the star's infrequent posts follow the same formula as The Rock's. They borrow some elements of the 'authentic' YouTube aesthetic while also making sure to promote whatever blockbuster the actor is appearing in next.

Both Reynolds and Johnson's YouTube channels show how deftly Smith, despite the public hate for his YouTube presence, has managed to walk the line between the old-school Hollywood school of celebrity and the new, YouTube-enabled one. Smith still ladles on the schmaltz and barely a video goes by without some sort of sponsored content or promotion for an upcoming movie. However, you get the impression he cares about his YouTube presence, and that he probably likes the site. It's that passion – manifested in some sort of authenticity – that helps make him successful while other celebrities fail.

Small snippets that punctuated the much-maligned 2018 *Rewind* video also show how some of traditional television's biggest stars have a home on YouTube, too. The hosts of America's late night television shows, including James Corden and Jimmy Fallon, have significant profiles on the site – a combined 35 million subscribers – through official channels branded with the logos of their programmes. Corden's *Carpool Karaoke* series of videos regularly feature on the site's trending page, as do videos posted by Ellen DeGeneres, the queen of daytime TV in the United States. Her YouTube channel, which posts some of the most heart-tugging moments from her television chat show, has nearly 30 million subscribers alone.

It makes sense for these people to be the faces of YouTube. They've been trained not to say or do anything stupid – unlike YouTubers, who regularly put their foot in it. That has become more important than ever as YouTube becomes a big corporation, rather than a platform for creativity. As a result, YouTubers are starting to act more like the businesses that are trying to replace them in order not to be left behind by the race towards safe harbours like Will Smith. They're clubbing together and giving off the veneer of professionalism under management, rather than as sole traders.

But there's more to YouTube embracing Will Smith and his Hollywood friends quite so tightly. As James Whatley, an advertising and branding expert who at the time worked at Ogilvy told me in May 2018, it helps YouTube diversify and expand its audience from the billions of young people it already had to an older generation of viewers. 'Why would a viewer, a 45-year-old parent, who has grown up with big Hollywood stars, prefer to watch Netflix rather than YouTube?' Whatley said. 'Premium content featuring the stars they recognise.' Getting Hollywood stars on YouTube helps redress that problem.

Still, the perfectly preened presentation of celebrities and stars has taken a dent in recent years. Marlene Dietrich, one of the highest paid actresses of her era, famously said that glamour was her stock-in-trade. Jennifer Lawrence, perhaps the highest-profile actress in the Hollywood system today, is totally different in her approach. 'In Hollywood, I'm obese,' she says. 'I eat like a caveman.'

The lid has been lifted on celebrities' lifestyles, and we've become more aware of the botox, silicon and figure-hugging Spanx that make Hollywood's biggest names look quite so perfect – in part thanks to the new wave of 'authentic' influencers who are willing to open up about their fears and foibles. But it's not just in the way famous people approach the pretence of perfection that shows a cross-pollination between YouTube and the traditional celebrity system.

Big-name stars from a past era of media have started encroaching on the new media space. They're people like superstar rapper Wiz Khalifa, who uploads semi-regular vlogs about his lifestyle that he calls *DayToday*. The video series was initially conceived of as a way to boost his Twitter followers, and was first posted to YouTube in March 2009. Ten years later, he's still continuing to post his *DayToday* videos, giving a glimpse into how he lives his life. Several scenes are filmed at home; in a recent example he fools around with his friends besides a pool table and beneath the neon green glow of a sign that reads 'High Life' underneath a marijuana leaf. (Weed plays a big part in Khalifa's videos: lingering close-ups of cannabis buds in a giant grinder the size of a small bin and elaborately crafted bongs are commonplace.) The rapper hovers around the top 100 most-subscribed channels, peers with UK children's nursery rhyme animation channel *Little Baby Bum*, classic YouTuber Liza Koshy and Jake Paul.

Khalifa's *DayToday* vlogs are often as popular as some of his official music videos uploaded to the same channel that 17 million people subscribe to. Khalifa uses his YouTube channel as a way of extending the connection with his fanbase, offering them a glimpse behind the scenes of the glitz and glamour of a rap lifestyle. It's a conscious attempt to pull back the curtain and humanise the figure: rather than being put on a pedestal, Khalifa engenders more loyalty from his fans by seeming – at least – to be one of us. That said, the gold chains and super-fast super cars undercut the message somewhat.

Others use YouTube as another outlet to publish repackaged snippets of their traditional media persona. Celebrity chefs Gordon Ramsay and Jamie Oliver have both dabbled with

YouTube channels. Embracing YouTube fully at the start, Oliver even partook in collaboration videos with big name YouTubers such as Alfie Deyes, Hannah Hart and Grace Helbig as an attempt to boost his credentials on the platform. Don't be fooled: they're carving out a place for themselves on the world's biggest online video platform. But it's generally with older viewers who see YouTube as an extension of traditional linear TV, rather than a standalone media entity.

Both Oliver and Ramsay's YouTube channels (which combined have 12 million subscribers) look too much like TV to really hit home with a viewership used to honesty and a certain raw aesthetic. They're still too polished, too wary of letting people too close into their lives for fear they'll find something unvarnished. As a result, their channels – while still popular – appeal more to the older users of YouTube. They're places to publish offcuts from their back catalogue and present them as prime cuts. The younger, YouTube-savvy fanbase that will promise them future income know something's not right, and shun them.

And that's the main issue with mainstream celebrities migrating to YouTube. Young viewers are attuned to what they see as authentic and are slavishly devoted to promoting their own. When a mainstream celebrity – or more accurately, their management – sets up a YouTube channel to offer a veneer of authenticity and a half-hearted attempt to get 'down with the kids', smart viewers see right through it. So it is with YouTube's own star-studded series, announced on the same stage that graced Madonna and the Rockettes. Just a few months after unveiling its latest series of shows to much ballyhoo at Radio City Music Hall, YouTube quietly announced it would be opening up access to its Originals to everyone – though those who didn't pay the $11.99 per month subscription fee would be served adverts throughout the programmes.

28.

IS YOUTUBE

KILLING

TRADITIONAL TV?

Around three years ago, forty-somethings Derek Holder and his wife Cannis bought a new Sony television. On the remote, alongside the standard volume and channel controls, was a bright red button, emblazoned with the word 'Netflix'. Holder says: 'I predict in the future there'll be a YouTube button. Once they get to that point – and I don't think it's far off – it will really kill TV.'

Holder has the credibility to make the prediction. He and his wife set up a booming YouTube business, El Bebe Productions, which posts 3D animated educational videos under the brand name *Little Baby Bum*. If you have small children, you might know it. If you don't, you should. It's the 13th biggest channel on all YouTube based on views (18 billion at the time of writing, and with another 200 million views added every month).

The Holders personify the rapid growth of YouTube better than any statistics. In 2011, they were not even in the media. They were simply parents looking for some children's nursery rhymes. Derek Holder, 48, recalls: 'I was looking on YouTube for some nursery rhyme videos for my own kid, who was one at the time, and couldn't really find too many that were good. I was comparing quality to *CBeebies* or something like that. *CBeebies* is generally speaking excellent quality and everything online was awful.' Many of these slap-dash YouTube productions had tens of millions of views.

Holder had worked in IT and teleconferencing, from which he had learned the principles of search engine optimisation. 'I knew, looking at these views, that they would translate into revenue.' Over a meal with another friend, he began sketching out the plan for the YouTube channel, telling him: 'I can't see how it can fail.' His 45-year-old wife was a graphic designer who had worked on corporate rebranding projects. They founded El Bebe with a hope and a dream – and a payment to a Ukrainian animator on Holder's personal credit card.

That animator was a precursor to the vast array of gig economy workers of freelance video editors, graphic designers and videographers now working in the YouTube space. More than 6,000 people offer YouTube video editing services on Fiverr, a work-for-hire website, while top videographers working for YouTube's biggest names can earn six figures a year, and video editors thousands a week working for established channels.

The result of the Ukrainian's handiwork was a simple first video that put visuals to a 29-second version of *Twinkle Twinkle Little Star*. Within a month of being posted on 29 August 2011, it had racked up 17,000 views. 'It doesn't sound like a lot, but it indicated to me that there was probably something here,' says Holder. He was thinking bigger: if 10, 50 or 100 videos were each seen 17,000 times every month, the advertising revenue would add up. 'To be honest, our aspirations at the beginning were pretty modest: all we wanted was to get a holiday out of it a year. That's what we were shooting for – spare cash.'

Holder went back to the animator to ask him to do some further videos. The animator had just landed a big contract with L'Oréal, and now wanted four times the money. Instead, Holder approached another company and suggested that it make the animations for a below-market price in return for Holder using his search engine expertise to get its website on the front page of Google. 'When I look back, I don't know how we got that rate,' Holder admits. 'But we got them on page one of Google, so they did well out of it, we did well out of it, and it gave us the chance to build up something.' By the time the bargain-basement agreement had ended, El Bebe had more than a dozen videos.

It now produces its videos in English, Spanish, Portuguese, German and Russian. By 2017, its shareholder funds had swelled to £8 million. 'We just kept reinvesting the money, throwing it back in and creating that kind of continual loop between the revenue and the investing,' explains Holder. 'Then the compilations came along and it was like fuel on the fire. It went ballistic. View numbers went through the roof.' In July 2018, the channel was bought by a media agency, Moonbug, for millions of pounds. Moonbug was one of five bids for the company, according to Holder. The investment was a smart one: *Little Baby Bum* is a major player on YouTube.

Its most popular video is a 54-minute medley of some of the most popular nursery rhymes uploaded in 2014: *Wheels On The Bus | Plus Lots More Nursery Rhymes | 54 Minutes Compilation from Little Baby Bum.* It has been viewed two billion times – more than half a billion more views than Justin Bieber's mega-hit *Baby*, which has been on YouTube for three years longer.

This is unsurprising given that primary-aged children and teenagers now watch more YouTube than traditional TV.

Three-quarters of five- and six-year-olds had used YouTube in 2016 — by 2018 that had risen to 89%. The youngest children spend around 80 minutes a day on the site. The statistics are almost a mirror image of traditional television, where elderly viewers watch daytime TV.

YouTube is increasingly being viewed on TV sets through apps. The number of viewers of *Little Baby Bum* videos accessing the channel through smart TV apps has increased from a decimal point-sized rounding error the year before we spoke to up to 10% of its total viewers on some days. But the more telling metric isn't the total number of views – it's total view time. Derek Holder says: 'By number of minutes, TV is the second-most popular way our videos are viewed now, which is really significant because [12 months earlier] it was way down the list.'

What's happening is what has always happened in households across the world since televisions first arrived in our front rooms: people are turning on their TVs, looking for something to watch. They're just doing it with YouTube videos now and the algorithm is constantly serving up video after video. This increases view time, YouTube's all-important goal. When viewers watch the latest YouTube video on their mobile phone on a bus, there is always the danger of a text message alert or the lure of Instagram's timeline to snap them out of their glassy-eyed, passive consumption. Unlike traditional broadcast TV, however, YouTube essentially is a TV channel just for the individual, tailored algorithmically to tickle their tastes, and with an endless, ever-expanding pool of videos to pick from. We don't know how vast the YouTube ecosystem is because the site refuses to give out numbers, but based on prior growth rates, around 12 million videos could be uploaded every day.

YouTube has attempted to embed itself in normal TV-viewing habits through a combination of specialist services and original programming. As well as purportedly giving parents confidence that their children won't accidentally come across unsuitable viewing, YouTube Kids also locks in those all-important eyeballs at a young age, creating a link in children's minds between entertainment and YouTube. YouTube Kids operates in at least 37 countries worldwide.

Another service is YouTube TV, which is available on smart TVs, smartphones and tablets, and through Roku Players and Chromecast dongles. Launched in summer 2017, YouTube TV serves up shows from US networks *ABC*, *NBC*, *CBS* and *FOX* alongside its own videos for $35 a month. In January 2019, it was available to 98% of US households. Before launching the service YouTube monitored more than 500 people's viewing habits at home: how they flicked through the channels, how and where they sat on their couch, and the kinds of things they wanted to watch.

In a report in 2017 on the future of online video, analysts at Barclays Capital explained that even when people were watching the television in the living room, they were watching different content than before. Interestingly, they didn't see a difference between online and traditional TV in the quality of programming; 54% of people saw no gap in quality, while 22% of people thought online streaming video was better than traditional TV. 'TV is not as much about the large screen in the living room or live programming anymore,' the report explained. Barclays estimated that 31 million American homes could stop watching normal TV (or severely cut back on paid TV channels) in the next decade.

Linear, programmed broadcast TV, arranged by channel directors and appointment-to-view, is dying. Instead time-shifted viewing (anything that isn't live) is becoming the dominant way we consume video nowadays. 70% of video viewing by millennials is time-shifted. In 2015, just under a third of people, 32%, used a connected device to stream video daily. In 2017, more than 46% of people did. As connected TVs, smartphones and tablets become more commonplace, that will rise further.

As a long-standing TV executive, Bastian Manintveld believes the last time such a big shift in viewing habits happened was back in the 1980s – when the world began moving from analogue terrestrial to digital television. 'Any home could receive two or three channels,' he says. 'And then all of a sudden you had analogue cable, but there was nobody to make those 15-20 channels. This is when *HBO* or *MTV* or Viacom were created. They were all born in that time. Why? Because all of a sudden there was more space available to put that content.' A similar shift – albeit in an increasingly quick world, at an increasingly quick pace – is occurring now.

'What's happening with YouTube is two things,' he says. 'One: the amount of space to put new content is unlimited. And, two, there's been a complete democratisation between creator and audience. You and I can take our phone, record something and they can see it in Australia in real time. The only thing that stands between us and winning that audience is making content people want to see... which, if you think about it, is very threatening to the TV industry.'

Unlike Netflix, where all the content is professionally produced at a cost of millions of dollars, anyone can pitch up to YouTube with no money and basic equipment. Although the biggest YouTubers are generally supported by agents, have cutting-edge technology and make significant incomes, their content is served alongside that from committed amateurs.

And the platform's intimacy is appealing. Although creators are broadcasting to hundreds, thousands or sometimes millions of people at once, the videos feel personal – like you're dropping in on a conversation meant only for you. For a viewer, that can be thrilling. YouTube videos are those in-depth teenage conversations behind locked bedroom doors so that your parents don't hear; they're the snatched discussions in nightclub bathrooms before heading back out onto the dance-floor; they're stepping into the confession booth as the priest, sitting down and hearing the person on the other side pouring out their heart and soul.

Some big YouTubers are understandably bullish about the future of the site. 'Hank and I have been saying for eight or nine years consecutively, surely this can't go on,' says John Green. 'Surely now is the moment of retraction, the moment when things stop growing at this crazy pace. But maybe not. When I look at where online video is compared to where what is called television is, I think I'd be a lot more nervous being those guys than being us.'

Derek Holder says: 'The younger generation basically don't watch TV at all now, and you can see why.' He 'absolutely' thinks that YouTube will soon replace TV. 'Why would you watch TV when you've got everything at a click, on any device you want, anywhere you want, at any time you want?'

Despite TV's last rites being read by some, Bastian Manintveld is not so sure. As he tears down the highway near Madrid in his BMW, I ask him when we will see TV die and YouTube take over. There's a brief pause as he scans the road sign rapidly approaching, then takes the turning off the highway onto a mazy, winding road leading up to the university campus. His surprising answer is: 'Never.

'At the end of the day, I think you need to separate the platform from the talent,' he says. 'And you know, talent will just go wherever they can express themselves in the best way, and/or make the best money. So I don't think TV is going to die. I think some of the YouTube talent will make the transition to TV, but TV is more like an image than a reality.'

Manintveld's a TV man at heart. Understandably, he has some warmth for television people. 'They're the best at monetising their audience – many times better than online or in a digital world,' he says. 'For me, the appeal of the TV business is its ability to create, acquire and aggregate programming, and monetise it better than anyone else in the world.' Never taking his eyes off the road, he says: 'The challenge for a digital platform like a Facebook or YouTube or Twitter or Snapchat is to get to the point where they can monetise like television.'

The online platforms are currently waging this battle – with TV and with each other.

29.

ONLINE VIDEO WAR:
YOUTUBE v FACEBOOK

YouTube may be on the brink of overtaking mainstream television for viewing hours, but in the febrile world of 21st-century media, there is no room for complacency. More than a decade after its foundation, and after years of little real rivalry for online video, YouTube now faces some serious competition. That is a big challenge at a time when its creators are restless and unhappy with the changing whims of a website that – some argue – has lost its way.

Facebook is the only website to outgun YouTube in the number of users, with 2.3 billion. The site is still growing despite the data privacy and advertising rows surrounding the election of US President Donald Trump and the UK's referendum to leave the European Union. Facebook has also decided that video is crucial to its future: in tech parlance it has 'pivoted' to video. Mark Zuckerberg, Facebook's chief executive, made this explicit in a widely reported conference call in July 2017 when he told investors: 'We've talked about how video will continue to be a big focus and area of investment for us... The biggest trend that we see in consumer behaviour is definitely video.'

Worryingly for YouTube, some YouTubers are willing to jump aboard Facebook. If any Google executive was present among the 47 people who attended a panel discussion with Facebook creators at the Summer in the City conference in London in August 2017 they would have heard the disenchantment with YouTube loud and clear.

Becca Lammin, who has left YouTube, found it easier to build up a fanbase on Facebook. She said: 'I find it is harder to get [YouTube] subscribers just because you have to watch the videos then subscribe, whereas Facebook you just click the like button.' The barrier to entry for fans was also lower because Facebook encouraged creators to make videos for viewing on the go that lasted seconds. By contrast, Lammin's YouTube videos were designed to receive the viewer's undivided attention and were around 10 to 15 minutes.

Fellow panelists Goubran 'Goubtube' Bahou, who has 1.6 million likes, and his girlfriend Jahannah James, who has a futher million likes, who are both comedians, agreed. Bahou, too, drew on his own experience: the year before the panel, his Facebook page had just 20,000 likes. 'I got recognised once in real life, had hardly had any views.' But then viral video skits had sent his popularity on Facebook rocketing. 'The last few years on Facebook have changed so dramatically it's unreal. A year ago, if you scrolled down your Facebook feed, you'd really only have seen stuff from your friends and family. Statuses, pictures. You look now, and it's videos.'

By contrast, YouTube was 'incredibly hard.' Bahou said: 'It's not just a case of liking someone's channel; you have to subscribe. Having a million followers on Facebook and a million followers on YouTube, YouTube is worth more, but we get way more views, we get seen way more. In an advertising and exposure sense, someone on Facebook is the way to go.' Jahannah James was equally definitive. 'It feels like Facebook is what YouTube was three years ago. Facebook is about to become a video platform. It's going to happen. Facebook is going to become one of the competitors for video.'

Less than a week after James made her prediction, it happened. In a blog post on 9 August 2017, Daniel Danker, Facebook's director of product, announced Facebook Watch – a tab on the homepage for viewing videos. While Facebook had learned that people like the serendipity of discovering videos in their news feed, Danker said, they also wanted a dedicated place to watch videos.

Facebook announced that Watch would feature video from major traditional media providers, such as Hearst, the A&E network, and Major League Baseball, along with more personalised creators, such as the travel blogger Nas Daily. Daily left YouTube in August 2016 after five years, leaving a message saying: 'I don't use YOUTUBE because I hate this place. Please find me on Facebook.'

By brokering simple, easy-to-manage deals with traditional content providers like Major League Baseball, Facebook Watch seems to be YouTube in reverse. While Google's video platform hosts millions of personal content creators (who receive attention from mass media if they are successful), Facebook aims to build a big audience first, before luring more independent video creators.

In March 2019, it made the first step towards that, announcing a programme called Facebook Match, which pairs big brands such as Viacom with independent creators. Each project, which would make videos for Facebook Watch, would get up to $200,000 to spend.

Facebook is aiming big: one of the first projects it announced under the Facebook Match funding was a partnership between BuzzFeed – which has a huge presence on YouTube – and Hannah Hart, who made her name on YouTube, and who was so nervous of telling the Google-owned platform she was making a movie.

Mark Zuckerberg's play for video still lags significantly behind YouTube. Four hundred million Facebook users spend at least one minute a month on Watch, and 75 million watch at least a minute a day. But Facebook has more work to do than simply attracting eyeballs: it has to build out the behind-the-scenes support network creators now expect. While approving of Facebook's easy audience-building format, the Summer in the City panellists highlighted that Facebook lags behind YouTube in supporting creators. YouTube offers advice from a dedicated staff liaison to those with more than 100,000 subscribers, intellectual property protection, more analytics information, and, crucially, significant amounts of money from advertising revenue. In its early days, Facebook creators could not make money from their videos, relying on sponsors paying for product placement in videos and other tie-ins, such as merchandise and sales away from Facebook. But that is changing. Facebook has introduced a revenue-sharing programme from new adverts of up to 15 seconds run in the middle of videos. Creators with more than 10,000 followers who have generated at least 30,000 one-minute views on videos that last longer than three minutes can claim 45% of revenue from these mid-roll ads.

Facebook is also allowing creators to legally license music in the background of their videos. And it bought copyright identification platform Source3 in order to encourage brands to its own video platform, safe in the knowledge that any pirated video content uploaded to the site will be tracked down and removed, just like YouTube uses its own ContentID system.

In putting video at the centre of its strategy for future growth, Facebook has materially changed the infrastructure of the internet. Watching a video requires passing packets of data downstream using your internet connection. In 2012, around a third of all the downstream video traffic going to North American mobile internet consumers was from YouTube, and just around 7% was from Facebook. In 2016, YouTube's share of the downstream video bandwidth had dropped to about a fifth – while Facebook's share doubled.

Facebook has taken a similarly aggressive approach with its other big platform, Instagram. When Instagram Stories was announced in August 2016, tech journalists, analysts and every teen around the world groused about how the company had simply copied Snapchat's own Stories function. Within seven months, 200 million users a day used the Stories function in Instagram – supplanting Snapchat, which at the time had 158 million users.

This is no accident. All the big social media platforms are coalescing in format, by liberally borrowing each other's innovations. They are seeking one simple thing: what works in driving traffic and all-important dwell time. Open up any of the big video and photo sharing platforms – whether Facebook,

Instagram, Snapchat or YouTube – and they look increasingly alike.

In the weeks before and during VidCon 2018 in Anaheim, California, every social network was announcing new features which looked like ones their competitors already had. Facebook announced a plan to support creators – 'whether they're just getting started or already have millions of fans.' In the hope of luring YouTubers fed up with the constantly changing algorithm and community guidelines, Instagram announced IGTV, a standalone video app that can be used to post long-form vertical videos lasting up to an hour. This was both an attempt to poach some unhappy YouTubers who already have a sizeable presence on Instagram and to kill off Snapchat, which declared it was beginning to invest more in video.

At the same time, YouTube looked to defend its own turf. After years of being buffeted by negative headlines and finally acting on the growing discontent of the creators, it announced YouTube Stories, ephemeral logs of creators' daily lives. The concept wasn't the only thing directly lifted from Snapchat and Instagram: even the name is used on both platforms. YouTube also announced YouTube Premieres – an added extra for big creators that combines interactive chat around pre-recorded video, like Facebook Premieres. Neal Mohan, YouTube's chief product officer, said: 'Creators should have as many ways and opportunities to make money as possible,' as he declared that YouTube's pre-existing channel membership programme, its version of Patreon, would be available to more smaller creators.

'It's clear that YouTube's been paying attention to third parties like Twitch, Patreon, Facebook, and Amazon,' says Internet Creators Guild executive director Anthony D'Angelo. 'They've been working rapidly to essentially copy all the things that draw creators to those platforms.'

Matt Gielen of Little Monster Media Co says: 'YouTube has suffered from a lack of competition. They've not innovated a tremendous amount in a meaningful way for three or four years. But now it looks like Facebook and Amazon and a host of other potential sites are starting to force their hands to innovate a little more.'

Amazon is the big unknown. It is the ultimate owner of Twitch, the livestreaming website best known for hosting some of the world's biggest gamers – but it takes a hands-off approach to running the site. Twitch has recently made moves to increase the proportion of 'IRL' (non-gaming) streams on its site. If that sounds a bit like YouTube to you, that's because it is.

In absolute numbers, Twitch is nowhere near YouTube. The total amount of video watched on Twitch in a month – 880 million hours in February 2019 – is lapped up by YouTube viewers in less than a day. But it's still a threat.

Also coming around the corner is TikTok, the short-form video sharing app also known as Douyin in China. TikTok has 800 million monthly active users worldwide (compared to YouTube's 1.9 billion). Its rise has been prodigious – 660 million of the app's billion installs came in 2018 alone. And while the app is still relatively young, in the first few months of 2019 it was simultaneously rolling out detailed analytics to its users, allowing them to secure brand deals by promoting their viewers' characteristics, and sounding out brands on advertising formats.

TikTok also has another thing working in its favour: its demographics. A quarter of the app's downloads come from India, opening it up to a massive, growing consumer market lapping up new platforms. And its users are also young. In the same way that YouTube stole television's audience, TikTok is building loyalty among a younger userbase than even YouTube can claim.

Some of the biggest YouTubers, including Tyler Oakley and Hannah Hart, have built mini-media empires off the website, securing their future for the long run if YouTube starts to wane. Laura Chernikoff says: 'I can't tell you how many creators I've talked to have just cracked their 10 year anniversary and they are bored and want to do something else. They want to grow off the platform, so if their channels are dying they're okay with that, sometimes. If they're lucky they've started pivoting enough that they have other opportunities.'

Sarah Weichel, the top Los Angeles talent manager, foresees a future where, like Netflix ('premium, original and millennial-focused content') and Hulu ('catalogues of classic television'), YouTube establishes its own brand. She's just not sure she will like what it will be. 'It'll be known for a very specific kind of content,' she says, 'and my biggest fear is that the algorithm will dictate that.' She is worried that the daily vlog, reality-style content – videos which have brought forth Jake Paul, his millions of subscribers and mainstream recognition – will become YouTube's calling card. Weichel says: 'And that it won't be a good home for the talent I represent long-term.'

Weichel has to make a simple calculation on behalf of those she represents: whether or not to advise them to spend hours planning, shooting and editing daily vlogs (and risk burnout) or devote that time to an equally beneficial but less demanding medium. If her clients can spend 10% of their time on a different platform, whether traditional TV, a competing website or another medium entirely, while still earning the same amount of money, she would advise them to do so.

She believes few creators are taking risks, knowing that being on the wrong side of the algorithm can make or break a career. In its place, quicker, less challenging content is taking precedence. Weichel says: 'I can't imagine it's sustainable for anybody: the creator, the platform, or the brand partners who are investing so much money in media space to keep investing in this low-budget reality-style content. We are desperate for a shift in the algorithm.'

PART VIII

CONCLUSION

30.

A FLAWED WINNER

YouTube is a volcano of creativity. Its arrival a decade and a half ago has led to an outpouring of inventiveness and chaos that has entertained, informed and amused nearly two billion people. It's a place where anyone can freely watch factual, educational content, where previously ignored minorities have a voice. It is horizontal, peer-to-peer TV, rather than the hierarchical top-down old industry; and that's undeniably democratic in intent, if not always in practice.

Events like Summer in the City and VidCon show that YouTube has real and tangible benefits: whether it's children grinning ear to ear at a glimpse of their favourite creator, adults sitting rapt at a panel discussion, or a group of highly motivated, highly intelligent, self-starting entrepreneurs gathering in the same place to discuss their latest successes and how to avoid the pitfalls. YouTube connects people who would not ordinarily ever talk, and provides more meritocratic opportunities in the creative industries than traditional occupations. If the gig economy is destroying the traditional job, and precarity in employment is the new norm, at least YouTubers can have fun expressing themselves while settling into the future of work.

And yet behind every positive headline there is a worry, often a legitimate one. In YouTube's brief life, we have sporadically seen shootings, suicides, sex scandals, discredited celebrities and advertising frauds. If you take your hands off the wheel, the site's algorithm dangerously veers off into the realm of false far-right conspiracy theories. It is an engine of unabashed, environmentally destructive consumerism. Until recently, parts of its comment sections have been co-opted as an unchecked forum for child abuse rings.

Arguably, YouTube has been negligent in failing to tackle the worst abuses. While no one who sets up a platform to host home videos in 2005 believes it will mutate into a viper's nest of extremist belief and unsavoury behaviour a decade later, YouTube has not taken its role as a policeman seriously enough. YouTube's global reach and untrammelled power are in part why I wrote this book. And if third-party observers like me have known about these problems for years, then those within the walls of its California campus have certainly known for longer. They are the ones with the data about how long people watch, what they watch, and how they swirl into stagnant pools that radicalise them into counter-factual beliefs.

YouTube's tendency is to ignore its problems until they are identified by others. Journalists, rather than its team of human and algorithmic moderators, have increasingly caught unsavoury content and alerted the site's bosses. I myself have flagged up dangerous prank videos, transphobia on YouTube's algorithm, and the availability of videos proffering advice on how to make drugs which are seen by millions. Others have pointed out child pornography, bestiality and disturbing content targeted at children. These are only the scandals that we know about: the ones discovered by journalists probing the limits, reach and responsibility of YouTube as a public forum. There are likely to be far more toxic and deeper-rooted problems that outsiders simply don't know about yet. It seems to take the risk of negative headlines or the abandonment of big advertisers for the site to act, rather than any sense of moral responsibility. And when it does act – or rather, react – it often addresses the manifestation, rather than the root cause of the problem, and frequently over-reacts.

It is fair to point out that many of the problems arise as a result of user-generated content over which YouTube has little control. But it has a responsibility as a major media platform not only to its advertisers, but to its users – which increasingly, means society as a whole. And I'm not alone in thinking that: as the polling conducted for this book shows, three-quarters of us think YouTube has partial or total responsibility for the videos hosted on its platform.

It is not yet doing nearly enough. Whether we're talking about the first adpocalypse, the second adpocalypse, Elsagate, terrorist content, extreme content, pranks, conspiracy theories or any other of the numerous scandals the site has been the subject of, YouTube's response can be summed up in one simple sentence: its actions are always too little, too late.

The biggest problem of all is that it's now too late to do much about YouTube's worst legacy: the creation of a generation with a distrust of commonly held beliefs. Within a few hours, You-Tube's algorithm can plant the germ of a seed that transforms a functioning member of society into a loner who trusts no one. It has conditioned a generation of children to think that they aren't living life unless the red light above the lens is on, and that you need to be more daring, more maverick, more extreme than anyone else. It has blurred the lines between what is editorial and what is advertising, and raised people who pretend to be in demand with big brands until they eventually get a call for a brand deal. That's all already happened. Undoing that will take years – and may not work.

Some things are out of the site's control, though. And most disconcertingly, YouTube may change our lives and our culture in ways that we haven't yet understood. We're still uncertain as to the long-term impacts of a life watching YouTube, or pursuing a career as a full-time YouTube creator. In large part, that's because of the site's relative youth: YouTube is still in the heart of its terrible teens. But early research by academics – much of it anecdotal – agrees that there will be some effect.

In a widely shared essay about children's content on YouTube, technology writer James Bridle went as far as to say that 'to expose children to this content is abuse'.

Researcher Alice Marwick worries about what she calls 'the fantasy of social media': the pursuit of the perfect lifestyle in front of the camera, which actually results in a cavalcade of behind-the-scenes stresses. 'We know that child stars don't have the easiest lives later on. I think that goes double for these young people that are becoming stars through other media that don't have the financial upside that broadcast celebrities have had.'

Nor are the long-term effects of the first flourishes of fame on YouTube on creators known. Burnout is a risk that has faced child stars since Hollywood's glory years, but the unrelenting pace of life, and the onward march of technology, has made the peaks and troughs of fame more pronounced.

And what will become of YouTube itself? It seems likely that it'll coexist with, and potentially eventually displace, television. Just as Netflix has upended traditional TV by providing glossy, high-budget professional products on demand, there will be a demand for a rougher but readier digital video platform – even if the likes of Amazon, TikTok, Facebook or Spotify improve their acts.

YouTube has more than 10 years' headstart and the backing of one of the world's most valuable and intelligent companies. It has created a range of new stars that we laud as celebrities. We hang on their every word. We empty our bank accounts and spend hours of our lives watching theirs. That is probably too enmeshed in our lives to disappear like a here-today-gone-to-morrow viral sensation. Even with other social media giants breathing down its neck, YouTube still rules.

Rather than reaching the end of an era, we're just at the beginning. When I started writing this book, YouTube was an afterthought, a curio to be brought out and prodded. As I put the final touches to it, there was barely a day when a national newspaper or international magazine didn't headline a YouTube personality or problem. In a viral world, we're still waiting for the greatest wave to crest. When we get past that point, who knows what path the platform will take? One thing is for certain: YouTube is far more influential, far more powerful, and far richer than most people realise. As Kevin Allocca, head of culture and trends at YouTube, says: 'It's the first global medium that's as rich, inventive, odd, and individual as we are.'

It's tapped into the human algorithm: our brains; what we enjoy, what we need. It reflects back our best aspects and our worst, amplifying them at the same time. It makes us laugh and cry. It's maddening and enchanting. It's YouTube, MeTube, UsTube. We can barely live with it, and yet we can't imagine a life without it. It's always on. Always uploading.

GLOSSARY

algorithm: the notoriously opaque set of code that helps promote videos to YouTube users, which Guillaume Chaslot now regrets helping make so powerful. The algorithm has gained a semi-mythical status among YouTubers who see their purpose on the platform as appeasing it. But much like an ancient god, it moves in mysterious ways.

authenticity: the dictionary definition of 'authenticity' is being 'genuine'. YouTubers are praised for their authenticity, but as discussed throughout the book, the extent to which they're playing a character is up for debate. See 'parasocial relationships' below.

content: a nebulous way to describe anything created and posted on the internet. While previously the preserve of marketers and one of those horrible business words, people have mostly lost the arched eyebrow when saying they produce 'content'. Digital journalists create content, rather than stories (often sarcastically toiling away in the 'content mines', reflecting the hard working conditions they suffer under); influencers and creators produce content, rather than videos.

creator: a catch-all term used to define those who post videos to YouTube (or other types of content – see above – to other social media platforms such as Instagram, TikTok, Snapchat and Twitter). A shortened version of 'content creator', many people uploading videos to YouTube prefer 'creator' to 'vlogger' or 'YouTuber', believing it gets across the creative side of their work better.

drama: in the same way that schoolyard arguments would devolve into the biggest thing that has ever happened – ever, so drama happens on YouTube. For the last several years, drama has been the biggest commodity on the platform. Often-confected conflicts between creators help promote both, and is stoked by dedicated personalities with their own channels who report on the latest developments, including Daniel 'Keemstar' Keem's *DramaAlert* channel, which Keem groused in January 2019 pays him 'only' $4,000 a day.

Facebook: Mark Zuckerberg's massive social network has been written about plenty of times, and is seen as among YouTube's biggest competitors (alongside Twitch).

fans: a contentious term in the YouTube world, some believe that calling subscribers or viewers of a certain creator 'fans' draws an old-fashioned us-versus-them distinction between the person in front of the camera and those behind the camera. In the early days of YouTube, preferred terms were 'creators' and 'viewers', who were involved in a 'relationship'. However, as the platform has matured, and new celebrities earn similar money to old ones, the barriers between them and fans have often been pulled up once more.

haul: beloved by beauty and shopping vloggers, 'haul' videos involve YouTubers showing their audience items they have purchased on a shopping trip. Often filmed in bedrooms, each item is taken out of the bag and the YouTuber passes comment on it, explaining why they bought it and how much it was. Can get expensive. A distant cousin of the unboxing video (see below).

influencer: a woolly term that nonetheless helps draw the distinction between old-school celebrities and the new series of content creators publishing on social media, 'influencers' are so named because of the outsized influence they wield on their fans (or viewers, depending on your standpoint). More on that influence can be read in 'parasocial relationships' below.

Instagram: many YouTubers have parallel Instagram accounts as well as profiles on other social networks, all of which help increase and diversify their reach. Interestingly, big YouTubers such as the Paul brothers will often silo their personalities on each platform. An apology for a misstep may be sneaked out on Instagram, rather than sullying the massive advertising storefront that is the main YouTube channel.

merch: whether it's T-shirts (often sold through e-commerce websites like Fanjoy) or hoodies, hats or trinkets, one of the best ways that viewers can show their appreciation for their favourite creator is by buying their merch (or merchandise).

parasocial relationships: besides drama, the most important contributor to the success of creators on YouTube. The term was first coined in the 1950s to fit obsessive fans' slavish following of their favourite TV or Hollywood celebrities, but better fits the YouTube generation. Fans (or viewers) know everything about their favourite YouTuber, and often support them financially by buying their merch (see above), supporting them on Patreon (see below) or simply stanning them (see below). But while the semblance of a a deep personal relationship is there, it's one-sided. While the YouTuber talks into the lens – and as a result, into your eyes – they probably don't know you.

Patreon: a platform that allows users ('patrons', see below) to support their favourite creators with regular stipends, often for privileged access to content.

patron or Patreon backer: the name for people who support creators via Patreon.

Snapchat: a social network where users share impermanent photos and videos with friends.

stanning: tracing its lineage back to Eminem's 2000 hit *Stan*, stanning is a term used to encapsulate the obsessive fandom many users feel for their favourite creators.

streamer: a type of content creator who livestreams video (often playing video games) to viewers. Rather than pre-recorded content, the videos go out live and unfiltered. One major streaming company is Twitch, which is largely focused on users playing video games.

subscriber: people who subscribe to a YouTube channel have asked YouTube to let them know when a YouTuber uploads a new video. Creators want subscribers, even though the metric's usefulness has been brought into question in the last few years as many people have lapsed accounts subscribing to old, inactive YouTubers. Creators often call on viewers to smash or hit that subscribe button at the end of a video. YouTube has changed the way in which it notifies viewers a new video is uploaded by creators, meaning many do not know when new content is available.

TikTok: a spiritual successor to Vine (see below) popular with children and teenagers, TikTok is driven by users participating in memes (a type of behaviour or video trope shared within a community).

unboxing: videos involving people taking items out of boxes. Really.

Vine: a six-second video sharing app, owned by Twitter, which closed in January 2017. It was the original stepping stone for some of YouTube's biggest names, including Jake and Logan Paul. The 'Vine invasion' of YouTube that occurred after its closure ushered in a new era for the platform.

vlogger: a person who uploads 'vlogs' (video blogs) to sites such as YouTube.

YouTuber: a content creator on YouTube.

ACKNOWLEDGEMENTS

Writing a book is far from easy, and it takes the combined effort of more than one person to produce the finished product. Martin Hickman, my publisher at Canbury Press, took a chance on a debut author and a book proposal written on a train journey back from a conference. He helped turn my manuscript into the finished work you see today. Canbury's publicist Nicola Burton joined the book in its final stages, helping get word out about the importance of the first independent, in-depth look at the site to the media. Thank you to both.

Finding people to talk to about YouTube and its impact on society is difficult to do, which is why I'm hugely thankful for those who spent several hours of their time discussing their thoughts with me on and off the record. In the early stages of the process Laura Chernikoff gave up far more time than was necessary to hear my odd prognostications and gave back plenty of her own. Anthony D'Angelo, another crucial part of the Internet Creators Guild, has been equally generous with his time. But as I began to dig deeper into this world, more people have proven willing to put up with my questions and theories:

Zoë Glatt, Harry Hugo and Matt Gielen in particular should be singled out.

This book would not have come about without the ability to report iteratively on YouTube and its broader effect on the world. The editors at Wired UK, under Greg Williams, have been far and away the most willing, and most longstanding supporters of my reporting on the massive power of YouTube. A story they commissioned also put me in touch with Bastian Manintveld, who has proven a hugely useful contact for understanding the world of YouTube outside the English language. However, I'm glad to say the more recent support of editors elsewhere, including at Bloomberg and *New Scientist*, has helped shift the tone of coverage of YouTube in the mass media.

I'd like to thank Tom Rowley for taking a look at an early draft of this book and patiently posting back hundreds of printed pages of text with scribbled notes that helped inform this book – and let me know who and what an ordinary reader knew about YouTube. I hope that the significant changes from that draft to the finished product are a pleasant surprise to you – and if you pick this up on publication day, happy birthday.

Oli Franklin-Wallis, Sam Parker, Tom Banham and Jo Stashko – collectively, founding members of The Queue – have also been an enormous support by simply talking through troubles. Oli in particular has taken on the role of unofficial editor, mentor, PR and career advisor throughout the process of producing this book, and during my career, in a way that has made a real difference and helped keep up my confidence in the book, and my wider reporting, throughout the process.

Angelika Strohmayer has been a tireless supporter in this and all aspects of my professional and personal life, while also juggling a massive writing project of her own over the last few years. That makes her support all the more valuable and meaningful. 2019 is a big year for both of us professionally, and an exciting one, too.

My parents and grandparents have been equally supportive, patiently reading every story I write about this and other odd technological developments before setting down the newspaper or magazine and explaining that they barely understood any of it, but they enjoyed it and were proud. I hope you feel as proud about this – and perhaps understand a little more of it than normal.

NOTES

PART I: POWER AND BEGINNINGS

1. Uploading: Casey Neistat and the power of YouTube

1. a video lasting five minutes and twenty-two seconds: *"Success" on YouTube Still Means a Life of Poverty*, Casey Neistat, YouTube, accessible at https://www.youtube.com/watch?v=xyVdZrL3Sbo

2. four billion people: everyone on Earth with an internet connection: Internet World Stats, accessible at https://www.internetworldstats.com/stats.htm

3. millions of Neistat's subscribers: Casey Neistat, YouTube, accessible at https://www.youtube.com/user/caseyneistat

4. load up Lofty Pursuits: Lofty Pursuits, YouTube, accessible at https://www.youtube.com/user/LoftyPursuits

5. meticulously scratch away the foil on 200 lottery playing cards: Moorsey Scratchcards, YouTube, accessible at https://www.youtube.com/channel/UCu1on9folR_LFkpQ2HWFpaA

6. YouTube's 1.9 billion registered users: YouTube for Press, accessible at https://www.youtube.com/intl/en-GB/yt/about/press/

7. elite influencers make millions of dollars every year: Highest-Paid YouTube Stars 2018: Markiplier, Jake Paul, PewDiePie And More, Forbes, accessible at https://www.forbes.com/sites/natalierobehmed/2018/12/03/highest-paid-youtube-stars-2018-markiplier-jake-paul-pewdiepie-and-more/#23f0eccb909a

8. becoming a YouTuber is the job children most covet: *Forget being a nurse or doctor, three quarters of today's children would rather be YouTubers and vloggers, Daily Mail*, accessible at https://www.dailymail.co.uk/news/article-4532266/75-cent-children-want-YouTubers-vloggers.html

9. 576,000 hours of video are added daily: Susan Wojcicki, YouTube CEO, speaking at VidCon 2015, accessible at https://www.tubefilter.com/2015/07/26/youtube-400-hours-content-every-minute/

10. Netflix released 781 hours of original content: analysis by John Blackledge, Cowen & Co., accessible at https://variety.com/2019/digital/news/netflix-q4-2018-earnings-preview-price-hike-1203109621/

11. YouTube viewing has rocketed from 100 million hours a day to one billion hours: *People now watch 1 billion hours of YouTube per day, Techcrunch*, accessi-

ble at https://techcrunch.com/2017/02/28/people-now-watch-1-billion-hours-of-youtube-per-day/

12. seen by nearly 69% of all internet users every month: Ampere Analysis Top Online Video Services Barometer Q3 2017, accessible at https://www.digitaltveurope.com/2017/10/05/ampere-study-highlights-shifting-online-video-pattern/

13. it's the internet's second-most visited site: Alexa data, accessible at http://www.alexa.com

14. YouTube was watched by an estimated 91 million Americans and by 21 million people in Britain: Alexa data, accessible at http://www.alexa.com

15. batteries in iPods irreplaceable: *iPod's Dirty Secret* – from 2003, Casey Neistat, YouTube, accessible at https://www.youtube.com/watch?v=SuT-cavAzopg

16. he joined YouTube in 2010...he has 10 million subscribers: Casey Neistat, YouTube, accessible at https://www.youtube.com/user/caseyneistat

17. 368 Broadway...the location of an independent co-working studio space: 368 THE FIRST EPISODE Casey Neistat, YouTube, accessible at https://www.youtube.com/watch?v=MA_zTtF5WDc

18. a story I had written for Bloomberg: *"Success" on YouTube Still Means a Life of Poverty*, accessible at https://www.bloomberg.com/news/articles/2018-02-27/-success-on-youtube-still-means-a-life-of-poverty

19. 96% of those who upload to YouTube don't make enough money: YouTube channels, uploads and views: A statistical analysis of the past 10 years, Matthias Baertl, Offenburg University

20. two million people watched the video: *"Success" on YouTube Still Means a Life of Poverty*, Casey Neistat, YouTube, accessible at https://www.youtube.com/watch?v=xyVdZrL3Sbo

21. review copies of its latest devices to YouTubers: *Apple Prioritized YouTubers Over Mainstream Tech Press for iPhone X Reviews*, *Variety*, accessible at https://variety.com/2017/digital/news/apple-youtube-iphone-reviews-1202603276/

22. 74 entrepreneurs used those titles: data collated via freedom of information requests for YouTubers from Companies House

23. names that are instantly recognised by young people – but not by their parents, YouGov survey of 1,625 British adults commissioned for YouTubers, 13-14 December 2017

2. Jake Paul: cars, money, and a burning swimming pool

1. a mountainside home in California: *EXCLUSIVE TOUR OF THE NEW TEAM 10 HOUSE *amazing**, Jake Paul, YouTube, accessible at https://www.youtube.com/watch?v=gDFh-ocrBkQ

2. 15,000 square foot, eight-bedroom mansion...\$6.9 million: *A 20-year-old YouTube star just bought a \$6.9 million mansion — take a look inside*, Business Insider, accessible at https://www.businessinsider.com/jake-paul-new-home-photos-2017-11?r=US&IR=T

3. is a high-school drop-out: *DRAW MY LIFE – JAKE PAUL*, Jake Paul, YouTube, accessible at https://www.youtube.com/watch?v=whOlQ9Z4Iz4

4. Paul left school and the family home in Westlake, Ohio: *DRAW MY LIFE – JAKE PAUL*, Jake Paul, YouTube, accessible at https://www.youtube.com/watch?v=whOlQ9Z4Iz4

5. Zoosh, inspired by the Smosh name: *DRAW MY LIFE – JAKE PAUL*, Jake Paul, YouTube, accessible at https://www.youtube.com/watch?v=whOlQ9Z4Iz4

6. when Vine closed in late 2016: *Why Vine Died*, The Verge, accessible at https://www.theverge.com/2016/10/28/13456208/why-vine-died-twitter-shutdown

7. \$17,000-a-month home: *Social media 'star' Jake Paul renting \$17K/month McMansion and driving neighbors mad*, Curbed Los Angeles, accessible at https://la.curbed.com/2017/7/19/16001358/jake-paul-house-neighbors-youtube

8. Ellis Barbacoff later sued Paul: *A YouTube star honked a car horn at strangers for a prank video. Now he's being sued*, The Sacramento Bee, accessible at https://www.sacbee.com/entertainment/celebrities/article178469816.html

9. class action lawsuit against him: *Jake Paul's Neighbors Hate Him And Are Considering A Class Action Lawsuit*, Tubefilter, accessible at https://www.tubefilter.com/2017/07/18/jake-paul-neighbors/

10. he has 17 million subscribers: Jake Paul, YouTube, accessible at https://www.youtube.com/channel/UCcgVECVN4OKV6DH1jLkqmcA

11. interviewed a United States senator: *It's Time To End School Shootings.*, Jake Paul, YouTube, accessible at https://www.youtube.com/watch?v=1Xp-CfxBSaUo

12. invited to – then illicitly stayed over night in – the White House: *WHITE HOUSE 24 HR OVERNIGHT CHALLENGE *NOT CLICKBAIT**, Jake Paul, YouTube, accessible at https://www.youtube.com/watch?v=KAAkWbTsS5g

13. he owns two absurdly expensive Audemars Piguet Swiss watches: *WIFE*

ERIKA ACTUALLY BOUGHT ME THIS $100K GIFT... {EMOTIONAL}, Jake Paul, YouTube, accessible at https://www.youtube.com/watch?v=38J2cidkr-Wg&t=788s

14. earn anything between £250,000 and £4 million per year: Jake Paul, Socialblade, accessible at https://socialblade.com/youtube/user/jakepaul-productions

15. banned from filming in the building: *The police won't let me vlog anymore...*, Jake Paul, YouTube, accessible at https://www.youtube.com/watch?v=oSSd-FDlYMOg

16. a toddler called Mini Jake Paul: *MEETING THE MINI JAKE PAUL?!*, Jake Paul, YouTube, accessible at https://www.youtube.com/watch?v=duNWzH-gisP4

17. $42 shorts, and a windbreaker that costs $90: Fanjoy, Jake Paul, accessible at http://www.fanjoy.co/jakepaul

18. 50 videos uploaded by Jake and Logan Paul: *Jake and Logan Paul are YouTube Merch Monsters*, *New York Magazine*, accessible at http://nymag.com/selectall/2018/04/jake-paul-and-logan-paul-are-youtube-merch-monsters.html

19. less than 24 hours after its release, it had been seen 2.4 million times: *Jake Paul – Litmas (feat. Slim Jxmmi)*, Jake Paul, YouTube, accessible at https://www.youtube.com/watch?v=nXUWK8oTOTI

20. Fanjoy to the World: *Fanjoy to the World*, Jake Paul, YouTube, accessible at https://www.youtube.com/watch?v=iPrqO6jC1HY

21. Paul was the second-highest-earning YouTuber: *Highest-Paid YouTube Stars 2018: Markiplier, Jake Paul, PewDiePie And More*, Forbes, accessible at https://www.forbes.com/sites/natalierobehmed/2018/12/03/highest-paid-youtube-stars-2018-markiplier-jake-paul-pewdiepie-and-more/#23f0eccb909a

22. $64 to learn more about Paul's business model: Edfluence, accessible at http://www.edfluence.com

3. Me At the Zoo: Jawed Karim and the worst video of all time

1. Me At The Zoo: *Me At The Zoo*, Jawed Karim, YouTube, accessible at https://www.youtube.com/watch?v=jNQXAC9IVRw

2. 60 million people have seen Me At The Zoo: *Me At The Zoo*, Jawed Karim, YouTube, accessible at https://www.youtube.com/watch?v=jNQXAC9IVRw

3. super-fast fibre broadband was out of the reach of many: *A history of UK*

broadband roll out: BT, Openreach and other major milestones, Computerworld UK, accessible at https://www.computerworlduk.com/galleries/infrastructure/history-of-uk-broadband-2000-now-3629899/

4. Apple's touch-screen iPhone was two years away: *Today in Apple history: Fans line up to get their hands on the very first iPhone, Cult of Mac*, accessible at https://www.cultofmac.com/489390/today-apple-history-iphone-launch-day/

5. Israeli entrepreneurs launched Metacafe in 2003: *Metacafe vs. YouTube? Metacafe CEO talks 'The Real Deal' in exclusive interview, ZDNet*, accessible at https://www.zdnet.com/article/metacafe-vs-youtube-metacafe-ceo-talks-the-real-deal-in-exclusive-interview/

6. in November 2004 came Vimeo: About Vimeo, accessible at https://vimeo.com/about

7. The True Story of Grouper, a.k.a. Crackle, Re:code, accessible at https://www.recode.net/2015/1/9/11557604/the-true-story-of-grouper-a-k-a-crackle

8. Vimeo's co-founder Jake Lodwick was among those video visionaries: accessible at http://vloggercon.blogspot.com/

9. Vloggercon began on the fourth-floor of an 11-floor block at 721 Broadway, New York: The Web Ahead, accessible at http://thewebahead.net/76

10. 'our intimate gathering has become a bit of a spectacle': *Final Info for Vloggercon*, Vloggercon, accessible at http://vloggercon.blogspot.com/2005/01/final-info-for-vloggercon.html

11. a TV journalist at CNN International: The Web Ahead, accessible at http://thewebahead.net/guest/jay-dedman

12. 'The thing about video blogs is it's not television': *VloggerCon 05 Session: Content is King*, Vloggercon, accessible at http://archive.org/details/VloggerCon05VloggerCon05SessionContentisKing

13. Google...also entered the fray: We're tuning into TV, Google official blog, accessible at https://googleblog.blogspot.com/2005/01/were-tuning-in-to-tv.html

14. Jawed Karim had arrived in the United States as a teenager...at the University of Illinois: YouTube Founders Steve Chen, Chad Hurley, and Jawed Karim, Patricia Wooster (2014)

15. Chen, whose family had emigrated...from Taiwan: YouTube Founders Steve Chen, Chad Hurley, and Jawed Karim, Patricia Wooster (2014)

16. Hurley...who had designed PayPal's original logo: Chad Hurley, Web 2.0 Summit, accessible at https://web.archive.org/web/20110309022538/http://www.web2con.com/cs/web2006/view/e_spkr/2843

17. Chen also worked briefly at...Facebook: *Here's where Facebook's first 20 employees are now, Business Insider*, accessible at https://www.businessinsider.com/first-20-facebook-employees-where-are-they-working-now-2017?r=US&IR=T#steve-chen-left-facebook-after-a-few-short-months-to-start-youtube-11

18. Late on Valentine's night 2005: YouTube.com Whois info, accessible at http://whois.domaintools.com/youtube.com

19. 'We're the ultimate reality TV': *Video websites pop up, invite postings, USA Today*, accessible at https://usatoday30.usatoday.com/tech/news/techinnovations/2005-11-21-video-websites_x.htm

20. in November 2005...Anthony Padilla and Ian Hecox launched a new comedy channel: Smosh: Smosh, YouTube, accessible at https://www.youtube.com/channel/UCY3oJRSgfhYXA6i6xX1erWg

21. Within a few months, Smosh was the most popular channel on YouTube: 'The History of the YouTube Most Subscribed – Visualized', Imgur, accessible at https://imgur.com/gallery/soDTn

22. running through $3.5 million of investment Sequoia Capital had pumped into the business: *YouTube Receives $3.5M in Funding From Sequoia Capital, MarketWire*, accessible at http://www.marketwired.com/press-release/youtube-receives-35m-in-funding-from-sequoia-capital-736129.htm

23. content creators who uploaded their videos didn't earn any money: *First ads appear on YouTube clips, The Guardian*, accessible at https://www.theguardian.com/media/2007/aug/22/advertising.digitalmedia

24. they created Freenet, the world's first decentralised peer-to-peer network: Interview with Ian Clarke

25. in October 2005, they founded Revver: Interview with Ian Clarke

26. tech pioneers, including Skype's inventors, were working on downloadable software to play videos: the product was called Joost, and was set up by Niklas Zennström and Janus Friis

27. they decided, early on, to split any money 50/50 with creators: Interview with Ian Clarke

4. Viral comedy: YouTube laughs all the way to the bank

1. in December 2005... *Saturday Night Live* broadcast a digital video sketch... called *Lazy Sunday*: *Nerds in the Hood, Stars on the Web, New York Times*, accessible at https://www.nytimes.com/2005/12/27/arts/nerds-in-the-hood-stars-on-the-web.html

2. in its first week it received two million views: *Did "Lazy Sunday" make YouTube's $1.5 billion sale possible?, Ars Technica*, accessible at https://arstechni-

ca.com/uncategorized/2008/11/did-lazy-sunday-make-youtubes-1-5-billion-sale-possible/

3. NBCUniversal, who owned the intellectual property, hadn't uploaded it: Viacom International Inc v YouTube Inc, case 10-3270 in the United States Court of Appeals for the Second Circuit

4. Smosh's... existence on YouTube is because they tracked down an unapproved upload: *The History Of Smosh | A Brief History*, FootofaFettet, YouTube, accessible at https://www.youtube.com/watch?v=v-wIiiTFgNg

5. 'We were watching numbers on a site we had never heard of': *'Lazy Sunday' Turns 10: 'SNL' Stars Recall How TV Invaded the Internet*, Variety, accessible at https://variety.com/2015/tv/news/lazy-sunday-10th-anniversary-snl-1201657949/

6. Grouper and other sites were quick to tackle copyrighted material: The True Story of Grouper, a.k.a. Crackle', Re:code, accessible at https://www.recode.net/2015/1/9/11557604/the-true-story-of-grouper-a-k-a-crackle

7. Revver had audio fingerprinting and a team of manual reviewers: Interview with Ian Clarke

8. it eventually pulled the *Lazy Sunday* clip, in February 2006: 'Lazy Sunday Viral Video', accessible at http://googlesystem.blogspot.com/2006/02/lazy-sunday-viral-video.html

9. Copyright owners complained that YouTube was slow to take down videos: Viacom International Inc v YouTube Inc, case 10-3270 in the United States Court of Appeals for the Second Circuit

10. in its two months online, *Lazy Sunday* was viewed seven million times: *Did 'Lazy Sunday' make YouTube's $1.5 billion sale possible?*, Ars Technica, accessible at https://arstechnica.com/uncategorized/2008/11/did-lazy-sunday-make-youtubes-1-5-billion-sale-possible/

11. *Lazy Sunday* was just one of at least 150,000 unauthorised clips: Viacom International Inc v YouTube Inc, case in the United States District Court for the Southern District of New York

12. the lawsuit was settled: *Google, Viacom settle landmark YouTube lawsuit*, Reuters, accessible at https://www.reuters.com/article/us-google-viacom-lawsuit/google-viacom-settle-landmark-youtube-lawsuit-idUSBREA2H11220140318

13. YouTube exploded on the backs of *Saturday Night Live*'s *Lazy Sunday* clip and a ton of 'illegally' shared copyrighted content: *The True Story of Grouper, a.k.a. Crackle*, Re:code, accessible at https://www.recode.net/2015/1/9/11557604/the-true-story-of-grouper-a-k-a-crackle

14. uploading her first video to YouTube on 16 June 2006: *First Blog / Dorkiness*

Prevails, lonelygirl15, YouTube, accessible at https://www.youtube.com/watch?v=-goXKtd6cPo

15. fans would find her MySpace page and send her messages. She would respond: *Lonelygirl15: how one mysterious vlogger changed the internet, The Guardian*, accessible at https://www.theguardian.com/technology/2016/jun/16/lonelygirl15-bree-video-blog-youtube

16. Michael Buckley, an administrative assistant from Connecticut: *YouTube Videos Pull In Real Money, New York Times*, accessible at https://www.nytimes.com/2008/12/11/business/media/11youtube.html?hp&mtrref=en.wikipedia.org&gwh=8089BDDE9EC44B915DB34D1BA64C6B35&gwt=pay

17. "a bitchy, rambling pop culture expert talking head": Interview with Michael Buckley

18. YouTube... traffic quadrupled between January and July 2006: *YouTube is World's Fastest Growing Website, Mashable*, accessible at https://mashable.com/2006/07/22/youtube-is-worlds-fastest-growing-website/?europe=true#u6KLFzCe.Zqo

19. it broke into the top 50 most-visited websites: *Online Video Officially Goes Mainstream as YouTube.com Breaks Into the Comscore MMX Top 50, Comscore*, accessible at https://www.comscore.com/Insights/Press-Releases/2006/08/YouTube-Breaks-into-Top-50-Websites

20. By September 2006 Smosh's subscriber numbers had rocketed to 17,500 subscribers, making it the fourth-most popular channel on the site: *The History of the YouTube Most Subscribed – Visualized, Imgur*, accessible at https://imgur.com/gallery/s0DTn

21. Metacafe... gave creators $5 for every 1,000 US views above 20,000: *Metacafe's Producer Rewards™ Program Continues to Deliver Real Income to Short Video Creators, BusinessWire*, accessible at https://www.businesswire.com/news/home/20070110005439/en/Metacafes-Producer-Rewards-TM-Program-Continues-Deliver

22. Google had floated some of its shares in an Initial Public Offering in 2004: *2004 Founders' IPO Letter, Google*, accessible at https://abc.xyz/investor/founders-letters/2004-ipo-letter/

23. valuing it at $23 billion: *A look back in IPO: Google, the profit machine, TechCrunch*, accessible at https://techcrunch.com/2017/07/31/a-look-back-in-ipo-google-the-profit-machine/

24. a single room above a Japanese restaurant and pizza parlour: *Ready for Its Close-Up, Washington Post*, accessible at http://www.washingtonpost.com/wp-dyn/content/article/2006/10/06/AR2006100600660.html

25. In September 2006... it partnered with Cingular Wireless: Cingular

Sponsors YouTube Underground Talent Hunt, press release, accessible at https://www.clickz.com/cingular-sponsors-youtube-underground-talent-hunt/81062/

26. struggled to field calls from media around the world: *Ready for Its Close-Up, Washington Post*, accessible at http://www.washingtonpost.com/wp-dyn/content/article/2006/10/06/AR2006100600660.html

27. Karim...was studying for a master's degree at nearby Stanford University: *With YouTube, Student Hits Jackpot Again, New York Times*, accessible at https://www.nytimes.com/2006/10/12/technology/12tube.html?hp&ex=1160712000&en=c6ddbc2fdb0a4dea&ei=5094

28. Google decided.. it would snap up YouTube... for $1.65 billion in October 2006: *Google buys YouTube for $1.65bn, BBC News*, accessible at http://news.bbc.co.uk/1/hi/business/6034577.stm

29. netted Hurley, Chen and Karim between $100 million and $200 million each: *Sequoia could take $480 million from Google/YouTube deal, TechCrunch*, accessible at https://techcrunch.com/2006/10/09/sequoia-could-take-480-million-from-googleyoutube-deal/

30. YouTube was seeing 100 million video views daily and 65,000 new videos uploaded daily: *YouTube serves up 100 million videos a day online, Reuters*, accessible at https://usatoday30.usatoday.com/tech/news/2006-07-16-youtube-views_x.htm

31. 'It was a bad business decision for Google': *Schmidt: We paid $1 billion premium for YouTube, CNET*, accessible at https://www.cnet.com/news/schmidt-we-paid-1-billion-premium-for-youtube/

32. Mark Cuban called the purchase "crazy": *A Decade Ago, Google Bought YouTube — and It Was the Best Tech Deal Ever, The Ringer*, accessible at https://www.theringer.com/2016/10/10/16042354/google-youtube-acquisition-10-years-tech-deals-69fdbe1c8a06

33. today, YouTube is estimated to be worth $140 billion: Needham estimate, accessible at https://www.barrons.com/articles/alphabet-google-spin-off-youtube-51551795837

34. in June 2007, YouTube went global: *YouTube makes international move, BBC News*, accessible at http://news.bbc.co.uk/1/hi/technology/6757525.stm

35. in August 2007 the first adverts from 1,000 official partners... rolled out across the site: *First ads appear on YouTube clips, The Guardian*, accessible at https://www.theguardian.com/media/2007/aug/22/advertising.digitalmedia

5. Grace Helbig and the first stars of vlogging

1. MyDamnChannel... had its own web presence:MyDamnChannel, accessible at http://mydamnchannel.com/

2. in April 2008 it signed up... Grace Helbig: *Grace Helbig, Stated Magazine*, accessible at http://www.statedmag.com/articles/interview-vlogger-daily-grace-helbig-of-attack-of-the-show.html

3. she uploaded her first videos in 2007: *GracieHInABox*, YouTube, accessible at https://www.youtube.com/user/graciehinabox/

4. Helbig liked to describe herself as 'the internet's awkward older sister': *Grace Helbig's Digital Path to Fame, New York Times*, accessible at https://www.nytimes.com/2014/11/16/arts/television/grace-helbigs-digital-path-to-fame.html

5. Helbig's first video for MyDamnChannel was about champagne and toast: 'CHAMPAGNE TOAST', DailyGrace, YouTube, accessible at https://www.youtube.com/watch?v=iwwnA4f4qYg

6. over five-and-a-half years, she uploaded more than 1,500 videos: *The Stars of YouTube Rewind 2012: Where Are They Now?*, Tubefilter, accessible at https://www.tubefilter.com/2017/12/21/youtube-rewind-2012-where-are-they-now/

7. she received a salary from MyDamnChannel: *Why the Outrage over Daily Grace and My Damn Channel Matters, Medium*, accessible at https://medium.com/@fruzse/why-the-outrage-over-daily-grace-and-my-damn-channel-matters-3bac86166b62

8. juggling his day job at the music promoter Live Nation: *YouTube Videos Pull In Real Money, New York Times*, accessible at https://www.nytimes.com/2008/12/11/business/media/11youtube.html?hp&mtrref=en.wikipedia.

9. by September 2008, Buckley was earning more than $100,000 a year from YouTube: *YouTube Videos Pull In Real Money, New York Times*, accessible at https://www.nytimes.com/2008/12/11/business/media/11youtube.html?hp&mtrref=en.wikipedia.

10. YouTubers bring in $20 million a year: *Highest-Paid YouTube Stars 2018: Markiplier, Jake Paul, PewDiePie And More, Forbes*, accessible at https://www.forbes.com/sites/natalierobehmed/2018/12/03/highest-paid-youtube-stars-2018-markiplier-jake-paul-pewdiepie-and-more/#23f0eccb909a

11. he gave up his job to become a full-time YouTuber: *YouTube Videos Pull In Real Money, New York Times*, accessible at https://www.nytimes.com/2008/12/11/business/media/11youtube.html?hp&mtrref=en.wikipedia.

12. he began shooting videos promoting Pepsi: *Meet YouTube's Most In-Demand Brand Stars, AdAge*, accessible at https://adage.com/article/digital/meet-youtube-s-demand-brand-stars/145844/

13. Vidcon... acquired by the American media firm Viacom for an undisclosed amount: *Viacom Announces Acquisition of VidCon Internet-Video Conference, Variety,* accessible at https://variety.com/2018/digital/news/viacom-acquires-vidcon-conference-official-1202690303/

14. At its second conference in 2011, Green was listening to two major YouTubers: Interview with John Green

15. Green posted an advert on the website Craigslist... one of the respondents was Stan Muller: Interview with John Green

16. with the Green brothers co-founded Crash Course: *Crash Course,* YouTube, accessible at https://www.youtube.com/user/crashcourse

6. From Russia to Latin America: YouTube goes global

1. on the wall of Martin Dominguez's office is a blackboard, two metres wide by one-and-a-half metres tall: Interview with Martin Dominguez

2. one of the biggest Spanish-language YouTube channels, *Enchufe.tv*: Enchufetv, YouTube, accessible at https://www.youtube.com/channel/UCoG-Dh1Xa3kUCp0k24JN5DKA

3. 20 million subscribers: *Enchufetv,* YouTube, accessible at https://www.youtube.com/channel/UCoGDh1Xa3kUCp0k24JN5DKA

4. Enchufe now employs 20 people: Interview with Martin Dominguez

5. in its basement are the editing and recording suites... upstairs are the meeting rooms: Interview with Bastian Manintveld

6. the channel was founded in 2011 by a group of Ecuadorean film students... they hawked it around TV companies: Interview with Martin Dominguez

7. in 2011 60% of YouTube's views came from non-English language users: *60% Of YouTube Views Come From A Non-English Speaking Audience, AdWeek,* accessible at https://www.adweek.com/digital/youtube-views-non-english-speaking-audience/

8. their first video, El peor casting: *El peor casting, Enchufetv,* YouTube, accessible at https://www.youtube.com/watch?v=TyiMl5doLwU

9. Dominguez pressed the upload button on a bank holiday weekend... the video racked up 600 views in a few weeks: Interview with Martin Dominguez

10. one based around a popular festival in Ecuador: *Misión: Carnaval (FPS Ecuatoriano), Enchufetv,* YouTube, accessible at https://www.youtube.com/watch?v=m6Z3UbK_63Q

11. Enchufe is among the top 100 most subscribed channels: *Enchufe,* Social-

Blade, accessible at https://socialblade.com/youtube/channel/UCoGDh1X-a3kUCpok24JN5DKA

12. A majority stake in the company behind *Enchufe* was bought by Spanish MCN-turned-digital media group 2btube: *YouTube channels are selling for millions, The Verge*, accessible at https://www.theverge.com/2019/1/23/18192711/youtube-channel-sales-price-trends-millions

13. El Rubius... has nearly 30 million fans: elrubiusOMG, YouTube, accessible at https://www.youtube.com/user/elrubiusOMG/

14. ComRes asked adolescents... about their wider social media usage...91% of British 14-18-year-olds...93% in France and 95% or more in Germany: March 2017 ComRes survey for Como Meningitis, accessible at https://www.comresglobal.com/wp-content/uploads/2017/05/CoMO-Communicating-with-Adolescents-in-Europe-about-Vaccines-Survey-Data-Tables.pdf

15. video views tracked by Tubular Insights... increased by 17% in the UK... 25% in Spain; 32% in Italy; and 23% in Germany: 2018/19 European Social Video Trends Report, Tubular Insights, accessible at https://view.pointdrive.linkedin.com/presentations/14c8fe15-0bb4-4db0-99b4-85afd892e7a7?auth=1b28e892-7c02-4409-9c64-34b02452bbd6

16. around 100 localised translations of the site display YouTube in the home language of 95% of the internet's users: YouTube for Press, accessible at https://www.youtube.com/intl/en-GB/yt/about/press/

17. only three in 10 YouTube channels are based in English-language countries... around a third of YouTubers based in the United States and United Kingdom broadcast in a language other than English: Paladin data, accessed 1 March 2019

18. Brazil and Russia account for one in five views of all non-English language content with more than 10,000 views uploaded in 2018: Tubular Insights data provided exclusively for this book

19. Konrad Cunha Dantas... picked up cinematography when his mother died when he was 18: *Kondzilla* biografia, accessible at https://kondzilla.com/biografia.html

20. Cunha Dantas has the eighth-most subscribed YouTube channel... the sixth-most viewed: Kondzilla, SocialBlade, accessible at https://socialblade.com/youtube/c/kondzilla

21. Nunes Batista wanted to be a YouTuber from the age of 15: Globo G1 video interview, accessible at http://g1.globo.com/pi/piaui/noticia/2012/12/video-de-piauiense-vira-hit-na-internet-com-more-de-4-milhoes-de-acessos.html

22. his comedy sketches are seen by 35 million subscribers: whinderssonnunes, YouTube, accessible at https://www.youtube.com/user/whinderssonnunes

23. Felipe and Luccas Neto... have 55 million subscribers between them: Felipe Neto and Luccas Neto, YouTube, accessible at https://www.youtube.com/user/felipeneto and https://www.youtube.com/channel/UC_gV7oG_Y5iLTa3qhu8KiEA

24. Felipe... founded Paramaker: *Multinacional francesa Webedia assume controle acionário da Paramaker, CanalTech*, accessible at https://canaltech.com.br/mercado/multinacional-francesa-webedia-assume-controle-acion-ario-da-paramaker-49105/

25. India's YouTube community is dominated by... *T-Series* and *SET India*: Top 250 YouTubers in India, SocialBlade, accessible at https://socialblade.com/youtube/top/country/in

26. *T-Series*... was founded in 1984, filed an injunction... against YouTube in the Delhi High Court in 2010: Interview with Neeraj Kalyan

27. the first officially uploaded *T-Series* video went live on 1 January 2011: Interview with Neeraj Kalyan

28. one of 16 channels to cross the million subscriber mark even by 2014: *3 Indian content creators cross 10M subscriber mark on YouTube, Economic Times*, accessible at https://tech.economictimes.indiatimes.com/news/internet/3-indian-content-creators-cross-10m-subscriber-mark-on-you-tube/66980461

29. now there are more than 300 Indian channels with more than a million followers: *PewDiePie's Tumultuous Reign Over YouTube Almost Over, Bloomberg*, accessible at https://www.bloomberg.com/news/articles/2018-11-15/you-tube-king-pewdiepie-surrenders-crown-to-indian-record-label

30. *T-Series* now has 90 million subscribers: *T-Series*, YouTube, accessible at https://www.youtube.com/user/tseries/

31. due to the launch of Jio: Interview with Neeraj Kalyan

32. it uploaded 1,335 videos in 2018... 0.05% of all videos in India... a quarter of the 648 billion YouTube views: data provided by Tubular Insights for this book

33. Amit Bhadana... 14 million subscribers: Amit Bhadana, YouTube, accessible at https://www.youtube.com/channel/UC_vcKmg67vjMP7ciLnSxSHQ

34. *FROST* plays video games for his eight million subscribers: *FROST*, YouTube, accessible at https://www.youtube.com/user/YFrostA/videos

35. Nastya, whose two channels... have a combined 32 million subscribers: Like Nastya and Like Nastya Vlog, YouTube, accessible at https://www.youtube.com/channel/UCCI5Xsd_gCbZb9eTeOf9FdQ and https://www.youtube.com/channel/UCJplp5SjeGSdVdwsfb9Q7lQ

36. Iran and North Korea have made the site inaccessible: *Here Are the Countries that Block Facebook, Twitter and YouTube*, Mother Jones, accessible at https://www.motherjones.com/politics/2014/03/turkey-facebook-youtube-twitter-blocked/

37. Yuri Dud's long-form video interviews regularly reach millions of people in a week: вДудь, YouTube, accessible at https://www.youtube.com/channel/UCMCgOm8GZkHp8zJ6l7_hIuA

38. 82% of Russians aged 18-44 watch YouTube – nearly the same proportion that watch *Channel One*: *Putin tries to build an internyet, The Economist*, accessible at https://www.economist.com/europe/2019/03/09/russians-are-shunning-state-controlled-tv-for-youtube

39. Hikakin... founding one of Japan's biggest multi-channel networks: UUUM, accessible at https://en.uuum.co.jp

40. Banzz...eats inordinately large amounts of food on camera: *Banzz*, YouTube, accessible at https://www.youtube.com/channel/UCYx9lh-Cwou2-OoqVtEUoIMg

41. has to exercise 12 hours a day: *Extreme eating in Korea, BBC Minute*, accessible at https://www.bbc.co.uk/programmes/p063dclx

42. the amount of time spent in the video players and editors and entertainment categories on mobile app stories has tripled since 2015: App Annie report

43. Wengie... 13.4 million subscribers, who moved to Australia as a child: Wengie, YouTube, https://www.youtube.com/channel/UCD9PZYV5he-Aevh9vrsYmt1g

44. pick out a couple of hundred people in the UK, US or elsewhere, and you'll find at least one YouTuber: analysis of Paladin data on the number of YouTubers per country

45. China is the country with the lowest proportion of YouTubers: analysis of Paladin data on the number of YouTubers per country

46. Alexa estimates that around four percent of visitors worldwide still come from China: Alexa data

47. Google employees are worried that the company is secretly developing a censored search engine: *Google's secret China project 'effectively ended' after internal confrontation, The Intercept*, accessible at https://theintercept.com/2018/12/17/google-china-censored-search-engine-2/

48. the auto-play queue... only came to YouTube in 2015: *Autoplay is now the default on YouTube and that's ok*, Tubular Insights, accessible at https://tubularinsights.com/youtube-autoplay/

PART II

ENGINE ROOM: HOW YOUTUBE WORKS

7. The Algorithm: YouTube's secret sauce

1. YouTube's best-known star is PewDiePie: PewDiePie, SocialBlade, accessible at https://socialblade.com/youtube/c/pewdiepie

2. Bitch Lasanga has proved oddly popular: *bitch lasagna*, PewDiePie, YouTube, accessible at https://www.youtube.com/watch?v=6Dh-RL__uN4

3. In December 2016 PewDiePie posted a video in which he told viewers: 'YouTube is trying to kill my channel': *DELETING MY CHANNEL AT 50 MILLION.*, PewDiePie, YouTube, accessible at https://www.youtube.com/watch?v=6-_4U00_7Y4

4. Google Brain... powers those recommendations: *How YouTube perfected the feed*, The Verge, accessible at https://www.theverge.com/2017/8/30/16222850/youtube-google-brain-algorithm-video-recommendation-personalized-feed

5. in 2016 in a paper by three Google employees: *Deep Neural Networks for YouTube Recommendations*, Paul Covington, Jay Adams and Emre Sargin, accessible at https://ai.google/research/pubs/pub45530

6. watch time from the YouTube homepage has grown 20-fold... more than 70% of the time people spend: *How YouTube perfected the feed*, The Verge, accessible at https://www.theverge.com/2017/8/30/16222850/youtube-google-brain-algorithm-video-recommendation-personalized-feed

7. in February 2005, YouTube... launched a child-centric version, YouTube Kids: *Introducing the newest member of our family, the YouTube Kids app--available on Google Play and the App Store*, YouTube Official Blog, accessible at https://youtube.googleblog.com/2015/02/youtube-kids.html

8. unofficial videos of trademarked characters accidentally showed up in YouTube Kids' 'Now playing' feeds: *Something is wrong on the internet*, James Bridle, *Medium*, accessible at https://medium.com/@jamesbridle/something-is-wrong-on-the-internet-c39c471271d2

9. researchers at Cyprus University of Technology analysed 130,000 videos: *Children can find inappropriate videos on YouTube in just 10 clicks*, New Scientist, accessible at https://www.newscientist.com/article/2196040-children-can-find-inappropriate-videos-on-youtube-in-just-10-clicks/

10. just four in 20 parents monitor their child's YouTube usage – and one in 20 children aged 4-12 say their parents never check: data from The Insights People analysed for this book

11. he threatened to delete his channel when it hit 50 million... he was 200,000 subscribers short when he made his stand: *DELETING MY CHANNEL AT 50 MILLION.*, PewDiePie, YouTube, accessible at https://www.youtube.com/watch?v=6-_4Uoo_7Y4

12. he has reached a staggering 90 million subscribers: PewDiePie, YouTube, accessible at https://www.youtube.com/user/PewDiePie/

13. *T-Series* is matching PewDiePie subscriber for subscriber: *LIVE PewDiePie vs T-Series - Most Subscribed YouTube Channel Live Sub Count!*, SocialBlade, YouTube, accessible at https://www.youtube.com/watch?v=mSQIX_G3TjU

14. on 1 January 2018, *T-Series* had 31 million subscribers, compared to PewDiePie's 58 million. A year to the day later, they were almost equal: SocialBlade data, accessible at https://www.socialblade.com

15. At 1.38am on 3 April 2018, two police officers pulled up to a parked car at a Walmart in Mountain View, California: video released by Mountain View Police Department

16. Aghdam, a 38-year-old Iranian, had emigrated to the United States in her late teens: 'Bizarre online profiles reveal YouTube shooter's possible motive', Sky News, accessible at https://news.sky.com/story/what-we-know-about-shooter-who-hated-youtube-11316204

17. Aghdam walked through the door of a garage with a Smith & Wesson nine millimetre semi-automatic handgun: Mountain View Police Department statement

18. in January 2019, YouTube said it had made hundreds of tweaks to the algorithm to improve the standard of videos recommended to users: *Continuing our work to improve recommendations on YouTube*, YouTube Official Blog, accessible at https://youtube.googleblog.com/2019/01/continuing-our-work-to-improve.html

19. probably about 10 million videos: estimate based on YouTube having around 10 billion videos on the platform as of late March 2019. The figure comes from extrapolation of YouTube's growth as tracked in *YouTube channels, uploads and views: A statistical analysis of the past 10 years*, Matthias Baertl, Offenburg University

20. in March 2019 33-year-old Kyle Long stepped into his car... he was arrested for making criminal threats...he couldn't be held accountable for his actions: Mountain View Police Department statement, accessible at https://www.facebook.com/mountainviewpolicedepartment/photos/rpp.335059318193/10157048067683194/?type=3&theater

8. Policing YouTube: extremism and the Adpocalypse

1. The *David Zublick Channel* has more than 150,000 subscribers: *David Zublick Channel*, YouTube, accessible at https://www.youtube.com/channel/UCFtoNILvZnchz4ezQeh-Auw

2. 10,000 paid community moderators: *YouTube hires moderators to root out inappropriate videos, Financial Times*, accessible at https://www.ft.com/content/080d1dd4-d92c-11e7-a039-c64b1c09b482

3. automated monitoring... the collective brainpower of another 180,000 people: statement by Nicklas Berild Lundblad, Google vice president of public policy for Europe, to UK parliamentary committee

4. community guidelines and policies about copyright: Policies and Safety, YouTube, accessible at https://www.youtube.com/intl/en-GB/yt/about/policies/

5. Loose Change... alleges that the attacks on America on 11 September were an inside job: *Loose Change*, YouTube

6. since it was uploaded to Google Video... *Loose Change* has been seen at least 100 million times: *The '9/11 was an inside job' guy has some regrets, The Outline*, accessible at https://theoutline.com/post/2179/reflecting-on-loose-change-in-the-age-of-fake-news-9-11-inside-job?zd=2&zi=a66b6x6m

7. YouTube was the website most frequently cited as helping facilitate that transition to extreme beliefs: *From Memes to Infowars: How 75 Fascist Activists Were 'Red-Pilled', Bellingcat*, accessible at https://www.bellingcat.com/news/americas/2018/10/11/memes-infowars-75-fascist-activists-red-pilled/

8. Carl Benjamin...has nearly 900,000 subscribers: *Sargon of Akkad*, YouTube, accessible at https://www.youtube.com/user/SargonofAkkad100

9. another video-maker is Alex Jones... YouTube shut his channel in August 2018 for repeatedly violating its guidelines: *Alex Jones Banned by YouTube for Repeatedly Violating Community Guidelines, Variety*, accessible at https://variety.com/2018/digital/news/youtube-alex-jones-ban-1202896074/

10. 'The change in his attitude was like switching the light from bright to dark': accessible at https://twitter.com/shoofleye/status/1051826178275848192

11. David Copeland... detonated three nail bombs in London... in 1999: *Hate-filled nailbomber is jailed for life, The Independent*, accessible at https://web.archive.org/web/20091201133942/http://www.independent.co.uk/news/uk/this-britain/hatefilled-nailbomber-is-jailed-for-life-706785.html

12. in its early days, YouTube was vital viewing for jihadists: Interview with Rita Katz

13. of the 515 links shared over that period, 328... directed people to YouTube:

To Curb Terrorist Propaganda Online, Look to YouTube. No, Really., *Wired*, accessible at https://www.wired.com/story/to-curb-terrorist-propaganda-on-line-look-to-youtube-no-really/

14. a year later... just 15 of 258 total links... were to YouTube: *Technology & Terrorism, October 2018*, SITE Group

15. around 1,000 channels a month are removed from YouTube for 'promotion of violence and violent extremism': YouTube Community Guidelines enforcement, accessible at https://transparencyreport.google.com/youtube-policy/removals?hl=en

16. *The Times* uncovered that banner adverts for holiday resorts appeared on top of speeches from guerrilla terrorists: *Big brands fund terror through online adverts*, *The Times*, accessible at https://www.thetimes.co.uk/article/big-brands-fund-terror-knnxfgb98

17. Pepsi, Walmart and Johnson & Johnson were among the multinational firms who pulled their advertising: *Google's bad week: YouTube loses millions as advertising row reaches US*, *The Guardian*, accessible at https://www.theguardian.com/technology/2017/mar/25/google-youtube-advertising-extremist-content-att-verizon

18. YouTube purged 150,000 videos and 270 accounts in a single week: 'YouTube Has Deleted Hundreds Of Thousands Of Disturbing Kids' Videos', BuzzFeed News, accessible at https://www.buzzfeednews.com/article/blakemontgomery/youtube-has-deleted-hundreds-of-thousands-of-disturbing

19. the likes of Nestle and Epic Games... pulled their adverts from the site: *YouTubers facing second 'adpocalypse' as Nestle and Epic Games withdraw adverts*, *Metro UK*, accessible at https://metro.co.uk/2019/02/21/youtubers-facing-second-adpocalypse-nestle-epic-games-withdraw-adverts-8696292/?ito=cb-share

20. YouTube said it would ban comments on almost all videos featuring children: *YouTube bans comments on all videos of children*, BBC News, accessible at https://www.bbc.co.uk/news/technology-47408969

21. the site finally announced in a 485-word blogpost it would make conspiracy videos harder to find: *Continuing our work to improve recommendations on YouTube*, YouTube Official Blog, accessible at https://youtube.googleblog.com/2019/01/continuing-our-work-to-improve.html

22. Jill Walker Rettberg... was asked by her 10-year-old daughter: accessible at https://twitter.com/jilltxt/status/1052467331811762182

23. when software engineer Keziyah Lewis dines with her family in Central Florida she debates with relatives who believe the flat earth theory because of YouTube videos: accessible at https://twitter.com/KeziyahL/status/1064687432224989184

24. Guillaume Chaslot... now feels intense remorse at the algorithm he helped optimise for watch time in 2011, along with 14 others: Interview with Guillaume Chaslot

25. his website AlgoTransparency scrapes the recommended videos of more than 1,000 major YouTube channels: accessible at https://algotransparency.org/

26. *Christmas at GITMO...* was recommended by 16 of those 1,000 channels: accessible at https://algotransparency.org/

27. *RedPill78...* has 126,000 subscribers: RedPill78, YouTube, accessible at https://www.youtube.com/user/votezaktaylor/

28. Hundreds of thousands of people watched the video before it was removed from YouTube: RedPill78, YouTube, accessible at https://www.youtube.com/user/votezaktaylor/

29. the 2017 Las Vegas shooting, where gunman Stephen Paddock killed 58 and injured more than 850 by firing more than 1,000 rounds from his hotel room on the 32nd floor of the Mandalay Bay hotel: *Mandalay Bay attack: everything we know about the deadliest mass shooting in US history in Las Vegas, The Telegraph*, accessible at https://www.telegraph.co.uk/news/2017/10/02/mandalay-bay-attack-everything-know-aboutthe-deadliest-mass/

30. YouTube's near-two billion monthly active users: YouTube for Press, accessible at https://www.youtube.com/intl/en-GB/yt/about/press/

9. Sponsored content: the tale of Dodie Clark and Heinz beans

1. came out as bisexual to her followers in a six-minute vlog: *I'm bisexual WOO*, doddleoddle, YouTube, accessible at https://www.youtube.com/watch?v=SXJnkNA2z38

2. just over a year later Clark... uploaded a two-minute song: *I'm bisexual – a coming out song!*, doddleoddle, YouTube, accessible at https://www.youtube.com/watch?v=SH_NwvdbecE

3. Clark uploaded another two-minute video in September 2016... more than a million people have watched that video: *BEANZ | ad*, doddleoddle, YouTube, accessible at https://www.youtube.com/watch?v=MESqkLGC-Lk

4. 'covert advertising', according to a study in 2016 by German academics: *Consumer responses to covert advertising in social media, Marketing Intelligence & Planning*, accessible at https://www.emeraldinsight.com/doi/abs/10.1108/MIP-11-2016-0212?journalCode=mip&

5. Nielsen and Carat Global... found that collaborations brands make with You-Tubers result in four times the increase: *How YouTube influencers are rewriting the*

marketing rulebook, Think with Google, accessible at https://www.thinkwithgoogle.com/advertising-channels/video/youtube-influencer-marketing-rulebook/?utm_medium=email-d&utm_source=content-alert-A-&utm_team=twg-us&utm_campaign=20171011-twg-us-video-alert-OT-OT-OT&utm_content=cta

6. Hannah Hart... struck a TV deal with the Food Network: *YouTuber Hannah Hart Dishes on New Food Network Series 'I Hart Food', Variety*, accessible at https://variety.com/2017/tv/news/hannah-hart-food-network-series-i-hart-food-youtube-1202477740/

7. Hart, who first won fans in 2011 when she recorded a drunken, late-night webcam conversation with a friend while trying hopelessly to make a grilled cheese sandwich: *The Pleasures of Cooking While Drunk with Hannah Hart, Time*, accessible at http://content.time.com/time/arts/article/0,8599,2079263,00.html

8. she now has 2.4 million subscribers: MyHarto, YouTube, accessible at https://www.youtube.com/channel/UCJQL1Fai-9GlVunsbP4x8Pg

9. the Vlogbrothers now make less than a fifth of their total revenue from advertising against their videos: John Green tweeted in June 2017 that 'We're making around 10% of our YouTube revenue from [YouTube] Red [since renamed YouTube Premium] now. Which is around 2% of our [total] content revenue. Big creators are pretty diversified'. Accessible at: https://twitter.com/hankgreen/status/876465975096422400

10. Hank Green... publishing his first novel in September 2018: *An Absolutely Remarkable Thing* was published on 25 September 2018

11. views alone account for just 30% of the income of Jordi van den Bussche... he told a Dutch TV documentary: *YouTube, YouTubers and You - VPRO documentary – 2017, VPRO*, YouTube, accessible at https://www.youtube.com/watch?v=--VqhKD3WxI

12. Boston Consulting Group... forecasts that spending on branded content will hit $25 billion in 2019: *Branded Content: Growth for Marketers and Media Companies*, Boston Consulting Group, accessible at https://www.bcg.com/en-gb/publications/2015/media-entertainment-branded-content-growth-for-marketers-and-media-companies.aspx

13. Kate Orseth told a gathering of businesses and developers in 2017: Presentation at Facebook's F8 2017 conference, accessible at https://developers.facebook.com/videos/?filters%5B0%5D=f8&filters%5B1%5D=2017

14. just four percent of British PR and marketing professionals wouldn't pencil in any money to spend on social media influencers: *How much do PRs spend on influencer marketing?, PR Week*, accessible at https://www.prweek.com/article/1443619/prs-spend-influencer-marketing?utm_content=buffercdfb-f&utm_medium=social&utm_source=twitter.com&utm_campaign=buffer

15. Ruxandra Maria, Chupa Chups product manager, said: *Chupa Chups on demystifying the smoke and mirrors around influencers, Digiday*, accessible at

https://digiday.com/marketing/chupa-chups-demystifying-smoke-mirrors-around-influencers/?utm_medium=email&utm_campaign=digidaydis&utm_source=uk&utm_content=170816

16. among the first 15 YouTubers it worked with in its first three years was Dodie: *Chupa Chups on demystifying the smoke and mirrors around influencers*, *Digiday*, accessible at https://digiday.com/marketing/chupa-chups-demystifying-smoke-mirrors-around-influencers/?utm_medium=email&utm_campaign=digidaydis&utm_source=uk&utm_content=170816

17. Jan-Frederik Grave... concluded: *Exploring the Perception of Influencers vs. Traditional Celebrities: Are Social Media Stars a New Type of Endorser?*, Jan Frederik Grave, accessible at https://www.dropbox.com/s/gt1795faxief-7dt/10.1145@3097286.3097322.pdf?dl=0

18. just 44% of British adults knew that the main source of funding was advertising: *Adults' Media Use and Attitudes Report 2018*, Ofcom, accessible at https://www.ofcom.org.uk/__data/assets/pdf_file/0011/113222/Adults-Media-Use-and-Attitudes-Report-2018.pdf

19. 61% of Generation Z... said that they didn't actually care whether a celebrity who marketed a brand in a video didn't declare it as an advert: *Adweek*, accessible at http://www.adweek.com/digital/infographic-50-of-gen-z-cant-live-without-youtube-and-other-stats-that-will-make-you-feel-old/

20. 'creators and brands are responsible for understanding and complying with their legal obligations to disclose Paid Promotion in their content': Paid product placements and endorsements, YouTube, accessible at https://support.google.com/youtube/answer/154235?hl=en-GB

21. Britain first tightened the rules on branded content in 2014: ASA Adjudication on Mondelez UK Ltd, ASA, accessible at https://www.asa.org.uk/rulings/mondelez-uk-ltd-a14-275018.html

22. Britain's Competition and Markets Authority (CMA) has censured a dozen or so influencers for breaching the rules, and in late 2018 began an investigation into the world of influencer marketing: *Celebrities pledge to clean up their act on social media*, gov.uk, accessible at https://www.gov.uk/government/news/celebrities-pledge-to-clean-up-their-act-on-social-media

23. similar guidance was issued by the United States Federal Trade Commission... after it claimed two YouTubers: *FTC Settles Complaint Against 'Let's Play' YouTube Stars, Sends Warning Letters To Other Influencers And Demands Responses*, Tubefilter, accessible at https://www.tubefilter.com/2017/09/07/ftc-influencers-youtube-syndicate-tmartn-csgo-lotto-warning-letter/

24. the FTC also wrote to 21 influencers: *FTC Settles Complaint Against 'Let's Play' YouTube Stars, Sends Warning Letters To Other Influencers And Demands Responses*, Tubefilter, accessible at https://www.tubefilter.com/2017/09/07/ftc-influencers-youtube-syndicate-tmartn-csgo-lotto-warning-letter/

25. a UK industry body set up in December 2018... the Business of Influencers: Interview with Ian Shepherd

26. three in 10 adult internet users didn't know that vloggers could be paid by a company to endorse a product: *Adults' media use and attitudes*, Ofcom, accessible at https://www.ofcom.org.uk/__data/assets/pdf_file/0020/102755/adults-media-use-attitudes-2017.pdf

27. YouTube's own survey of teenagers and millennials found 40% believed YouTubers understood them better than their friends or family. And 60% said that a creator had changed their view of the world – or life: *Why YouTube stars are more influential than traditional celebrities*, Think with Google, accessible at https://www.thinkwithgoogle.com/consumer-insights/youtube-stars-influence/

28. BuzzFeed...has regularly faced brickbats... for juxtaposing content created by its news and editorial staff and that produced by its 'creative' (advertising) staff: *Sponsored content is compromising media integrity*, openDemocracy, accessible at https://www.opendemocracy.net/en/sponsored-content-is-blurring-line-between-advertising-and-editorial/

29. the *Texaco Star Theatre* or the *Camel News Caravan*... companies would fund the production: *Social Media Influencers: A Lesson Plan for Teaching Digital Advertising Media Literacy*, Cynthia B Meyers, accessible at https://muse.jhu.edu/article/663708/summary

30. the audience for the *Maxwell House Show Boat*... was let into all aspects of the production: *Social Media Influencers: A Lesson Plan for Teaching Digital Advertising Media Literacy*, Cynthia B Meyers, accessible at https://muse.jhu.edu/article/663708/summary

31. in 2017 an academic survey of German YouTubers... found that two-thirds of creators had taken advantage of product placement... they did so frequently – half more than 10 times a year: *Product placement on YouTube: An explorative study on YouTube creators' experiences with advertisers*, Claudia Gerhards, Convergence, accessible at https://www.dropbox.com/s/3cd7gs-vooyw2q4g/10.1177@1354856517736977.pdf?dl=0

32. 'Idols of Promotion': *Idols of Promotion: The Triumph of Self-Branding in the Social Media Age*, Brooke Erin Duffy and Jefferson Pooley, accessible at https://www.dropbox.com/home/Book/Social%20Media%20%26%20Society%20conference%20papers?preview=10.1145%403097286.3097339.pdf

33. in 2016, 1,000 YouTube channels hit the one million subscriber mark: *On average, about four YouTube channels hit 1 million subscribers every single day*, SocialBlade blog, accessible at https://socialblade.com/blog/youtube-milestones-four-channels-hit-one-million-subscribers-every-day/

PART III

CHARTING THE STARS

10. Know your YouTube: elite, macro-influencer and micro-influencer

1. YouTube has also deprioritised the importance of being a subscriber by reducing the efficacy of notifications: *YouTube exploring changes to notification system after subscriber alert kerfuffle*: *Polygon*, accessible at https://www.polygon.com/2018/4/2/17181876/subscriber-notifications-youtube-creator-insider

2. four categories of influencer: *Introducing the Standard Terminology in Influencer Marketing (STIM)*, *MediaKix*, accessible at http://mediakix.com/influencer-tiers/?utm_campaign=Weekly%20Blog%20Newsletter&utm_source=hs_email&utm_medium=email&utm_content=68907355&_hsenc=p2ANqtz-8_

3. smaller influencers... hold more sway over their fans: *The rise of micro-influencers and how brands use them. Clickz*, accessible at https://www.clickz.com/the-rise-of-micro-influencers-and-how-brands-use-them/216503/

4. Get less than 1,000 views... you're not even a nano-influencer: *Introducing the Standard Terminology in Influencer Marketing (STIM)*, *MediaKix*, accessible at http://mediakix.com/influencer-tiers/?utm_campaign=Weekly%20Blog%20Newsletter&utm_source=hs_email&utm_medium=email&utm_content=68907355&_hsenc=p2ANqtz-8_

5. the last time the average YouTube video got more than 1,000 views in its lifetime was in 2011. Videos uploaded in 2016... averaged just 89 views: *YouTube channels, uploads and views: A statistical analysis of the past 10 years*, Matthias Baertl, Offenburg University

6. break through the 1,000 view mark and you are a nano-influencer... a micro-influencer might get between 10,000 and 25,000 views per video... above that and... you're considered a bona fide influencer: *Introducing the Standard Terminology in Influencer Marketing (STIM)*, *MediaKix*, accessible at http://mediakix.com/influencer-tiers/?utm_campaign=Weekly%20Blog%20Newsletter&utm_source=hs_email&utm_medium=email&utm_content=68907355&_hsenc=p2ANqtz-8_xnG14mgBHd3lCTOwGn33kkxugR4SHO9nbL4WSWgXFcisGL618HhUxoEhJUSj9_wMwGujqL4sZprQgnq4Zesx_JM9gw&_hsmi=68907355#gs.24w1ak

11. Elite influencers: fighting their way to the top

1. Copper Box Arena in London where British super heavyweight boxer Anthony Joshua saw off Roberto Cammarelle to take gold at the 2012 Olympics: *91kg Super Heavyweight Men, Olympics*, accessible at https://www.olympic.org/london-2012/boxing/91kg-super-heavyweight-men

2. this is the world's first ever boxing match between big YouTubers: Interview with Stuart Jones

3. all 7,000 seats sold out: Interviews with Stuart Jones and Liam Chivers

4. hundreds of thousands of pounds had changed hands on the betting market: Interview with Alex Apati, Ladbrokes

5. special fight merchandise... was shifting so fast that one person maintaining a stall staid they couldn't keep count of the value: Interview with unnamed merch stall worker

6. an estimated 1.6 million were watching on a pay-per-view live stream: *Rival gamers have a real ding-dong*, *The Sunday Times*, accessible at https://www.thetimes.co.uk/article/rival-gamers-have-a-real-ding-dong-lsw2kk5zs

7. after three rounds, the match was stopped due to a technical knockout: *Rival gamers have a real ding-dong*, *The Sunday Times*, accessible at https://www.thetimes.co.uk/article/rival-gamers-have-a-real-ding-dong-lsw2kk5zs

8. KSI attended a £15,000-a-year private school, Berkhamsted: Berkhamsted School, accessible at https://www.berkhamsted.com

9. KSI flunked his A-Levels...he locked himself in the toilet until he could steel himself to tell his furious parents: *KSI - MOST HONEST INTERVIEW EVER | True Geordie Podcast #18*, *True Geordie Podcast*, YouTube accessible at https://www.youtube.com/watch?v=8ea6zww6DtY

10. his younger brother Deji is also a YouTuber: ComedyShortsGamer, YouTube, accessible at https://www.youtube.com/user/ComedyShortsGamer

11. a novelty rap about footballer Emile Heskey: *HESKEY TIME - Official KSIOlajidebt + Randolph - Music Video*, TheKSIOlajidebtMUSIC, YouTube, accessible at https://www.youtube.com/watch?v=D3pnaWMfV9g

12. he released his first proper album in 2016: *YouTuber, rapper, actor: KSI Olatunji is the new triple threat*, *Wired UK*, accessible at https://www.wired.co.uk/article/youtube-star-ksi-olatunji-fifa

13. his first feature film, Laid in America... it bombed – in part, KSI believes, because his fanbase preferred to pirate rather than buy the production: 'KSI gets smart: what YouTube's biggest star is planning next', Esquire, accessible at https://www.esquire.com/uk/culture/a19481583/ksi-interview/

14. sold-out matches that see an all-star team of YouTubers play a glorified Sunday league kick-about in top-flight stadiums: Interview with Stuart Jones

15. KSI grabbed the microphone and challenged Jake Paul, Logan Paul or their father, Greg, to a boxing match: *KSI vs Joe Weller – Copper Box Arena February 3rd 2018*, KSI, YouTube, accessible at https://www.youtube.com/watch?v=Sl9npEDYeLk

16. when KSI next entered the boxing ring six months later, he faced Logan Paul: *The Logan Paul vs KSI fight was the weirdest event in internet history, Wired UK*, accessible at https://www.wired.co.uk/article/who-won-the-ksi-logan-paul-fight-analysis

17. Logan Paul... uploaded a tasteless video from Japan's Aokigahara 'suicide' forest: *Logan Paul's disastrous YouTube video is just a symptom of very modern problem*, *The Telegraph*, accessible at https://www.telegraph.co.uk/business/2018/01/05/logan-pauls-disastrous-youtube-video-just-symptom-far-bigger/?WT.mc_id=tmg_share_tw

18. tickets cost between £30 and £495: Manchester Arena, accessible at https://www.manchester-arena.com/events/ksi-v-logan-paul/9352/

19. almost 20,000 filled Manchester Arena: Interview with Stuart Jones

20. some 865,000 people watched the event live, with at least a million more following along on pirated streams: *KSI vs Logan Paul: YouTube fight shows the danger of pirated, free streams to future of vloggers*, *The Independent*, accessible at https://www.independent.co.uk/life-style/gadgets-and-tech/features/ksi-logan-paul-fight-youtube-video-watch-live-free-stream-piracy-channel-a8510296.html

21. the event ended in a draw: *The Logan Paul vs KSI fight was the weirdest event in internet history*, *Wired UK*, accessible at https://www.wired.co.uk/article/who-won-the-ksi-logan-paul-fight-analysis

22. watched by an average of 1.5 million people: Latest overnights, Broadcast, accessible at https://www.broadcastnow.co.uk/ratings/overnights

23. according to Forbes, the top 10 earning YouTube stars pulled in $180 million in 2018, a rise of 42% on the previous year: *Highest-Paid YouTube Stars 2018: Markiplier, Jake Paul, PewDiePie And More*, *Forbes*, accessible at https://www.forbes.com/sites/natalierobehmed/2018/12/03/highest-paid-youtube-stars-2018-markiplier-jake-paul-pewdiepie-and-more/#23f0eccb909a

24. more than 330 separate YouTube channels had more than 10 million subscribers... at least 4,000 had more than two million: Top 5,000 YouTube channels, SocialBlade, accessible at https://socialblade.com/youtube/top/5000/

25. PewDiePie is only recognised by a quarter of British adults... Zoella is recognised by a third... ask those aged 18-24, though, and things change: YouGov survey of 1,625 British adults commissioned for YouTubers, 13-14 December 2017

26. Five of the top 10 earners on YouTube are men who play video games for a living: *Highest-Paid YouTube Stars 2018: Markiplier, Jake Paul, PewDiePie And More*, *Forbes*, accessible at https://www.forbes.com/sites/natalierobehmed/2018/12/03/highest-paid-youtube-stars-2018-markiplier-jake-paul-

pewdiepie-and-more/#23f0eccb909a

27. Since 2012, gaming has had the second highest number of channels on the platform... for comparison, one in 10 views goes to vloggers: *YouTube channels, uploads and views: A statistical analysis of the past 10 years*, Matthias Baertl, Offenburg University

28. since 2010, the gaming industry has been bigger than both Hollywood and the music industry combined: *The Video Games' Industry is Bigger Than Hollywood*, *LPE Esports*, accessible at https://lpesports.com/e-sports-news/the-video-games-industry-is-bigger-than-hollywood

29. in absolute numbers YouTube's gamers blow their competition out of the water: Twitch Viewers Statistics, TwitchTracker, accessible at https://twitchtracker.com/statistics/viewers

30. PewDiePie earns a fortune - $15.5 million in 2018: *Highest-Paid YouTube Stars 2018: Markiplier, Jake Paul, PewDiePie And More*, *Forbes*, accessible at https://www.forbes.com/sites/natalierobehmed/2018/12/03/highest-paid-youtube-stars-2018-markiplier-jake-paul-pewdiepie-and-more/#23f0ecc-b909a

31. PewDiePie's Tuber Simulator... reached number seven overall in the US iPhone charts (in the UK, it was a top-ranking game): App Annie, accessible at https://www.appannie.com/apps/ios/app/pewdiepies-tuber-simulator/intelligence/

32. watch time on beauty videos increased by more than 60% year-on-year between 2015 and 2016: YouTube data, Think with Google

33. born in Oklahoma to Iraqi immigrants, Kattan... used to ask her classmates to call her Heidi: *HBD! 9 Things You Didn't Know About Huda Kattan*, *Vogue*, accessible at https://en.vogue.me/culture/huda-kattan-9-facts-about-her/

34. Kattan has three million subscribers: Huda Beauty, YouTube, accessible at https://www.youtube.com/channel/UCRSvEADlY-caz3sfDNwvRiA

35. she has her own line of beauty products stocked in 1,500 stores... and turnover at her company is around $300 million: *How Huda Kattan Built A Billion-Dollar Cosmetics Brand With 26 Million Followers*, *Forbes*, accessible at https://www.forbes.com/sites/chloesorvino/2018/07/11/huda-kattan-huda-beauty-billion-influencer/#11e836156120

36. invited to have breakfast with Kattan alongside 20 other influencer at a London department store: *BREAKFAST WITH HUDA BEAUTY AND MONA KATTAN !!!*, *Modest Street*, YouTube, accessible at https://www.youtube.com/watch?v=LA6lU7ToNiw

37. Huda Beauty sends review products from Kattan's latest beauty ranges to Rana and other beauty influencers: Interview with Eniyah Rana

38. the highest earning influencer is a child...eight-year-old Ryan: *Highest-Paid YouTube Stars 2018: Markiplier, Jake Paul, PewDiePie And More*, Forbes, accessible at https://www.forbes.com/sites/natalierobehmed/2018/12/03/highest-paid-youtube-stars-2018-markiplier-jake-paul-pewdiepie-and-more/#23f0eccb909a

39. Ryan also has a branded line of merchandise sold through the US supermarket Walmart, and his own line of toys available on Amazon: *Ryan Toy Hunt for his own toys Ryan's World at Walmart!!!*, Ryan ToysReview, YouTube, accessible at https://www.youtube.com/watch?v=o_8VwSlyxuA

40. Hearts by Tiana... will be stocked in Asda's 400 stores later this year: Interview with Ian Shepherd

41. *CKN Toys*... particularly popular in Indonesia: Paladin data, accessed 1 March 2019

42. *CKN Toys* has 11.6 million subscribers, who watch the videos 460 million times in a month: *CKN Toys*, YouTube, accessible at https://www.youtube.com/channel/UCfaZw8XH_zmAVkBst_MPD6w/

43. the channel signed a deal with Haven Global: *CKN Toys appoints Haven Global*, License Global, accessible at https://www.licenseglobal.com/agency-appointments/ckn-toys-appoints-haven-global

12. Child stars: meet MattyB, who gets two million views a day

1. in 2007 a mother uploaded a video of her 12-year-old son singing to YouTube: *Justin Singing So Sick by Ne-yo*, Justin Bieber, YouTube, accessible at https://www.youtube.com/watch?v=csymVmm1xTw

2. he's worth $200m: *How Much Money Does Justin Bieber Have?*, Cosmopolitan, accessible at https://www.cosmopolitan.com/entertainment/a22103870/justin-bieber-net-worth/

3. the pop stars Troye Sivan and Dua Lipa started on YouTube at the age of 12 and 14 respectively: Troye Sivan and Dua Lipa, YouTube, accessible at https://www.youtube.com/channel/UCWcrr8Q9INGNp-PTCLTzc8Q and https://www.youtube.com/channel/UC-J-KZfRV8c13fOCkhXdLiQ

4. Mini Jake Paul... started at the age of four: *MEETING THE MINI JAKE PAUL?!*, Jake Paul, YouTube, accessible at https://www.youtube.com/watch?v=duNWzHgisP4

5. Ben Hampton... joined YouTube when he was six: Ben Hampton, YouTube, accessible at https://www.youtube.com/channel/UCNpbTBAGC2aYfqfos-9DDyAw

6. Russian-born brother and sister Mister Max, and Miss Katy, are seen by 25 million subscribers across four separate channels: Mister Max and Miss Katy, YouTube

7. Matthew David Morris was just 11 when he surpassed one billion views for his covers of pop songs in 2014: Interview with Blake Morris

8. his first officially-released single, Friend Zone, has been watched 87 million times since mid-April 2016: *MattyBRaps – Friend Zone*, MattyBRaps, YouTube, accessible at https://www.youtube.com/watch?v=9vbddLNUOMs

9. in June 2016 his memoir became an Amazon bestseller: 'That's a Rap', MattyB

10. peeing in buckets in hotel kitchens: *Justin Bieber defends urinating in bucket*, *Toronto Sun*, accessible at https://torontosun.com/2015/09/29/justin-bieber-defends-urinating-in-bucket/wcm/79ff13cb-1eb6-447f-8221-fa08051bb372

11. a survey in 2014 asking US teenagers aged 13-18 to name influential figures demonstrated the pulling power of the video streaming website: the top five most recognisable names were all YouTubers: *Survey: YouTube Stars More Popular Than Mainstream Celebs Among U.S. Teens*, *Variety*, accessible at https://variety.com/2014/digital/news/survey-youtube-stars-more-popular-than-mainstream-celebs-among-u-s-teens-1201275245/

12. with his 11 million subscribers: MattyBRaps, YouTube, accessible at https://www.youtube.com/channel/UCmdYipHB-KbFYxOyhwjVeQw

13. Jacob Sartorius tweets superficially profound statements like I'm into you" and "YOU'RE IMPORTANT': accessible at https://twitter.com/jacobsartorius/status/752164705079136262 and https://twitter.com/jacobsartorius/status/751924140135813120

14. his three million subscribers on YouTube, nine million followers on Instagram and 1.6 million followers on Twitter: Jacob Sartorius social media accounts

15. MattyB LLC: accessible at http://mattybraps.com/

16. funniflix, where children perform comedy sketches: funniflix, YouTube, accessible at https://www.youtube.com/channel/UCex83nRMBJRBx8pHLxojntA

17. the Haschak sisters... were introduced to the world in a video with MattyB: *Kanye West - Clique (Haschak Sisters & MattyBRaps Cover)*, MattyBRaps, YouTube, accessible at https://www.youtube.com/watch?v=5MwM-KZB36Tk

18. The Haschak Sisters are still going strong...now have six million subscribers: Haschak Sisters, YouTube, accessible at https://www.youtube.com/channel/UCMkfcYouNTa7hccthSooPnQ

13. Macro-influencers: beauty, crime and DIY

1. Eleanor Neale...has 500,000 subscribers: *Eleanor Neale*, YouTube, accessible at https://www.youtube.com/channel/UCFMbX7frWZfuWdjAMLoba-bA

2. watch time on 'shop with me' videos... grew 10 times on mobile in the last two years alone: Think with Google data, accessible at https://www.think-withgoogle.com/data/shop-with-me-youtube-mobile/

3. Neale... spent £1,000 on blushers, mascara and other products for one video: *BIGGEST MAKEUP HAUL ON YOUTUBE 2018?!*, Eleanor Neale, YouTube, accessible at https://www.youtube.com/watch?v=vEBHWK3Q2Jk

4. Neale's beauty video uploads tend to average only 10,000 or 20,000 views. Her mega-haul, however, topped 100,000 views: *Eleanor Neale*, YouTube, accessible at https://www.youtube.com/channel/UCFMbX7frWZfuWd-jAMLobabA

5. it costs £23,000 to get Neale to plug your product... 94% are women, and 65% under the age of 24. One in every eight viewers is aged between 13 and 17: Social Circle data

6. her crime videos generally hit hundreds of thousands of views... her first two dozen videos were almost exclusively about looking good: *Eleanor Neale*, YouTube, accessible at https://www.youtube.com/channel/UCFMbX7frWZ-fuWdjAMLobabA

7. nearly two million tuned in when she swapped her makeup bag with her 12-year-old cousin: *MAKEUP BAG SWAP with a 12 YEAR OLD!*, Eleanor Neale, YouTube, accessible at https://www.youtube.com/watch?v=UqvvEIN9Xyg

8. Lucy Moon... chanced upon a career on YouTube after graduating from university: Interview with Lucy Moon

9. she has grown from 3,000-odd subscribers to 310,000, and her videos are seen by anywhere between 25,000 and 250,000 people: Lucy Moon, YouTube, accessible at https://www.youtube.com/user/meowitslucy

10. priced at £12,000: Social Circle data

11. in a video in early 2019, she admitted she really only feels comfortable endorsing a product that she already loves: *How YouTubers Actually Make Money | Forbes Highest-Paid YouTube Stars 2018 | Lucy Moon*, Lucy Moon, YouTube, accessible at https://www.youtube.com/watch?v=NTKgHAXoP-c

12. Chez Rossi, a 47-year-old living in Darwen: Interview with Chez Rossi

13. Rossi had built a following of 300,000 subscribers on YouTube for his DIY videos: *Ultimate Handyman*, YouTube, accessible at https://www.youtube.com/user/ultimatehandyman

14. in 2004... Rossi started a website: Interview with Chez Rossi

15. Rossi set up his... channel on 22 January 2008: *Ultimate Handyman*, SocialBlade, accessible at https://socialblade.com/youtube/user/ultimatehandyman

16. only around four percent of his total views come from those who have actually asked YouTube to serve them up his videos: Interview with Chez Rossi

17. 70% of millennials saying they log onto the site to learn how to do something new...videos that had 'how-to' in their titles were watched for more than a billion hours: YouTube data supplied by press office

18. Tim Blais...A Capella Science... his video on evolutional development to the tune of Justin Bieber's *'Despacito': 'Evo-Devo (Despacito Biology Parody) | A Capella Science', A Capella Science*, YouTube, accessible at https://www.youtube.com/watch?v=ydqReeTV_vk

19. Laci Green talking about how to have anal sex safely (two million views) or explaining what to do if you have herpes: Laci Green, YouTube, accessible at https://www.youtube.com/watch?v=83lo7OqruJI and https://www.youtube.com/watch?v=yi8AwEnYdPo

20. how to remove a broken bolt from a deep hole racked up five million views: *How to remove a broken bolt in a deep hole | remove broken bolt in recessed hole*, Ultimate Handyman, YouTube, accessible at https://www.youtube.com/watch?v=dJfkCj3FWBs

21. he moved to Cyprus: Interview with Chez Rossi

22. 225,000 people subscribe to... 74-year-old American Peggy Glenn: Granny PottyMouth, YouTube, accessible at https://www.youtube.com/channel/UCGUCiifwWCd_DCroi3nc-vQ/about

23. Glenn uploaded her first YouTube video, sliding down a hill on an inner tube: Interview with Peggy Glenn

24. she shoots her videos in a computer room in front of three shower curtains: Interview with Peggy Glenn

25. a day after the video was uploaded, it had been viewed by just 1,100 people: *Thanks GIVING Love, Granny PottyMouth*, YouTube, accessible at https://www.youtube.com/watch?v=OAiisqdqlaM

14. Micro-influencers: speaking to a devoted audience

1. In February 2014 Eniyah Rana was at a loose end....she wanted to be a flight attendant: Interview with Eniyah Rana

2. the seven-minute video... was filmed as she sat on a dining room chair... the £15 scarf she'd bought from Next: *maxi hijab tutorial, Modest Street*, YouTube,

accessible at https://www.youtube.com/watch?v=gremYjZ-jm8&t=64s

3. 48,000 subscribers on YouTube and 110,000 followers on Instagram: Eniyah Rana social media accounts

4. she has bought a PO box near her home in Birmingham: Interview with Eniyah Rana

5. Rincey Abraham found YouTube an escape from her job. She majored in journalism at Marquette University... and began working part-time as a copywriter: Interview with Rincey Abraham

6. Abraham's first video came out in 2012: *Intro Post, rinceyreads*, YouTube, accessible at https://www.youtube.com/watch?v=03jpcRiNCtQ

7. her 32,000 subscribers: rinceyreads, YouTube, accessible at https://www.youtube.com/user/rinceyreads

8. two videos for *Book Riot*: *Book Riot*, YouTube, accessible at https://www.youtube.com/user/BookRiotVideo

9. an online hardware store in Illinois between 7.30am and 4.30pm: Interview with Rincey Abraham

10. most of her viewers are in their mid-20s, 30s or 40s... more than half are women: Interview with Rincey Abraham

11. Mats Stigzelius... has said: '9% of UK marketing professionals plan to spend £100,000 on influencers', *Digital Marketing Briefing*, accessible at https://digitalmarketingsolutionssummit.co.uk/all/9-uk-marketing-professionals-plan-spend-100000-influencers/

PART IV

BEHIND THE SCENES: SNAPSHOTS

15. Summer in the City: a gathering of influencers

1. Summer in the City... is a three-day summer jamboree for fans and creators: Summer in the City, accessible at https://www.sitc-event.co.uk/

2. around 1,200 people already attended the first day of the 2017 event... around 8,000 people are expected on the second day and slightly fewer on the closing Sunday: Discussions with ExCel and Summer in the City staff

3. 30-page pamphlet... an advert for an upcoming movie, and a handful of Chupa Chups lollies: Summer in the City goody bag

4. VidCon attracts more than 20,000 fans annually in California, and 7,500 to its European outing in Amsterdam: Wired UK story on VidCon Europe

5. HelloWorld!... proved a flop: *Furious parents slam Hello World Live as rip-off after spending more than £200 just to queue for hours*, The Sun, accessible at https://www.thesun.co.uk/news/4801044/hello-world-live-event-parents-complaints/

6. the 150 members of the press are given a pink paper wristband: on-the-ground reporting at Summer in the City

7. yellow speaker/featured creator lanyards get you almost everywhere bar the exclusive YouTube Creators Lounge backstage, for which you need a fabric band: on-the-ground reporting at VidCon London

8. along the length of the 77-foot far wall: ExCel London floor plan, accessible at https://www.excel.london/organiser/venue-spaces/event-halls

9. he founded Summer in the City aged 16 in 2009 as a gathering of 200 YouTubers in Hyde Park in central London: Interview with Tom Burns

10. Burns added one in 2012: Interview with Tom Burns

11. that same year also saw a step change in how YouTube marketed itself: the platform's motto, 'Broadcast Yourself', was dropped from the logo: YouTube, Logopedia, accessible at https://logos.fandom.com/wiki/YouTube

12. both YouTube and Facebook have extensive lounges backstage above the busy show floor: on-the-ground reporting at Summer in the City

16. Collaboration: Sapphire builds a career

1. Sapphire has played Wembley two times. She has brand endorsements and is on a retainer with an American sponsor. And she's been flown out to Germany: Interview with Nick Upshall

2. Sapphire first got the itch for performing when she joined a stage school near London at the age of four. The school had around 80 pupils...draw crowds of 3,000 or more: Interview with Nick Upshall

3. Sapphire performed a song from the Disney musical *Camp Rock* in her front hall: *Sapphire singing This is Me Demi Lovato Camp Rock – 7yrs*, Sapphire, YouTube, accessible at https://www.youtube.com/watch?v=Ly6Lb-eUvPOU

4. most of Sapphire's fans are 13-17-year-olds, and around 70% are girls. However, a significant number fall into the 35-45-year-old demographic: Interview with Nick Upshall

5. Sapphire has been followed around a Claire's Accessories by young fans: Interview with Sapphire

6. Sapphire has uploaded hundreds of videos online, some of which have more than six million individual views: Sapphire, YouTube, accessible at https://www.youtube.com/user/444jet

7. in 2019, she's started testing out medleys, cramming 12 songs into a three-minute video: *Ariana Grande MEDLEY! FULL ALBUM 'Thank u, Next' - ALL 12 SONGS!*, Sapphire, YouTube, accessible at https://www.youtube.com/watch?v=2w40ojOssP4

8. Musical.ly (which has since merged with the all-encompassing super short-form video app, TikTok): *The popular Musical.ly app has been rebranded as TikTok, The Verge,* accessible at https://www.theverge.com/2018/8/2/17644260/musically-rebrand-tiktok-bytedance-douyin

9. Zoomin' TV, a video production company founded in 2000 by two Dutch entrepreneurs in Amsterdam: Zoomin' TV, accessible at http://zoomin.tv/video/#!l/eng_gb/latestvideos

17. Management: Sarah Weichel, star agent

1. Sarah Weichel initially wanted to be a talent manager in the music industry: Interview with Sarah Weichel

2. The Collective (now known as Studio 71): *Collective Digital Studio Rebrands as Studio71, The Hollywood Reporter,* accessible at https://www.hollywoodreporter.com/news/collective-digital-studio-rebrands-as-859844

3. she became one of five people in the digital department in 2011: Interview with Sarah Weichel

4. representing some of the world's biggest YouTubers, including Lilly Singh: Sarah Weichel Management, accessible at https://www.sarahweichelmanagement.com

5. Singh earned an estimated $10.5 million in 2017: *The World's Highest Paid YouTube Stars 2017, Forbes,* accessible at https://www.forbes.com/pictures/5a275d6931358e286471a7e8/the-worlds-highest-paid-y/#5c5118b12583

6. has 14 million subscribers: *IISuperwomanII*, YouTube, accessible at https://www.youtube.com/user/IISuperwomanII

7. she'd be replacing Carson Daly as a late-night TV talk show host: *I'm Getting My Own TV Show!, IISuperwomanII,* YouTube, accessible at https://www.youtube.com/watch?v=9RkJ-67xqwo

8. Weichel also represents Jon Cozart... and *Smosh* co-founder Anthony Padilla: Sarah Weichel Management, accessible at https://www.sarahweichelmanagement.com

9. YouTubers are taking on mini-empires of support staff: *Feeding algorithms*

is a full-time job, BBC Capital, accessible at http://www.bbc.com/capital/story/20190307-the-hidden-armies-that-power-the-internets-new-stars

10. Zoe Sugg... and her boyfriend, Alfie Deyes, have a company, A to Z Creatives, to look after their burgeoning business interests: A to Z Creatives, accessible at https://www.atozcreatives.com/

11. Zoella has 4.8 million subscribers: Zoe Sugg, YouTube, accessible at https://www.youtube.com/user/MoreZoella

12. A to Z Creatives employs a creative manager...and an office manager. (Alfie has his own staff too.): *The Team,* A to Z Creatives, accessible at https://www.atozcreatives.com/

13. ICC Capital Suite rooms 3-4 at the 2019 edition of VidCon held at London's ExCeL conference centre: VidCon London, accessible at https://vidconlondon.com/full-agenda/

14. (real name Patrick Simondac): *Patrick Starrr Reveals How He Went From Makeup-Loving Teen to YouTube Businessman, People,* accessible at https://people.com/social-media-stars/patrick-starrr-bio/#

15. who previously worked at US sandwich chain Panera Bread and on the make-up counter of MAC cosmetics in Orlando: *This Is My Team with Patrick Starrr,* VidCon London, accessible at https://vidconlondon.com/full-agenda/

16. more than four million subscribers and collaborations with supermodels and Hollywood royalty: Patrick Starrr, YouTube, accessible at https://www.youtube.com/channel/UCDHQbU57NZilrhbuZNbQcRA

17. he's walked the red carpet at big mainstream awards ceremonies: *This Is My Team with Patrick Starrr,* VidCon London, accessible at https://vidconlondon.com/full-agenda/

18. Patrick Starrr Inc: accessible at https://vidconlondon.com/people/10265/peter-simondac-business-manager-patrickstarrr-inc/

19. in July 2018 she joined Anonymous Content: *Anonymous Content Taps Sarah Weichel to Lead Emerging Platforms Division (Exclusive), The Hollywood Reporter,* accessible at https://www.hollywoodreporter.com/news/anonymous-content-taps-sarah-weichel-lead-emerging-platforms-group-1126916

20. Hart had just won a Streamy award for best female performance in comedy: *Hannah Hart Wins Best Female Performance: Comedy,* Streamy Awards, accessible at https://www.streamys.org/2013/02/hannah-hart-wins-best-female-performance-comedy/

21. a two-year veteran of the site: MyHarto, YouTube, accessible at https://www.youtube.com/user/MyHarto

22. asking fans to crowdfund the trip... would go on to raise more than

$220,000 in a month: Hello Harto, Indiegogo, accessible at https://www.indiegogo.com/projects/hello-harto#/

23. she, Helbig and Mamrie Hart had been approached by Michael Gold-fine... who wanted to make a movie starring the trio: *YouTube's Holy Trinity Goes to 'Camp Takota'*, *The Daily Beast*, accessible at https://www.thedaily-beast.com/youtubes-holy-trinity-goes-to-camp-takota

24. called *Camp Takota*: *Camp Takota*, accessible at http://www.camptakota.com/

25. in Hart's hotel room, the YouTuber and her manager were deep in thought: Interview with Sarah Weichel

26. YouTube launched YouTube Red: *Red Dawn: An inside look at YouTube's new ad-free subscription service*, *The Verge*, accessible at https://www.theverge.com/2015/10/21/9566973/youtube-red-ad-free-offline-paid-subscription-service

27. (since renamed YouTube Premium): *YouTube Red rebrands as Premium ahead of global rollout*, *Screendaily*, accessible at https://www.screendaily.com/news/youtube-red-rebrands-as-premium-ahead-of-global-roll-out/5129565.article

18. Training camp: with the 11-year-old YouTubers

1. in a villa 20 miles from Madrid: *Inside the "University of YouTube" where children are transformed into YouTubers*, *Wired UK*, accessible at https://www.wired.co.uk/article/become-youtuber-2btube

2. Bastian Manintveld, a long-haired Dutch entrepreneur: Interview with Bastian Manintveld

3. being a YouTuber was the main career option of British youngsters: *Forget being a nurse or doctor, three quarters of today's children would rather be YouTubers and vloggers*, *Daily Mail*, accessible at https://www.dailymail.co.uk/news/article-4532266/75-cent-children-want-YouTubers-vloggers.html

4. YouTube viewing is growing among continental Europeans at a greater rate than the UK: *2018/19 European Social Video Trends Report, Tubular In-sights*, accessible at https://view.pointdrive.linkedin.com/presentations/14c8fe15-0bb4-4db0-99b4-85afd892e7a7?auth=1b28e892-7c02-4409-9c64-34b02452bbd6

5. a survey in Japan in 2017: *Japan's YouTuber Academy Teaches Kids How To Be Better YouTubers*, *Kotaku*, accessible at https://kotaku.com/japans-youtuber-academy-teaches-kids-how-to-be-better-y-1798421158?utm_medium=e-mail&utm_source=flipboard

6. some of the 150 influencers Manintveld's operation represented in 2016 (500 today): interviews with Bastian Manintveld in 2016 and 2019

7. he's a TV man at heart: Interview with Bastian Manintveld

8. Disney had just bought a company specialising in YouTube videos, Maker Studios, for $675 million in 2014: *Inside Disney's troubled $675 mil. Maker Studios acquisition, Digiday*, accessible at https://digiday.com/media/disney-maker-studios/

9. founded five years earlier by a number of early YouTubers: *Lights, Camera, YouTube: Studio Cashes In On An Entertainment Revolution, NPR*, accessible at https://www.npr.org/sections/alltechconsidered/2012/06/18/155300875/lights-camera-youtube-a-new-studio-cashes-in-on-an-entertainment-revolution

10. Manintveld moved quickly and set up 2btube later in 2014: Interview with Bastian Manintveld

11. the hundreds of millions of people who subscribe to 2btube talent: 2btube data published in 2019

12. Francisco de Vitoria University was thrown up quickly in the 1990s: Universidad Francisco de Vitoria website, accessible at https://www.ufv.es/

13. their parents have paid between €650... and €1,705: information published by 2btube in marketing materials for its summer camp

14. Tubers Academy... operating since 2017: Tubers Academy, accessible at http://www.tubers.uk

15. Camp17...held its first events in the United States in summer 2016: Camp17 website, accessible at http://www.gocamp17.com

16. iD Tech Camps: *Digital Video Production: Start a YouTube Channel*, iD Tech Camps, accessible at https://www.idtech.com/courses/digital-video-production-start-a-youtube-channel

17. SocialStar Creator Camp: *Take a trip to Los Angeles' new internet celebrity summer camp, The Verge*, accessible at https://www.theverge.com/2017/7/20/15992846/socialstar-creator-camp-la-teen-internet-celebrity

18. Japan has its own YouTuber Academy: *Japan's YouTuber Academy Teaches Kids How To Be Better YouTubers, Kotaku*, accessible at https://kotaku.com/japans-youtuber-academy-teaches-kids-how-to-be-better-y-1798421158?utm_medium=email&utm_source=flipboard

19. Jonathan Saccone-Joly...1.9 million subscribers: SACCONEJOLYs, YouTube, accessible at https://www.youtube.com/channel/UCxJrnvfqSSvly5hiq2Fe68g

19. YouTube school: with the adult entrepreneurs

1. Mi Elfverson... has lived in New York and London... a former commercial photographer and video director: Interview with Mi Elfverson

2. on the sixth floor of the Hilton Metropole hotel in Brighton: Vlog on the Beach 2016, accessible at http://www.vlogacademy.com/vlog-on-the-beach-2016/

3. the Folkhogskola in Kalix... began classes to teach students how to make YouTube videos in October 2017: *Action! School offers first course on YouTube, The Local*, accessible at https://www.thelocal.se/20170928/action-school-offers-swedens-first-course-in-youtube

4. participants have paid £45 each to attend Elfverson's 'Vlog on the Beach': Vlog on the Beach 2016, accessible at http://www.vlogacademy.com/vlog-on-the-beach-2016/

5. Barrie runs a Chichester-based coffee company: Harrie's Coffee, accessible at http://www.harries-coffee.com/

6. A former accountant... outside Arundel train station: Interview with Heather Barrie

7. a 360-degree viewing platform: British Airways i360, accessible at https://britishairwaysi360.com/

CAUGHT IN THE MACHINE

20. Pranks for views: why Monalisa Perez shot her boyfriend

1. a glistening stud in each ear, and a camera in his right hand: video released by Norman County, Minnesota county attorney

2. the town of Halstad (pop: 597): 2010 US Census data for Halstad, Minnesota

3. in the background was his car, a white Toyota Celica. On the right side of its tail fin was a GoPro camera. On its roof sat a cheap red cushion. And on that red cushion was a gold .50-calibre Desert Eagle pistol :video released by Norman County, Minnesota county attorney and transcript of police interview with Monalisa Perez conducted by Minnesota Department of Public Safety Bureau of Criminal Apprehension (BCA case 2017-467)

4. aged 22... their three-year-old daughter Aleah: transcript of police interview with Monalisa Perez conducted by Minnesota Department of Public Safety Bureau of Criminal Apprehension (BCA case 2017-467)

5. a parenting and family channel called LaMonaLisa: La MonaLisa, YouTube, accessible at https://www.youtube.com/channel/UCYqSxhPHNY-CLnt6pgUq-pJA

6. starting in March 2017, her channel contained videos in which they had pranked each other, with titles such as *WORLDS HOTTEST PEPPER PRANK!! GONE MAJORLY GONE!!* [sic] and *SHE TOOK IT TO [sic] FAR...: La MonaLisa*, YouTube, accessible at https://www.youtube.com/channel/UCYqSxhPHNY-

CLnt6pgUq-pJA (author's note: as explained later in this chapter, Perez has since made those videos filmed with Ruiz private and inaccessible to the general public. Links to the video pages, which are now unavailable, will follow in subsequent end notes).

7. despite the couple's inventiveness, the channel hadn't taken off: its 18 videos had been viewed a total of 8,460 times, averaging just 470 views per video: *La MonaLisa*, SocialBlade, accessible at https://socialblade.com/youtube/c/lamonalisa

8. 'imagine when we have 300,000 subscribers': *DOING SCARY STUNTS AT THE FAIR | PART 1*, La MonaLisa, YouTube, accessible at https://www.youtube.com/watch?v=hr8VlTZMNno

9. he aimed to set up his own channel, calling himself Dammit Boy, because that's what everybody would say when they watched one of his stunts: video released by Norman County, Minnesota county attorney

10. Ruiz had been thinking about it for weeks, begging his girlfriend to help him, and eventually she had given in: transcript of police interview with Monalisa Perez conducted by Minnesota Department of Public Safety Bureau of Criminal Apprehension (BCA case 2017-467)

11. he test fired his pistol at an abandoned house three or four miles away, at one of several books he found there. The book – particularly thick – blocked a bullet: transcript of police interview with Monalisa Perez conducted by Minnesota Department of Public Safety Bureau of Criminal Apprehension (BCA case 2017-467)

12. with a black marker pen he drew a target in the centre of the hardback cover, and an arrow pointing to it, then wrote 'Plz Hit Here': images released by Norman County, Minnesota county attorney

13. Ruiz had just come home from work at BNSF Railways in nearby Hillsboro at 4pm on 26 June 2017 when he decided the time was right: transcript of police interview with Monalisa Perez conducted by Minnesota Department of Public Safety Bureau of Criminal Apprehension (BCA case 2017-467)

14. two video cameras would record the stunt: transcript of police interview with Monalisa Perez conducted by Minnesota Department of Public Safety Bureau of Criminal Apprehension (BCA case 2017-467)

15. 'Me and Pedro are probably going to shoot one of the most dangerous videos ever, HIS idea not MINE.': tweet by Monalisa Perez, accessible at https://twitter.com/MonalisaPerez5/status/879459393145888768

16. 'every vlogger on YouTube starts at 0 subscribers. Believe in what you do!': tweet retweeted by Monalisa Perez, accessible at https://twitter.com/VlogNationInc/status/618518426122784768

17. 'what's up everybody, it's Dammit Boy': video released by Norman County, Minnesota county attorney

18. inch-and-a-half thick: *Woman Who Fatally Shot Dead Boyfriend in YouTube Stunt Pleads Guilty*, New York Times, accessible at https://www. nytimes.com/2017/12/19/us/youtube-shooting-minnesota-guilty-plea. html

19. his heavily-pregnant girlfriend was reluctant: transcript of police interview with Monalisa Perez conducted by Minnesota Department of Public Safety Bureau of Criminal Apprehension (BCA case 2017-467)

20. 'I can't do this babe, I am so scared': transcript of YouTube video released by Minnesota Department of Public Safety Bureau of Criminal Apprehension (BCA case 2017-467)

21. Ruiz reassured her that she would not hurt him as long as she hit the book: transcript of YouTube video released by Minnesota Department of Public Safety Bureau of Criminal Apprehension (BCA case 2017-467)

22. Ruiz recoiled backwards... he said 'Oh shit'... his girlfriend rushed indoors to ring 911: transcript of police interview with Monalisa Perez conducted by Minnesota Department of Public Safety Bureau of Criminal Apprehension (BCA case 2017-467)

23. Curtis Combs, a 36-year-old former US Marine from Kentucky: *Secret Service nabs Pikachu-dressed man at WH*, CNN, accessible at https://edition. cnn.com/2017/10/19/politics/secret-service-white-house-pikachu/index. html

24. Combs 'wanted to become famous and thought jumping the White House fence and posting it to YouTube would make him famous': *Man seeking YouTube fame accused of jumping White House fence dressed as Pokémon's Pikachu*, USA Today, accessible at https://eu.usatoday.com/story/news/ nation-now/2017/10/19/man-seeking-youtube-fame-accused-jumping-white- house-fence-dressed-pokemons-pikachu/782197001/

25. in March 2017, five pranksters snuck into the *BBC*'s New Broadcasting House... gained just 184,000 views in its first seven months: *Sneaking into BBC NEWS Studio! (Invading LIVE TV)*, Carnage, YouTube, accessible at https://www.youtube.com/watch?v=2SSfJDyguKI

26. 'invaded' Facebook's London headquarters: accessible at https://www. youtube.com/watch?v=2IQzo2vkHE4

27. Fake Hand Ass Pinch Prank: *Fake Hand Ass Pinch Prank*, Anon Anonymous, YouTube, accessible at https://www.youtube.com/watch?v=qUSMSyr_oQE

28. Sex vlogger Laci Green... wrote Pepper an open letter, which was co-signed by 63 other YouTubers: *An Open Letter to Sam Pepper*, Tumblr, accessible at http://lacigreen.tumblr.com/post/98083811325/an-open-letter-to-sam-pepper

29. the Vlogbrothers banned Pepper from appearing at VidCon: Hank Green, Twitter, accessible at https://twitter.com/hankgreen/status/513776219574530048

30. Pepper later claimed his video was a "social experiment": *Sam Pepper Apology – 'Social Experiment', StopSam*, YouTube, accessible at https://www.youtube.com/watch?v=lBWnuYaGDJo

31. Heather and Mike Martin... garnered more than three-quarters of a million subscribers to their videos: YouTube has since deleted their channel

32. 'it started out as family fun,' Mike, the children's father, told *Good Morning America*: *Parents speak out about backlash over YouTube prank videos: 'We were going for shock value', ABC News*, accessible at https://abcnews.go.com/Lifestyle/parents-speak-backlash-youtube-prank-videos-shock/story?id=47072871

33. the Martins were sentenced in a Maryland county circuit court in September 2017 to five years probation for two counts of child neglect, and lost custody of their children: *YouTube star DaddyOFive and wife get probation for controversial video 'pranks' on kids, USA Today*, accessible at https://eu.usatoday.com/story/news/nation-now/2017/09/14/youtube-star-daddyofive-and-wife-get-probation-controversial-video-pranks-kids/665084001/

34. the sentence was reduced in January 2019, though the judge retained a probation condition preventing the couple from uploading new videos: *Dad and stepmom who were convicted of child neglect over cruel DaddyOFive YouTube 'prank' channel get their five-year probation REDUCED, The Daily Mail*, accessible at https://www.dailymail.co.uk/news/article-6580169/DaddyOFive-YouTube-couple-sentence-reduction-child-neglect.html

35. YouTube finally deactivated their ability to upload in 2018: *YouTube takes down controversial 'FamilyOFive' channel, New York Post*, accessible at https://nypost.com/2018/07/18/youtube-takes-down-controversial-family-ofive-channel/

36. on 7 December 2017, they uploaded a video called I cemented my head in a microwave and emergency services came.. (nearly died): *I cemented my head in a microwave and emergency services came.. (nearly died), TGFBro*, YouTube, accessible at https://www.youtube.com/watch?v=iY8gvu6h2Hc

37. five firefighters... the West Midlands Fire Service tweeted: 'We're seriously unimpressed.': West Midlands Fire Service, Twitter, accessible at https://twitter.com/westmidsfire/status/938831999770521600?lang=en

38. within 13 hours of being uploaded, the video was viewed 850,000 times. Within two days, two million people had seen it, with 25,000 leaving comments: *I cemented my head in a microwave and emergency services came.. (nearly died), TGFBro*, YouTube, accessible at https://www.youtube.com/watch?v=iY8gvu6h2Hc

39. it earned up to $8,000 from the video in its first two days online... another 17,247 subscribed: TGFBro, SocialBlade, accessible at https://socialblade. com/youtube/channel/UCOgUcv_9DaivXzsN9mcHIzQ

40. 'I think this shit's hilarious': *My Response.. (I cemented my head in a microwave), TGFBro*, YouTube, accessible at https://www.youtube.com/ watch?v=-47sqwkLEtk

41. 1,887 in 2013 to 3,172 in 2017: data gathered via Freedom of Information requests from UK police forces

42. West Yorkshire Police recorded 406 incidents in 2018: data gathered via Freedom of Information requests from UK police forces

43. Crazy Sumit, an Indian YouTuber, has 612,000 subscribers: *The Crazy Sumit*, YouTube, accessible at https://www.youtube.com/channel/UCsYka-wkbODbRl2hB-6Txm_g

44. Poli asked nearly 3,000 British adults whether they thought YouTubers are good role models for children. Half said they aren't... those same people were asked who is responsible for the content of videos: polling of 2,965 people by Poli, commissioned for this book

45. caused YouTube to crack down significantly... dangerous challenges and pranks... were banned from the platform in January 2019, with a two-month grace period: *YouTube's prank ban deepens the expanding rift with its creators, Wired UK*, accessible at https://www.wired.co.uk/article/youtube-prank-ban

46. in the first half of 2018, YouTube started to age-restrict Swingler and Henry's videos: Interview with Jay Swingler

47. Pedro Ruiz III... bled out through a bullet-hole: transcript of police interview with Monalisa Perez conducted by Minnesota Department of Public Safety Bureau of Criminal Apprehension (BCA case 2017-467)

48. Monalisa Perez... was charged with second-degree manslaughter, and sentenced to 180 days in jail: *Woman jailed for fatally shooting boyfriend in botched YouTube stunt, USA Today*, accessible at https://eu.usatoday.com/ story/tech/nation-now/2018/03/15/woman-jailed-fatally-shooting-boyfriend-botched-youtube-stunt/427423002/

49. three months after she shot her boyfriend, her account was stuck at 21,942 subscribers: *La MonaLisa*, YouTube, accessible at https://www. youtube.com/channel/UCYqSxhPHNYCLnt6pgUq-pJA

50. on 31 July 2018... she hid all the videos from her past life... and uploaded a new video entitled *Something to say...*: *Something to say..., La MonaLisa*, YouTube, accessible at https://www.youtube.com/watch?v=iKGGElNrAKM&t=357s

51. her son Rayden... was approaching his first birthday. She had found a

new boyfriend: *Something to say...*, *La MonaLisa*, YouTube, accessible at https://www.youtube.com/watch?v=iKGGElNrAKM&t=357s

52. she posted a vlog titled *THINGS AREN'T JUST EASY: 'THINGS AREN'T JUST EASY | Vlog 007*, *La MonaLisa*, YouTube, accessible at https://www.youtube.com/watch?v=ykUluQ-vBjw&t=243s

53. she gets a couple of thousand views a day now: *La MonaLisa*, SocialBlade, accessible at https://socialblade.com/youtube/channel/UCYqSxhPHNY-CLnt6pgUq-pJA

21. Authenticity: the fourth wall for YouTubers

1. she became the most followed individual on *YouTube: The History of the YouTube Most Subscribed – Visualized*, *Imgur*, accessible at https://imgur.com/gallery/soDTn

2. claimed that she was being targeted by a mysterious group called The Order: *The Order*, *LGPedia*, accessible at http://www.lg15.com/lgpedia/index.php?title=The_Order

3. the *Los Angeles Times* revealed that Avery... was not a real person... she was a 19-year-old actress, Jessica Lee Rose, who had been hired by... media company EQAL: *Lonelygirl15 Video Blog Is Brainchild of 3 Filmmakers*, *Los Angeles Times*, accessible at http://webcache.googleusercontent.com/search?q=cache:_Xye5TMI-ZgJ:articles.latimes.com/2006/sep/13/local/me-lonelygir13+&cd=3&hl=en&ct=clnk&gl=uk&client=firefox-b-d

4. they were snapped up by Creative Artists Agency: *Lonelygirl15: how one mysterious vlogger changed the internet*, *The Guardian*, accessible at https://www.theguardian.com/technology/2016/jun/16/lonelygirl15-bree-video-blog-youtube

5. as Tyler Oakley... seven million subscribers, told *Time* magazine: *Tyler Oakley on How He Became a Social-Media Star: 'It's Not in My Interest to Change Who I Am'*, *Time*, accessible at http://time.com/4074927/tyler-oakley-binge/

6. structured reality TV programmes... have been phenomenally popular: *The Reality Principle*, *The New Yorker*, accessible at https://www.newyorker.com/magazine/2011/05/09/the-reality-principle

7. Facebook now has more than 2.3 billion monthly active users: *In 15 years Facebook has amassed 2.3 billion users*, *Business Insider*, accessible at https://www.businessinsider.com/facebook-has-2-billion-plus-users-after-15-years-2019-2?r=US&IR=T

8. YouTube has topped 1.9 billion monthly logged-in users: YouTube for Press, accessible at https://www.youtube.com/intl/en-GB/yt/about/press/

9. Instagram has more than one billion users: *Instagram hits 1 billion monthly*

315

users, up from 800M in September, TechCrunch, accessible at https://tech-crunch.com/2018/06/20/instagram-1-billion-users/

10. mourners share funeral selfies on Snapchat or Facebook: *'Stop taking selfies at funerals' say funeral directors, The Telegraph*, accessible at https://www.telegraph.co.uk/news/2017/02/08/stop-taking-selfies-funerals-say-fu-neral-directors/

11. brought the camera with her into the shower as part of a Paris travelogue: *I Took Myself To Paris | 168 Hours | Lucy Moon*, Lucy Moon, YouTube, accessible at https://www.youtube.com/watch?v=XWEsZCVbmto

12. Maximiliane Frobenius of the University of Hildesheim found that You-Tubers insert vocal phrases and terms into their monologues in order to cajole viewers into interacting with them: *Audience design in monologues: How vloggers involve their viewers, Journal of Pragmatics*, accessible at https://doi.org/10.1016/j.pragma.2014.02.008

13. parasocial relationship – a definition coined in 1956 by Donald Horton and Richard Wohl: *Mass Communication and Para-Social Interaction: Observations on Intimacy at a Distance, Psychiatry*, accessible at https://www.tandfon-line.com/doi/abs/10.1080/00332747.1956.11023049

14. Chih-Ping Chen... described YouTube: *Forming digital self and parasocial relationships on YouTube, Journal of Consumer Culture*, accessible at https://journals.sagepub.com/doi/abs/10.1177/1469540514521081?journalCode=joca

15. a study of German YouTube viewers... concluded that the bonds between fan and creator where neither deep and emotional nor hierarchical: *YouTube celebrities and parasocial interaction: Using feedback channels in mediatized relationships, Convergence*, accessible at https://journals.sagepub.com/doi/abs/10.1177/1354856517736976

16. watch time on videos where creators let viewers into their morning routines has more than trebled between June 2016 and June 2018: *Trending now on YouTube: Halloween, morning and nighttime routines, and holiday travel planning*, Think with Google, accessible at https://www.thinkwithgoogle.com/advertising-channels/video/october-youtube-trends/

17. 57% of people said they believed Jennifer Lawrence was authentic; just 14% said they thought her inauthentic... 22% of people told the pollsters they thought Zoella was authentic: YouGov survey of 1,625 British adults commissioned for YouTubers, 13-14 December 2017

18. a money-grabbing advent calendar: *Zoella's £50 advent calendar has goods in it worth just £20, The Sun*, accessible at https://www.thesun.co.uk/fabu-lous/4904545/zoellas-50-advent-calendar-goods-20/

19. Will Smith has his YouTube channel: Will Smith, YouTube, accessible at https://www.youtube.com/channel/UCKuHFYu3smtrl2AwwMOXOlg

20. Jack Black plays games on YouTube: JablinskiGames, YouTube, accessible at https://www.youtube.com/channel/UCuriCa9loP_OsH75_5j8M5w

22. Burnout: Slaves to the algorithm

1. Kay (real name Olga Karavayeva) was discussing how best to break into showbusiness with some of her friends. She was a professional juggler with the Ringling Brothers circus: Interview with Olga Karavayeva

2. at first she thought they said U2.com: Interview with Olga Karavayeva

3. Lisa Donovan... eventually founded Maker Studios: *Lights, Camera, YouTube: Studio Cashes In On An Entertainment Revolution*, *NPR*, accessible at https://www.npr.org/sections/alltechconsidered/2012/06/18/155300875/lights-camera-youtube-a-new-studio-cashes-in-on-an-entertainment-revolution

4. filming videos from smoke-filled airport departure lounges in eastern Europe: *Moscow Airport*, Olga Kay, YouTube, accessible at https://www.youtube.com/watch?v=YxA63Ab-7G4&t=85s

5. by 2008, around two years into her time on YouTube, she had managed to build up a following of around 50,000 people: Interview with Olga Karavayeva

6. a tactic that Taylor Lorenz of *The Atlantic* has flagged up: *Rising Instagram Stars Are Posting Fake Sponsored Content*, *The Atlantic*, accessible at https://www.theatlantic.com/technology/archive/2018/12/influencers-are-faking-brand-deals/578401/

7. Ford was among the first... picking Kay as one of 100 YouTube influencers driving its cars across the country: Interview with Olga Karavayeva

8. a feature in the *New York Times* in 2014... she was producing more than 20 videos a week in return for around $100,000 a year: *Chasing Their Star, on YouTube*, *New York Times*, accessible at https://www.nytimes.com/2014/02/02/business/chasing-their-star-on-youtube.html

9. she had some help managing her channels from one or two other people she had hired: Interview with Olga Karavayeva

10. Buckley has left YouTube and returned time and again: Interview with Michael Buckley

11. Michelle Phan... joined the site in 2007: *Natural Looking Makeup Tutorial*, Michelle Phan, YouTube, accessible at https://www.youtube.com/watch?v=OB8nfJCOIeE

12. became the official make-up artist for the French beauty brand Lancome: *Michelle Phan first-ever YouTuber to be hired as beauty brand's 'video makeup*

artist', The Independent, accessible at https://www.independent.co.uk/life-style/fashion/news/michelle-phan-first-ever-youtuber-to-be-hired-as-beauty-brands-video-makeup-artist-1897709.html

13. L'Oreal released a range of cosmetics under her name: *L'Oréal Ends Beauty Deal With Michelle Phan*, *Refinery29*, accessible at https://www.refinery29.com/en-us/2015/10/95607/michelle-phan-loreal-split

14. Phan launched a multi-channel network: *Michelle Phan goes beyond YouTube with Icon multi-channel network*, *The Guardian*, accessible at https://www.theguardian.com/technology/2015/apr/01/michelle-phan-youtube-icon-endemol-beyond

15. a make-up subscription box service: Ipsy, accessible at https://www.ipsy.com

16. she published a book: *Make Up: Your Life Guide to Beauty, Style, and Success--Online and Off* by Michelle Phan

17. raised hundreds of millions of dollars in funding: *Michelle Phan's Makeup Subscription Service Raises $100 Million*, *Recode*, accessible at https://www.recode.net/2015/9/14/11618526/michelle-phans-makeup-subscription-service-raises-100-million

18. eight million subscribers followed her tips and advice: Michelle Phan, YouTube, accessible at https://www.youtube.com/michellephan

19. in July 2016 she posted a video providing advice about hair removal: *Mastering the Art of Hair Removal*, Michelle Phan, YouTube, accessible at https://www.youtube.com/watch?v=1-31plMisJ4

20. almost a year later she tried to explain: *Why I Left*, Michelle Phan, YouTube, accessible at https://www.youtube.com/watch?v=UuGpm01SPcA

21. the British vlogger said in a blog on her website in September 2017: *The Importance Of Self-Care Online*, accessible at https://iamlucymoon.com/importance-online-self-care/

22. I chaired a mental health panel with four big YouTubers: Let's Talk About Mental Health, VidCon London 2019

23. Hanna, who has 6.5 million subscribers: Gabbie Hanna, YouTube, accessible at https://www.youtube.com/channel/UCfBpv6ahDMg7kEClQuMpzzw

24. Laci Green... started making videos at the age of 19... while studying for an undergraduate degree in law, social sciences and education at the University of California, Berkeley: *Well Positioned*, *The Magazine*, accessible at https://books.google.co.uk/books?id=EFlfCgAAQBAJ&pg=PT643&lpg=PT643&dq=the+magazine+laci+green+chris+stokel-walker&source=bl&ots=Gd853gooVE&sig=ACfU3U225PrWEiVeiCzLtPK4jdmQr41mF-w&hl=en&sa=X&ved=2ahUKEwio68TVya_

25. Charlie McDonnell admitted to his fans he had stepped away from YouTube: Charlie McDonnell, Twitter, accessible at https://twitter.com/coollike/status/1103386836242702338

26. I watched her YouTube channel in the months since: Laci Green, YouTube, accessible at https://www.youtube.com/user/lacigreen/videos

27. from a maximum time of three to four minutes to 10-12 minutes: Interview with Matt Gielen

28. in 2015 the number of videos by individual creators more than 20 minutes long… was 6.3 million. Three years later, it had more than doubled: Tubular Insights data provided exclusively for this book

23. Fanatical fans: obsessive relationships

1. Christina Grimmie was a fan of… Hannah Montana: *Inside the Inspiring Life and Still Bizarre Death of Singer Christina Grimmie, E! News*, accessible at https://www.eonline.com/uk/news/1022095/inside-the-inspiring-life-and-still-bizarre-death-of-singer-christina-grimmie

2. aged 15 in 2009, Grimmie uploaded one of her first tracks to YouTube: *Me Singing 'Party in the USA' by Miley Cyrus*, Christina Grimmie, YouTube, accessible at https://www.youtube.com/watch?v=Mcj_Iitf9w4

3. in 2011 she released her first EP: *Find Me* by Christina Grimmie

4. then moved to Los Angeles… in 2014 she came third in the US talent show *The Voice*: *Christina Grimmie: thousands say farewell to slain Voice singer, The Guardian*, accessible at https://www.theguardian.com/world/2016/jun/18/christina-grimmie-thousands-say-farewell-to-slain-voice-singer

5. on 10 June 2016 after a concert in Orlando, Florida, Grimmie held a meet and greet for her fans: *The Voice star Christina Grimmie 'greeted killer with arms open for a hug' before being shot and killed after Orlando concert, The Telegraph*, accessible at https://www.telegraph.co.uk/news/2016/06/11/voice-star-christina-grimmie-dies-after-shooting-at-florida-conc/

6. one of them was Kevin James Loibl, a 27-year-old from nearby St Petersburg… arrived with two handguns and a hunting knife… Loibl shot her four times, then turned the gun on himself: *'Voice' singer Christina Grimmie's shooter identified, USA Today*, accessible at https://eu.usatoday.com/story/life/music/2016/06/11/voice-singer-christina-grimmie-shot-killed-orlando-concert/85741008/

7. the gunman had shown an 'unrealistic infatuation' with Grimmie: Orlando Police Department handout, accessible at http://i2.cdn.turner.com/cnn/2016/images/06/22/grimmie.investigative.supplement.pdf

8. John Lennon was assassinated in 1980: *John Lennon's killer says he feels*

'more and more shame' every year, Associated Press, accessible at https://www. theguardian.com/music/2018/nov/15/mark-david-chapman-john-lennon-killer-parole-hearing-transcript-shame

9. Gianni Versace in 1997: *Why Did Andrew Cunanan Go on a Killing Spree? American Crime Story Explores His Motives, Harper's Bazaar,* accessible at https://www.harpersbazaar.com/culture/film-tv/a15924270/why-did-andrew-cunanan-kill-gianni-versace/

10. more than a quarter of people aged 18-24 told the pollsters asking them for this book that they knew KSI well: YouGov survey of 1,625 British adults commissioned for YouTubers, 13-14 December 2017

11. 47% of millennials admitted in an Ipsos Connect survey that YouTube improved their mood or health: Ipsos Connect survey, accessible at https://www.thinkwithgoogle.com/data-gallery/detail/YouTube-millennial-marketing-trends/

12. in January 2019 the centre of Britain's second-biggest city was brought to a standstill when... James Charles appeared at... Birmingham's Bullring shopping centre: *Birmingham brought to standstill by YouTuber James Charles, The Guardian,* accessible at https://www.theguardian.com/uk-news/2019/jan/27/birmingham-brought-to-standstill-after-visit-from-youtuber-james-charles

13. a three-year-veteran of YouTube about to enter his 20s, Charles has more than 14 million subscribers who he calls sisters: James Charles, YouTube, accessible at https://www.youtube.com/channel/UCucot-Zp428OwkyRm2I7v2Q

14. eight thousand people poured into Birmingham to see him, many driven by their parents: *Why I waited four hours to catch a glimpse of YouTuber James Charles, The Telegraph,* accessible at https://www.telegraph.co.uk/technology/2019/01/30/waited-four-hours-catch-glimpse-youtuber-james-charles/

15. during the worst traffic jams at 2pm on the day, what would normally be a 15-minute bus journey took 75 minutes: Thomas Forth, Twitter, accessible at https://twitter.com/thomasforth/status/1089500646137647105

16. Tahj Deondre Speight decided to break into Paul's $7 million home in the San Fernando Valley: *Logan Paul Trespasser Sentenced to 45 Days Behind Bars, The Blast,* accessible at https://theblast.com/logan-paul-trespasser-sentenced-jail/

17. when the YouTuber returned home... at around 10pm... uploaded to Paul's YouTube channel: *I ARRESTED THE GUY WHO BROKE INTO MY HOUSE... IN MY HOUSE...,* Logan Paul, YouTube, accessible at https://www.youtube.com/watch?v=nWqorQsLndY

18. police confirmed the incident actually happened: *Police Confirm Logan Paul Really Did Citizen's Arrest an Intruder. Here's Who He Collared., The Daily Beast,* accessible at https://www.thedailybeast.com/police-confirm-logan-

paul-really-did-citizens-arrest-an-intruder-heres-who-he-collared

19. British newspapers... mocked the news that vlogger Joe Sugg was a contestant on... Strictly Come Dancing: *Joe Sugg might be a cynical ratings ploy, but he could change Strictly forever, The Telegraph,* accessible at https://www.telegraph.co.uk/tv/0/strictly-come-vlogging-joe-sugg-could-change-strictly-forever/ and Katie Deacon, Twitter, accessible at https://twitter.com/Curly_Katie/status/1029327676669128705

20. four months later, Sugg was in the final... because of a dedicated following who voted for him... some 30 or 40 times every week: *Strictly Come Dancing' Bosses Speak Out After Joe Sugg's Fans Attempt To Find Voting "Loophole", Huffington Post,* accessible at https://www.huffingtonpost.co.uk/entry/strictly-come-dancing-joe-sugg-fans-loophole

21. in 2017 Deyes told *The Telegraph* that he and his girlfriend face daily intrusions into their lives: *YouTube vlogging sensation Alfie Deyes: 'There's a very fine line between me filming my life and me living my life',* The Telegraph, accessible at https://www.telegraph.co.uk/men/thinking-man/youtube-vlogging-sensation-alfie-deyes-fine-line-filming-life/

22. major personalities on the site began bumping up their personal protection: Interview with Anthony D'Angelo

23. VidCon that year made major security changes to keep the talent attending the event safe: *Vidcon Enacts Drastic Security Changes In Wake Of Christina Grimmie's Death, Deadline,* accessible at https://deadline.com/2016/06/christina-grimmie-vidcon-orlando-massacre-1201772101/

PART VI

THE BATTLE FOR CONTROL

24. YouTubers found a union

1. for five years after she signed up with *MyDamnChannel*...Grace Helbig... uploaded more than 1,500 videos: *The Stars of YouTube Rewind 2012: Where Are They Now?,* Tubefilter, accessible at https://www.tubefilter.com/2017/12/21/youtube-rewind-2012-where-are-they-now/

2. DailyGrace... gained nearly two and a half million subscribers: *Grace Helbig's Digital Path to Fame, New York Times,* accessible at https://www.nytimes.com/2014/11/16/arts/.../grace-helbigs-digital-path-to-fame.html

3. Helbig's contract with *MyDamnChannel* gave her little say over the videos she posted... she explained to fellow YouTubers Rhett and Link later: *Episode 52 – Grace Helbig, Ear Biscuits,* accessible at https://soundcloud.com/earbiscuits/ep-52-grace-helbig-ear-biscuits

4. Helbig was on a simple salary for her channel: *Episode 52 – Grace Helbig,*

Ear Biscuits, accessible at https://soundcloud.com/earbiscuits/ep-52-grace-helbig-ear-biscuits

5. in December 2013, she posted a final video to DailyGrace: *SEE YOU NEXT YEAR*, *DailyGrace*, YouTube, accessible at https://www.youtube.com/watch?v=03IZQKy7DTo

6. MyDamnChannel announced that Helbig had elected not to renew her contract: *Grace Helbig Is Leaving My Damn Channel and 'Daily Grace' in 2014*, Tubefilter, accessible at https://www.tubefilter.com/2013/12/31/my-damn-channel-daily-grace-helbig/

7. Helbig's brother Tim posted on Twitter: Tim Helbig, Twitter, accessible at https://twitter.com/RaginBotanist/status/418858885944836098

8. within a month, Grace Helbig had more than a million subscribers. Now she has three million: Grace Helbig, YouTube, accessible at https://www.youtube.com/user/graciehinabox/videos

9. her own channel has shed 10% of its 2.2 million viewers since she left: DailyGrace, YouTube, accessible at https://www.youtube.com/user/dailygrace/

10. it was Helbig's experiences – and those of other YouTubers... that inspired the Green brothers to set up an industry union: Interview with Hank and John Green

11. replaced by Anthony D'Angelo: *ICG Announces New Executive Director*, *Internet Creators Guild*, *Medium*, accessible at https://medium.com/@internetcreatorsguild/icg-announces-new-executive-director-da71b-468de56

12. Sam Mollaei is a Californian lawyer who advises YouTubers... around a tenth of his caseload is focused on YouTube: Interview with Sam Mollaei

13. the November 2018 closure of *Defy Media*, an American MCN which left 50 creators among the talent it represented... owed a combined $1.7 million: *Multi-channel YouTube network Defy Media left 50 creators out of $1.7 million after closing*, 9to5 Google, accessible at https://9to5google.com/2019/01/29/youtube-defy-media-network-creators/

14. *Smosh* was bought by Mythical Entertainment... in February 2019: *the rumors are true... WE FOUND A HOME!*, Smosh, accessible at https://www.youtube.com/watch?v=NT4Pt8QWF5k

15. people can now earn a five-figure income from 100,000 subscribers: Interview with Sam Mollaei

25. Patreon: seeking independent support

1. in spring 2017... YouTube lost advertising clients because it promoted their brands against extremist and offensive content: *Google's bad week: YouTube loses millions as advertising row reaches US*, The Guardian, accessible at https://www.theguardian.com/technology/2017/mar/25/google-youtube-advertising-extremist-content-att-verizon

2. some YouTubers saw their ad revenue drop by 80%: Interview with Laura Chernikoff

3. Patreon was co-founded in May 2013 by Jack Conte of the band Pomplamoose, when they received a YouTube AdSense cheque for the million views... around $150: Interview with Tyler Sean Palmer

4. the company's first employee: Interview with Tyler Sean Palmer

5. half those who had joined the nascent site were YouTubers looking to earn additional funds... accounts for only one in three people... average of $12 a month: Interview with Tyler Sean Palmer

6. valuing the firm at $450 million: *Patreon raises big round at ~$450M valuation to get artists paid*, TechCrunch, accessible at https://techcrunch.com/2017/09/14/patreon-series-c/

7. in 2019, 100,000 creators on Patreon are receiving money from more than three million patrons, and the site expects to pay them $500 million: *Patreon Now Has Over 3 Million Patrons, Expects to Pay $500M to Creators in 2019*, Variety, accessible at https://variety.com/2019/digital/news/patreon-3-million-patrons-500-million-dollar-payout-1203114979/

8. in a blog post in May 2017... Sean Baeyens... appealed to YouTubers: *9 Ways to Make Money on YouTube Without Ads*, Patreon, accessible at https://blog.patreon.com/make-money-youtube-2017

9. DeFranco first uploaded videos... at university in Carolina: Philip DeFranco, YouTube, accessible at https://www.youtube.com/user/sxephil

10. he is senior vice president of his own company, Phil DeFranco Networks and Merchandise: *Philip DeFranco goes from Web host to network exec, Los Angeles Times*, accessible at http://webcache.googleusercontent.com/search?q=cache:x8v6Gf-pReMJ:articles.latimes.com/2013/may/30/business/la-fi-ct-discovery-defranco-20130530+&cd=14&hl=en&ct=clnk&gl=uk&client=firefox-b-d

11. his YouTube channels have more than 7.5 million subscribers: YouTube data

12. DeFranco has publicly estimated his annual income... as ranging between $100,000 and $250,000 a year: DeFranco has varied estimates of his income – accessible at https://www.tubefilter.com/2012/02/10/phil-de-

franco-pays-himself-100k-a-year/ and https://www.suicidegirls.com/girls/
nicole_powers/blog/2680080/philip-defranco-is-sxephil/

13. *People Outraged Over Now-Deleted Video* and *The Trump 'Witch Hunt' Rabbit
Hole: People Outraged Over Now-Deleted Video* and *The Trump 'Witch Hunt'
Rabbit Hole*, Philip DeFranco, YouTube, accessible at https://www.youtube.
com/watch?v=8q9_y16ckLA

14. DeFranco shared the mature demographics of his viewership: Phil De-
Franco, Twitter, accessible at https://twitter.com/PhillyD/
status/865562891126059010

15. Patreon had set up his Patreon page a couple of weeks before... 8,000
people pledged him money... today around 10,000 people fund DeFranco...
the 12th-most popular Patreon project, and is earning at least $26,000 every
month: Phil DeFranco, Graphtreon, accessible at https://graphtreon.com/
creator/DeFranco

16. fewer than one percent of YouTubers used its own abortive attempt at a
Patreon-style monthly subscription service... after its launch in 2013... in
September 2017 YouTube announced it was expanding its Sponsorships
programme: *YouTube Kills Paid Channels, Expands $4.99 per Month Sponsorship
Model, Variety*, accessible at https://variety.com/2017/digital/news/youtube-
kills-paid-channels-1202563599/

17. Revver's early attempts to reward creators directly in 2006: Interview
with Ian Clarke

18. in December 2017, it shifted the responsibility for paying transaction
fees: *We're Updating Patreon's Fee Structure. Here's Why.*, Patreon, accessible at
https://blog.patreon.com/updating-patreons-fee-structure

19. Patreon backed down: *We messed up. We're sorry, and we're not rolling out
the fees change.*, Patreon, accessible at https://blog.patreon.com/not-rolling-
out-fees-change

20. YouTube introduced new rules: *YouTube is cracking down on external links
in videos, Engadget*, accessible at https://www.engadget.com/2017/09/29/
youtube-links-end-cards-new-requirements/

21. seen by 160,000 subscribers: *Innuendo Studios*, YouTube, accessible at
https://www.youtube.com/c/InnuendoStudios

22. Danskin helps fund his essays... through Patreon: *Innuendo Studios*,
Patreon, accessible at https://www.patreon.com/InnuendoStudios

23. he tweeted: Ian Danskin, Twitter, accessible at https://twitter.com/Innu-
endoStudios/status/913507983610580992

24. he published a 22-minute video called *We Don't Talk About Kenny: Telltale's
Walking Dead: We Don't Talk About Kenny: Telltale's Walking Dead Season 2*,

Innuendo Studios, YouTube, accessible at https://www.youtube.com/watch?v=vGlI2Sv9SNs

25. for six months it did nothing outstanding... the numbers of views shot up: Interview with Ian Danskin

26. Susan Wojcicki, described the platform as 'an ecosystem between advertisers and creators and users': *Full transcript: YouTube CEO Susan Wojcicki on Recode Decode, Recode*, accessible at https://www.recode.net/2017/10/27/16560868/transcript-youtube-ceo-susan-wojcicki-video-recode-decode

26. Merchandise: From books to pop sockets

1. in its first week in the UK, 78,109 copies were sold, the biggest ever first-week sales figures for a first-time author: *Zoella and publishers confirm that Girl Online was ghostwritten, The Telegraph*, accessible at https://www.telegraph.co.uk/books/girl-online/zoella-girl-online-ghostwritten-zoe-sugg/

2. Sugg relied on a ghostwriter to write the book: *Zoella and publishers confirm that Girl Online was ghostwritten, The Telegraph*, accessible at https://www.telegraph.co.uk/books/girl-online/zoella-girl-online-ghostwritten-zoe-sugg/

3. 'told in Zoe's relatable, fresh and engaging voice': *YouTube star takes online break as she admits novel was 'not written alone', The Guardian*, accessible at https://www.theguardian.com/books/2014/dec/08/zoella-bestselling-girl-online-written-siobhan-curham-zoe-sugg

4. between £7,000 and £8,000: *Zoella under pressure to reveal whether Girl Online was ghostwritten, The Telegraph*, accessible at https://www.telegraph.co.uk/news/celebritynews/11278379/Zoella-under-pressure-to-reveal-whether-Girl-Online-was-ghostwritten.html

5. a second book in the *Girl Online* series was published in October 2015: *Girl Online: On Tour* by Zoe Sugg

6. *Cordially Invited* – a vapid guide to celebrating Christmas – was published in October 2018: *Cordially Invited: A Seasonal Guide to Celebrations and Hosting, Perfect for Festive Planning, Crafting and Baking in the Run Up to Christmas!* by Zoe Sugg

7. Deyes wrote his first book in 2014: *The Pointless Book: Started by Alfie Deyes, finished by you* by Alfie Deyes

8. it sold 30,000 copies in its first two weeks: *Alfie Deyes: Prince Pointless hits the spot for YouTube kids, The Sunday Times*, accessible at https://www.the-times.co.uk/article/alfie-deyes-prince-pointless-hits-the-spot-for-youtube-kids-f27kqxvmsk2

9. 'a two volume non-extravaganza': *Zoella and the YouTubers: they let us write*

pointless books!, *The Guardian*, accessible at https://www.theguardian.com/books/2015/dec/01/zoella-youtube-books-pewdiepie-tyler-oakley-dan-phil-jamie-curry-alfie-deyes

10. sold more than 600,000 copies, making nearly £4 million in sales. The first book was on *The Sunday Times* bestseller list for 11 straight weeks: *Blink to publish another Pointless Book from Deyes, The Bookseller*, accessible at https://www.thebookseller.com/news/blink-publish-vlogger-alfie-deyes-pointless-book-3-485081

11. a London book signing at Waterstones had to be abandoned after thousands more fans than expected turned up: *My First Book Signing!*, Alfie Deyes Vlogs, accessible at https://www.youtube.com/watch?v=FhHaZf41OyU

12. the two Pointless Books still sell more than a thousand copies per week: *Blink to publish another Pointless Book from Deyes, The Bookseller*, accessible at https://www.thebookseller.com/news/blink-publish-vlogger-alfie-deyes-pointless-book-3-485081

13. in July 2017... Gleam Futures... announced it was setting up its own book agency, Gleam Titles, poaching staff from established publisher Simon & Schuster: *Gleam Futures launches literary division, The Bookseller*, accessible at https://www.thebookseller.com/news/gleam-futures-launches-literary-division-digital-writers-583951

14. the Sidemen book rocketed to the top of the UK non-fiction book charts, selling 26,346 copies in its first three days... had outsold Jamie Oliver... and the diaries of Alan Bennett: *YouTube stars the Sidemen are frontrunners in race for Christmas books No 1, The Guardian*, accessible at https://www.theguardian.com/books/2016/oct/26/youtube-stars-the-sidemen-are-frontrunners-in-race-for-books-christmas-no-1

15. on Super Thursday 2015... Dan Howell and Phil Lester, better known as simply Dan and Phil, sold 26,744: Nielsen Bookscan press release, accessible at http://www.nielsenbookscan.co.uk/press.php?release_id=114

16. Boots released the 12 Days of Christmas Advent Calendar... a packet of confetti, two cookie cutters (one of which seemed to cost 77p to buy individually), seven stickers, two candles, a pen, a key ring, a notepad and a room spray, plus a bag: Zoella 12 Days of Christmas Advent Calendar, Boots, accessible at https://www.boots.com/zoella-12-days-of-christmas-advent-calendar-10235552

17. Twitter users discovered that the entire contents of the calendar could be bought separately for under £20: *Zoella's £50 advent calendar has goods in it worth just £20, The Sun*, accessible at https://www.thesun.co.uk/fabulous/4904545/zoellas-50-advent-calendar-goods-20/

18. 'literal tat': *Zoella advent calendar reviews slam £50 'tat', The Week*, accessible at https://www.theweek.co.uk/89717/zoella-advent-calendar-reviews-slam-50-tat

19. Zoella explained that she had worked on the calendar for a year: *CHRIST-MAS ADVERTS & HOW WE MET*, Zoe Sugg, YouTube, accessible at https://www.youtube.com/watch?v=A5TPOKoE1_M&feature=youtu.be

20. American YouTuber Johnny Orlando was advertising tickets to watch him and his sister Lauren take part in a photo shoot for a teen-focused magazine for $40: *Behind the Shoot with Johnny and Lauren Orlando*, Eventbrite, accessible at https://www.eventbrite.com/e/behind-the-shoot-with-johnny-and-lauren-orlando-tickets-39875361279

21. PewDiePie launched a clothing like... a cotton-polyester blend hoodie adorned with a small embroidered logo cost $100: Tsuki, accessible at https://tsuki.market/

22. on 23 August 2017, Alfie Deyes and Zoella broached a new boundary: *OPENING OUR SHOP!!*, Alfie Deyes Vlogs, YouTube, accessible at https://www.youtube.com/watch?v=Kex9qLHdBwI&feature=youtu.be

23. hiring the 1,450-square-foot store for 12 days was a gamble: rent cost £1,000 per day before VAT: 21 Slingsby Place, Covent Garden, Appear Here, accessible at https://www.appearhere.nyc/spaces/london/covent-garden/21-slingsby-place-covent-garden

24. Posters, tote bags and phone pop sockets started at £10... a sign for the broken staff toilet reading: 'It's free, unlike our pop sockets, which are £10 please': *OPENING OUR SHOP!!*, Alfie Deyes Vlogs, YouTube, accessible at https://www.youtube.com/watch?v=Kex9qLHdBwI&feature=youtu.be

25. T-shirts emblazoned with the Sugg Life and Pointless Blog logos cost £15, while a hoodie set buyers back £25... more than 4,000 people visited the shop on the first day: *OPENING OUR SHOP!!*, Alfie Deyes Vlogs, YouTube, accessible at https://www.youtube.com/watch?v=Kex9qLHdBwI&feature=youtu.be

26. they had to beat a hasty retreat: *Zoella, Alfie Deyes and Joe Sugg forced to leave shop launch after it gets 'dangerous'*, Metro UK, accessible at https://metro.co.uk/2017/08/24/zoella-alfie-deyes-and-joe-sugg-forced-to-leave-shop-launch-after-it-gets-dangerous-6875402/?ito=cbshare

27. 'Guys, remember this pop up isn't a meet & greet': Alfie Deyes, Twitter, accessible at https://twitter.com/AlfieDeyes/status/900325211589013504

28. the doors of the Los Angeles shop didn't open when planned for safety reasons: *Dear YouTube, I'm Sorry To Let You Down...*, Jake Paul, YouTube, accessible at https://www.youtube.com/watch?v=OYp2afqvM14

29. nine hundred fans attended the first day... in New York... paying $10 for a ticket: *Jake Paul Pop-Up Shop DRAMA... (behind the scenes)*, Fanjoy, YouTube, accessible at https://www.youtube.com/watch?v=wNiycENtrwo

30. Tiana... brought 11,000 people to Birmingham's Bullring shopping

centre for her own pop-up shop in September 2018: *TIANA'S BACK TO SCHOOL SUPPLIES MERCH HAUL!!*, Tiana, YouTube, accessible at https://www.youtube.com/watch?v=0xQob6txDcc

31. YouTube's London Creator Space... gave over part of its shop, which has since closed, to Dodie Clark for three weeks in November 2017: on-the-ground reporting at the shop

32. in an exclusive survey for this book... a third of adults aged between 18 and 24... told the pollster YouGov that they felt they knew her well: YouGov survey of 1,625 British adults commissioned for YouTubers, 13-14 December 2017

27. Invasion of the Hollywood stars

1. as well as the Rockettes, its famous in-house dance troupe, Madonna performed her infamous rendition of *Like A Virgin*... hundreds of films have premiered in the vast auditorium: *The best of Radio City Music Hall*, Rockefeller Center, accessible at https://www.rockefellercenter.com/blog/2014/04/29/great-performances/

2. its 5,376-square foot stage: *Radio City Music Hall*, Madison Square Garden, accessible at https://www.msg.com/radio-city-music-hall/history

3. on 3 May 2018... YouTube executives... unveiled their latest round of original, platform-supported programming at Brandcast: *Highlights from the Brandcast stage: New YouTube Originals and advertiser offerings*, YouTube Official Blog, accessible at https://youtube.googleblog.com/2018/05/highlights-from-brandcast-stage-new.html

4. Jack Whitehall... James Corden... Kevin Hart... Will Smith: *Highlights from the Brandcast stage: New YouTube Originals and advertiser offerings*, YouTube Official Blog, accessible at https://youtube.googleblog.com/2018/05/highlights-from-brandcast-stage-new.html

5. Smith... holds the record for the most consecutive $100 million-plus earning films: Will Smith, Box Office Mojo, accessible at https://www.boxofficemojo.com/people/chart/?id=willsmith.htm

6. opened his YouTube channel 10 days before Christmas 2017: Will Smith, YouTube, accessible at https://www.youtube.com/channel/UCKuHFYu3smtr-l2AwwMOXOlg

7. YouTube's 2018 Rewind video: *YouTube Rewind 2018: Everyone Controls Rewind | #YouTubeRewind*, YouTube, YouTube, accessible at https://www.youtube.com/watch?v=YbJOTdZBX1g

8. the most hated video in the history of YouTube: *How YouTube's 2018 PR stunt became even more hated than Justin Bieber*, The Telegraph, accessible at https://www.telegraph.co.uk/tv/2018/12/11/youtubes-2018-pr-stunt-became-even-hated-justin-bieber/

9. he uploads highlights of his Twitch streams to a separate YouTube channel, subscribed to by 21 million people: Ninja, YouTube, accessible at https://www.youtube.com/user/NinjasHyper/

10. 'Will Smith, my favourite YouTuber': *YouTube Rewind 2018: Everyone Controls Rewind | #YouTubeRewind*, YouTube, YouTube, accessible at https://www.youtube.com/watch?v=YbJOTdZBX1g

11. Smith... has 4.6 million subscribers: Will Smith, YouTube, accessible at https://www.youtube.com/channel/UCKuHFYu3smtrl2AwwMOXOlg

12. Dwayne 'The Rock' Johnson has more than 3.5 million subscribers: *The Rock*, YouTube, accessible at https://www.youtube.com/user/therock

13. Ryan Reynolds' YouTube channel... gaining 750,000 subscribers since it was set up at the end of 2015: Ryan Reynolds, YouTube, accessible at https://www.youtube.com/channel/UCA3-nIYWu4PTWkb6NwhEpzg

14. James Corden and Jimmy Fallon have... a combined 35 million subscribers: *The Late Late Show with James Corden* and *The Tonight Show Starring Jimmy Fallon*, YouTube, accessible at https://www.youtube.com/user/TheLateLateShow and https://www.youtube.com/user/latenight

15. Ellen DeGeneres... has nearly 30 million subscribers alone: *TheEllenShow*, YouTube, accessible at https://www.youtube.com/user/TheEllenShow

16. Marlene Dietrich... said that glamour was her stock in trade: Max Factor, accessible at https://www.maxfactor.com/ar-en/our-story/iconic-looks/marlene-dietrich

17. Jennifer Lawrence... 'In Hollywood, I'm obese': *Jennifer Lawrence: 'In Hollywood, I'm obese*, Today, accessible at https://www.today.com/news/jennifer-lawrence-hollywood-im-obese-1C6959715

18. Wiz Khalifa, who uploads semi-regular vlogs... he calls *DayToday*... initially conceived of as a way to boost his Twitter subscribers and was first posted to YouTube in March 2009: *Wiz Khalifa Youtube episode 1*, Wiz Khalifa, YouTube, accessible at https://www.youtube.com/watch?v=NBoflY2gkEk

19. in a recent example he fools around with his friends... lingering close-ups of cannabis buds... and elaborately-crafted bongs: *Wiz Khalifa - Daytoday: Gangsters Everywhere We Go*, Wiz Khalifa, YouTube, accessible at https://www.youtube.com/watch?v=Bro3j9hkY_0

20. the rapper hovers around the top 100 most subscribed channels: Top 100 YouTube channels, SocialBlade, accessible at https://socialblade.com/youtube/top/100

21. 17 million people subscribe to: Wiz Khalifa, YouTube, accessible at https://www.youtube.com/channel/UCVp3nfGRxmMadNDuVbJSk8A

22. Gordon Ramsay and Jamie Oliver have both dabbled with YouTube channels... which combined have 12 million subscribers: Gordon Ramsay and Jamie Oliver, YouTube, accessible at https://www.youtube.com/user/gordonramsay and https://www.youtube.com/user/JamieOliver

23. YouTube quietly announced it would be opening up access to its Originals to everyone: *YouTube Originals will soon be free to watch for everyone*, *Mashable*, accessible at https://mashable.com/article/youtube-originals-free-premium-strategy/?europe=true#Ytex2PMK.mqg

28. Is YouTube killing traditional TV?

1. around three years ago... Derek Holder and his wife Cannis bought a new Sony television: Interview with Derek Holder

2. forty-somethings... set up a booming YouTube business, El Bebe Productions: Companies House records for Derek and Cannis Holder

3. it's the 13th biggest channel on all YouTube based on views (18 billion at the time of writing, and with another 200 million views added every month): *Little Baby Bum*, SocialBlade, accessible at https://socialblade.com/youtube/user/littlebabybum

4. they were simply parents looking for some children's nursery rhymes: Interview with Derek Holder

5. more than 6,000 people offer YouTube video editing services on Fiverr: Fiverr, YouTube video editing, accessible at https://www.fiverr.com/search/gigs?acmpl=1&utf8=%E2%9C%93&source=top-bar&locale=en&search_in=everywhere&query=youtube%20video%20editing&search-autocomplete-original-term=&search-autocomplete-original-term=youtube&search-autocomplete-available=true&search-autocomplete-type=recent-gigs-suggest&search-autocomplete-position=0

6. videographers working for YouTube's biggest names can earn six figures a year: *Feeding algorithms is a full-time job*, *BBC Capital*, accessible at http://www.bbc.com/capital/story/20190307-the-hidden-armies-that-power-the-internets-new-stars

7. a 29-second version of *Twinkle Twinkle Little Star*... posted on 29 August 2011: *Twinkle Twinkle Little Star | Little Baby Bum | Nursery Rhymes for Babies | Videos for Kids*, *Little Baby Bum*, YouTube, accessible at https://www.youtube.com/watch?v=9HDeEbJyNK8

8. they had just landed a big contract with L'Oreal... holder approached another company... El Bebe had more than a dozen videos: Interview with Derek Holder

9. it now produces videos in English, Spanish, Portuguese, German and Russian: *About Us*, *Little Baby Bum*, accessible at http://littlebabybum.com/about-us/

10. by 2017 its shareholder funds had ballooned to £8 million: Companies House records

11. in July 2018, the channel was bought by a media agency, Moonbug, for millions of pounds: *One of the World's Biggest YouTube Channels Just Got Sold*, *Bloomberg*, accessible at https://www.bloomberg.com/news/articles/2018-09-14/youtube-channel-little-baby-bum-children-s-cartoons-sold

12. its most popular video is a 54-minute medley of some of the most popular nursery rhymes uploaded in 2014: *Wheels On The Bus | Nursery Rhymes for Babies | Little Baby Bum | Videos for Kids*, *Little Baby Bum*, YouTube, accessible at https://www.youtube.com/watch?v=HP-MbfHFUqs&t=7s

13. more than half a billion more than Justin Bieber's mega-hit *Baby*: *Justin Bieber - Baby ft. Ludacris (Official Music Video)*, Justin Bieber, YouTube, accessible at https://www.youtube.com/watch?v=kffacxfA7G4

14. three-quarters of five- and six-year-olds had used YouTube in 2016 – by 2018 that had risen to 89%. The youngest children spend around 80 minutes a day: Childwise reports, 2017 and 2019

15. YouTube is increasingly being viewed on TV sets: *YouTube is taking on TV on its home turf, and it's starting to win*, *Recode*, accessible at https://www.recode.net/2017/10/26/16527272/youtube-tv-viewing-100-million-google-alphabet-earnings-q3-october-google

16. accessing the channel through smart TV apps has increased: Interview with Derek Holder

17. around 12 million videos could be uploaded every day: estimate based on YouTube having around 10 billion videos on the platform as of late March 2019. The figure comes from extrapolation of YouTube's growth as tracked in *YouTube channels, uploads and views: A statistical analysis of the past 10 years*, Matthias Baertl, Offenburg University

18. YouTube Kids operates in at least 37 countries worldwide: *Introducing kid profiles, new parental controls, and a new exciting look for kids, which will begin rolling out today!*, YouTube Official Blog, accessible at https://youtube.googleblog.com/2017/11/introducing-kid-profiles-new-parental.html

19. YouTube TV... is available on smart TVs, smartphones and tablets, and through Roku Players and Chromecast dongles: YouTube TV, accessible at https://tv.youtube.com/welcome/

20. in January 2019 it was available to 98% of US households: *YouTube TV Expands to 95 New Markets, Now Has 98% U.S. Coverage*, *Streaming Media*, accessible at https://www.streamingmedia.com/Articles/ReadArticle.aspx?ArticleID=129546

21. YouTube monitored more than 500 people's viewing habits at home: *YouTube's Quest to Make TV Work Everywhere*, *Wired*, accessible at https://

www.wired.com/story/youtubes-quest-to-make-tv-work-everywhere/

22. analysts at Barclays Capital... in 2017 more than 46% of people did: *Testing YouTube TV*, Barclays Capital

29. Online video war: YouTube v Facebook

1. more than a decade after its foundation: YouTube.com Whois info, accessible at http://whois.domaintools.com/youtube.com

2. Facebook is the only website to outgun YouTube in the number of users, with 2.3 billion: *In 15 years Facebook has amassed 2.3 billion users*, Business Insider, accessible at https://www.businessinsider.com/facebook-has-2-billion-plus-users-after-15-years-2019-2?r=US&IR=T

3. Mark Zuckerberg... made this explicit in a widely-reported conference call: Facebook Q2 2017 conference call, Facebook, accessible at https://s21.q4cdn.com/399680738/files/doc_financials/2017/Q2/Q2-'17-Earnings-call-transcript.pdf

4. the 47 people who attended a panel discussion with Facebook creators at the Summer in the City conference: on-the-ground reporting at Summer in the City

5. Becca Lammin, who has left YouTube: Lammin at Facebook Video panel discussion at Summer in the City

6. Goubran 'Goubtube' Bahou, who has 1.6 million likes: Goubtube, Facebook, accessible at https://www.facebook.com/Goubtube/

7. his girlfriend, Jahannah James, who has a further million likes: Jahannah James, Facebook, accessible at https://www.facebook.com/jahannahjames/

8. his Facebook page had just 20,000 likes: Bahou at Facebook Video panel discussion at Summer in the City

9. in a blog post on 9 August 2017, Daniel Danker, Facebook's director of product, announced Facebook Watch – a tab on the homepage for viewing videos... would feature videos from traditional media providers... along with more personalised creators: *Introducing Watch, a New Platform For Shows On Facebook*, Facebook Newsroom, accessible at https://newsroom.fb.com/news/2017/08/introducing-watch-a-new-platform-for-shows-on-facebook/

10. Daily left YouTube in August 2016 after five years, leaving a message: Nas Daily Official, YouTube, accessible at https://www.youtube.com/channel/UCJsUvAqDzczYv2UpFmu4PcA

11. in March 2019... announcing a programme called Facebook Match... each project... would get up to $200,000 to spend: *Facebook Launches New*

Program to Fund Original Facebook Watch Shows, Social Media Today, accessible at https://www.socialmediatoday.com/news/facebook-launches-new-program-to-fund-original-facebook-watch-shows/550332/

12. four hundred million Facebook users spend at least one minute a month on Watch, and 75 million watch at least a minute a day: *Facebook Watch is finally growing as payouts get spread thin, TechCrunch*, accessible at https://techcrunch.com/2018/12/13/facebook-watch-is-finally-growing-as-payouts-get-spread-thin/

13. YouTube offers advice from a dedicate staff liaison to those with more than 100,000 subscribers: Interviews with various YouTubers

14. Facebook has introduced a revenue-sharing programme: *Facebook to share ad revenue with Indian content makers, Economic Times*, accessible at https://economictimes.indiatimes.com/articleshow/66884537.cms?from=mdr&utm_source=contentofinterest&utm_medium=text&utm_campaign=cppst

15. it bought copyright identification platform Source3: *Facebook acquires Source3 to get content creators paid, TechCrunch*, accessible at https://techcrunch.com/2017/07/24/facebook-source3/

16. in 2012, around a third of all the downstream video traffic... was from YouTube, and just around seven percent was from Facebook. In 2016, YouTube's share... had dropped to about a fifth – while Facebook's share doubled: Mary Meeker's internet trends 2017 report, Kleiner Perkins, accessible at https://www.slideshare.net/kleinerperkins/internet-trends-2017-report

17. when Instagram stories was announced in August 2016: *Introducing Instagram Stories*, Instagram Info Center, accessible at https://instagram-press.com/blog/2016/08/02/introducing-instagram-stories/

18. within seven months, 200 million users a day used the Stories function in Instagram – supplanting Snapchat, which at the time had 158 million users: *Instagram Stories is now more popular than the app it was designed to kill, The Verge*, accessible at https://www.theverge.com/2017/4/13/15279266/instagram-stories-facebook-200-million-users-snapchat-clone

19. all the big social media platforms are coalescing in format... IGTV, a standalone video app... at the same time, YouTube looked to defend its own turf: *Instagram's grand video plans are tediously familiar. Just ask Snapchat and YouTube, Wired UK*, accessible at https://www.wired.co.uk/article/vidcon-2018-igtv-instagram-youtube-premieres

20. Amazon... is the ultimate owner of Twitch: accessible at https://twitch.amazon.com

21. has recently made moves to increase the proportion of 'IRL' (non-gaming) streams on its site: Interview with Kitboga

22. the total amount of video watched on Twitch in a month – 880 million hours in February 2019: Twitch Tracker, accessible at https://twitchtracker.com/statistics/viewers

23. lapped up by YouTube viewers in less than a day: *People now watch 1 billion hours of YouTube per day*, TechCrunch, accessible at https://techcrunch.com/2017/02/28/people-now-watch-1-billion-hours-of-youtube-per-day/

24. TikTok has 800 million monthly active users worldwide: *Pitch deck: How TikTok is selling ads in Europe*, Digiday, accessible at https://digiday.com/marketing/pitch-deck-what-tiktok-is-offering-european-advertisers/

25. YouTube's 1.9 billion: YouTube for Press, accessible at https://www.youtube.com/intl/en-GB/yt/about/press/

26. 660 million of the app's billion installs came in 2018 alone: *TikTok Surpasses One Billion Installs on the App Store and Google Play*, SensorTower, accessible at https://sensortower.com/blog/tiktok-downloads-one-billion

27. simultaneously rolling out detailed analytics: Interviews with TikTok users

28. a quarter of the app's downloads came from India: *TikTok Surpasses One Billion Installs on the App Store and Google Play*, SensorTower, accessible at https://sensortower.com/blog/tiktok-downloads-one-billion

PART VIII

CONCLUSION

30. A flawed winner

1. its arrival a decade and a half ago: YouTube.com Whois info, accessible at http://whois.domaintools.com/youtube.com

2. nearly two billion people: YouTube for Press, accessible at https://www.youtube.com/intl/en-GB/yt/about/press/

3. shootings: Pedro Ruiz III, Christina Grimmie, Nasim Aghdam; the March 2019 Christchurch mosque attacks, which YouTube was criticised for not preventing reuploads of the gunman's Facebook livestream

4. suicides: 'Suicide instructions spliced into kids' cartoons on YouTube and YouTube Kids', Ars Technica, accessible at https://arstechnica.com/science/2019/02/youtube-kids-cartoons-include-tips-for-committing-suicide-docs-warn/

6. discredited celebrities: *Sam Pepper Apology – 'Social Experiment'*, StopSam, YouTube, accessible at https://www.youtube.com/watch?v=lBWnuYaGDJo and *Olivia Jade, the education-hating YouTuber at the heart of the US admissions scandal*, The Telegraph, accessible at https://www.telegraph.co.uk/tv/0/

olivia-jade-education-hating-youtuber-heart-us-admissions-scandal/ – plus plenty more

7. advertising frauds: *The Flourishing Business of Fake YouTube Views*, *New York Times*, accessible at https://www.nytimes.com/interactive/2018/08/11/technology/youtube-fake-view-sellers.html?mtrref=www.google.com&gwh=55004A0455311F401D304D4F82ED13AF&gwt=pay

8. the site's algorithm dangerously veers off into the realm of false far-right conspiracy theories: AlgoTransparency, accessible at https://algotransparency.org/

9. it is an engine of unabashed, environmentally-destructive consumerism: *Jake and Logan Paul are YouTube Merch Monsters*, *New York Magazine*, accessible at http://nymag.com/selectall/2018/04/jake-paul-and-logan-paul-are-youtube-merch-monsters.html

10. parts of its comment sections have been co-opted as an unchecked forum for child abuse rings: *On YouTube, a network of paedophiles is hiding in plain sight*, *Wired UK*, accessible at https://www.wired.co.uk/article/youtube-pedophile-videos-advertising

11. flagged up dangerous prank videos: *Police ire at YouTube stunt pranksters*, *The Sunday Times*, accessible at https://www.thetimes.co.uk/article/police-ire-at-youtube-stunt-pranksters-vgvhpqktz

12. transphobia on YouTube's algorithm: *Why Has 'Transgender' Become a Trigger Word for YouTube?*, *The Daily Beast*, accessible at https://www.thedailybeast.com/why-has-transgender-become-a-trigger-word-for-youtube?ref=author

13. the availability of how-to videos proffering advice on how to make drugs seen by millions: *Make crystal meth and crack cocaine the YouTube way*, *The Sunday Times*, accessible at https://www.thetimes.co.uk/article/make-crystal-meth-and-crack-cocaine-the-youtube-way-jqtcr528q

14. child pornography: *Google moves to fix YouTube glitch exploited for child porn*, *Phys.org*, accessible at https://phys.org/news/2019-02-google-youtube-glitch-exploited-child.html

15. bestiality: *YouTube Hosted Graphic Images of Bestiality For Months*, *BuzzFeed News*, accessible at https://www.buzzfeednews.com/article/charliewarzel/youtube-hosted-graphic-images-of-beastiality-for-months#.usp8OiNow
16. disturbing content targeted at children: *YouTube Has Deleted Hundreds Of Thousands Of Disturbing Kids' Videos*, *BuzzFeed News*, accessible at https://www.buzzfeednews.com/article/blakemontgomery/youtube-has-deleted-hundreds-of-thousands-of-disturbing

17. it often addresses the manifestation, rather than the root cause of the problem, and frequently over-reacts: *Banning comments won't fix YouTube's paedophile problem. Its algorithm is totally broken*, *Wired UK*, accessible at https://www.wired.co.uk/article/youtube-comments-disabled

18. three-quarters of us think YouTube has partial or total responsibility for the videos hosted on its platform: polling of 2,965 people by Poli, commissioned for this book

19. the first adpocalypse: *Google's bad week: YouTube loses millions as advertising row reaches US, The Guardian,* accessible at https://www.theguardian.com/technology/2017/mar/25/google-youtube-advertising-extremist-content-att-verizon

20. the second adpocalypse: *YouTubers facing second 'adpocalypse' as Nestle and Epic Games withdraw adverts, Metro UK,* accessible at https://metro.co.uk/2019/02/21/youtubers-facing-second-adpocalypse-nestle-epic-games-withdraw-adverts-8696292/?ito=cbshare

21. Elsagate: *Inside Elsagate, the conspiracy-fueled war on creepy YouTube kids videos, The Verge,* accessible at https://www.theverge.com/2017/12/8/16751206/elsagate-youtube-kids-creepy-conspiracy-theory

22. terrorist content: *Big brands fund terror through online adverts, The Times,* accessible at https://www.thetimes.co.uk/article/big-brands-fund-terror-knnxfgb98

23. extreme content: *Logan Paul's disastrous YouTube video is just a symptom of very modern problem, The Telegraph,* accessible at https://www.telegraph.co.uk/business/2018/01/05/logan-pauls-disastrous-youtube-video-just-symptom-far-bigger/?WT.mc_id=tmg_share_tw

24. pranks: *YouTube's prank ban deepens the expanding rift with its creators, Wired UK,* accessible at https://www.wired.co.uk/article/youtube-prank-ban

25. conspiracy theories: *Continuing our work to improve recommendations on YouTube,* YouTube Official Blog, accessible at https://youtube.googleblog.com/2019/01/continuing-our-work-to-improve.html

26. a widely-shared essay about children's content on YouTube: *Something is wrong on the internet,* James Bridle, *Medium,* accessible at https://medium.com/@jamesbridle/something-is-wrong-on-the-internet-c39c471271d2

27. burnout is a risk: *Why YouTubers are feeling the burn, The Observer,* accessible at https://www.theguardian.com/technology/2018/aug/12/youtubers-feeling-burn-video-stars-crumbling-under-pressure-of-producing-new-content

INDEX

Cingular Wireless 36
CKN Toys 101
Clark, Dodie 76, 81, 131, 226
Clarke, Ian 29, 33
click-bait 57
Clinton, Hillary 67
CNN International 26
Coca-Cola 57
collaborations 138
Collective, The 141
College Humor 45
College of Mount Saint Vincent 16
Combs, Curtis 167
comedy
     pilot 45
     skits 248
coming out 76
comments 12, 168
Communist ruling party 52
community guidelines 68
Companies House 17
Competition and Markets Authority 82
computer engineers 57
computers 57
ComRes 46
ComScore 36
connected TV 244
Connecticut 34, 154
conspiracy theories 57, 67, 69, 260
consumers, targeted with efficiency 36, 83
Conte, Jack 212
ContentID 251
conversation 179
Copeland, David 70
Copper Box Arena, London 92
copyright identification 251
copyright owners 32
Corden, James 231, 234
Cordially Invited 221
Cornell University 85
corporate-run channels 48
counselling 173
Covent Garden 224
Coward, Simon 13
Craigslist 42
Crash Course 42
Crazy Sumit, The 172
Creative Artists Agency 176
creativity 213, 234, 258
creators 15, 28, 32, 59, 82, 85, 109,
127, 132, 178, 195, 199, 206, 207, 211, 217, 248, 250, 252, 258
creator community 62
feeling of community among 35
creator/viewer divide 131
criminal threats 66
Cronkite, Walter 179
crowdfunding 146, 210
Cruikshank, Lucas 35
Cruise, Tom 199
CSGO Lotto 83
Cuban, Mark 37
Curham, Siobhan 221
Cyprus 113
     University of Technology 60
Cyrus, Miley 197

DaddyOFive 168
DailyGrace 204, 205
Daily Mail, The 122, 133
Daily, Nas 249
Daly, Carson 142
Dammit Boy 165
dance routines 138
D'Angelo, Anthony 192, 201, 206, 252
Danker, Daniel 249
Danskin, Ian 84, 198, 218, 219
Dantas, Konrad Cunha 47
Darwen 111
Dawn, Nataly 212
Dawson, Shane 195
DaxFlame 28
daytime TV 234
DayToday 236
Dedman, Jay 26
deep state movement 68
DeFranco, Philip 42, 151, 215, 216
Defy Media 209
DeGeneres, Ellen 234
Delhi High Court 48
demographics 84, 253
demonetise 63
Desert Eagle pistol 164
Deyes, Alfie 128, 142, 200, 201, 221, 222, 224, 237
Dietrich, Marlene 235
digital platform 246
Discovery Channel 193
Disney 60, 72, 106, 135, 148, 151, 197
    Disney Channel 150